This book will help you:

- Chart your ideal college education.

- Pick a major and a minor.

- Know which courses *not* to place out of.

- Optimize your day.

- Take really useful notes.

- Study effectively.

- Ace exams.

- Write great college-level essays.

- Stand out from the crowd (beyond making high grades).

- Develop mentoring relationships with your professors.

- Find research opportunities early in your college career.

- Build a strong foundation for your future profession.

- Apply for nationally competitive scholarships.

- Sharpen your interview skills.

- Achieve 15 college goals that will prepare you for a life of distinction.

Praise from students and scholarship winners

"Dr. Duban offers solid, straightforward advice on how to make the most out of the college experience. His emphases on fostering intellectual relationships with professors and on developing sound writing skills are right on the money, as is his framework for thinking about nationally competitive scholarships. As a former student of Dr. Duban, I benefited enormously from his approach. I highly recommend this book to any student who takes his or her educational investment seriously."

—MARK SOMERVILLE

Mark Somerville won a Rhodes Scholarship to earn his M.A. (first class honors) in Physics from Oxford University. He also holds M.S. and Ph.D. degrees in Electrical Engineering from MIT, where he earned the Joint Services Electronics Program Doctoral and Post Doctoral Fellowship, along with an Office of Naval Research Graduate Fellowship. Having taught at both MIT and Vassar College, he is now Assistant Professor of Electrical Engineering and Physics at Olin College.

"Dr. Duban's *Complete Guide to Academic Stardom* is a true treasure that provides a clear path for students to follow on their journey to become accomplished graduates. Dr. Duban unlocks several secrets every college student can benefit from as they strive to achieve academic excellence. Success is guaranteed for those who follow this guide."

—SHANNA WHITLEY

After winning a Harry S. Truman Scholarship, Shanna Whitley earned her Master of Social Work degree from the University of Texas at Arlington, where she did graduate-level research in the area of child welfare. As an undergraduate at the University of North Texas, she graduated number one in her class with a perfect grade point average. Shanna is now completing a law and business degree at Texas Tech University, where she has been honored with generous scholarship support.

"Dr. Duban and his expert academic and interview coaching changed my life. Thanks directly to the interview techniques he taught me, I won a British Marshall Scholarship and spent several eye-opening years studying and living abroad. Later, in law school, those same techniques helped me land prestigious judicial clerkships at the U.S. Court of Appeals and the U.S. Supreme Court. Now Professor Duban has made these techniques, *and much more*, available to students everywhere in this immensely useful book. What sets Dr. Duban apart from the pack is how concrete, specific, and practical his advice is. Mastering even a handful of the tactics described in this book will provide a huge head start toward success and fulfillment in college and beyond."

—J. C. ROZENDAAL

J. C. Rozendaal won a British Marshall Scholarship, which funded his B.A. (awarded with first class honors) and M.A. at Oxford University. After earning a law degree (with highest honors) from The University of Texas School of Law, he worked as a Law Clerk for Hon. Douglas H. Ginsberg, U.S. Court of Appeals, District of Columbia Circuit, and then clerked for Hon. Anthony M. Kennedy, U.S. Supreme Court. J. C. is now a partner with Kellogg, Huber, Hansen, Todd, Evans & Figel, P.L.L.C., a law firm based in Washington, D.C. He specializes in litigation, telecommunications, and antitrust.

"This is the most thorough book I've seen on the entire college experience, including what comes after college. This is a book that all students should read—and re-read each year to remind themselves of where they're going and how to get there. This book is an invaluable resource for college students and parents of college students."

—EMILY WITTEN

Emily Witten won both a Barry M. Goldwater Scholarship (in engineering research) and a Morris K. Udall Scholarship (in environmental public policy) during her final year at the Texas Academy of Mathematics and Science, at the University of North Texas. She then earned a B.S., with Distinction, at Stanford University, following which she worked for an engineering firm, designing pipelines for oil and gas companies. Emily then passed the Professional Engineer Examination to become a licensed mechanical engineer in California. But her intellectual journey didn't stop there. After scoring a 179 out of a possible 180 on the LSAT, she was accepted into a number of law schools, including Harvard, NYU, Berkeley, UCLA, USC, and UT-Austin. She chose Harvard.

"Well deserved praise goes to Dr. James Duban for writing the definitive manual for college-bound students. I highlighted this manuscript and had my daughter read it during the semester break of her sophomore year in college. I only wish it had been available when she was a senior in high school. *The Complete Guide to Academic Stardom* should be in the hands of every high school student who dreams of college, every parent who anticipates tuition payments, and every counselor who advises students bound for college....From one who blossomed under Dr. Duban's watchful mentoring, I can assure you that this book captures every ounce of his wisdom and insight. Success awaits any student who diligently applies the principles set forth in this comprehensive guide."

—Pier Larsen

The winner of a James Madison Fellowship, Pier Larson earned her master's degree in history (with an emphasis on the constitutional era). She now teaches AP U.S. History and is head of the Social Studies Department of Creekview High School in Carrollton, Texas. She's also the mother of a college student!

"When you apply for scholarships, your grades get you past the first cut, and your letters of recommendation get you invited to interviews; but your unique experiences are what make you stand out. This book is an insightful guide to strategies that all students can reference to get the grades, the experiences, the letters of rec, the interviews, and ultimately... the scholarships."

—Anna Cristina Taboada

Cristina Taboada majored in both Economics and Political Science, with minors in French and Spanish, graduating with a 4.0 GPA. She studied for two years at Université de Montpellier and Université D'Angers, France, before winning a Fulbright Scholarship to study at The Autonomous Technological Institute in Mexico. She now works as a new-business development analyst for Dupont.

Be a College Achiever™
★
The Complete Guide to Academic Stardom

James Duban, Ph.D.

Visit the Be a College Achiever™ website for additional learning opportunities designed for college and college-bound students at:
www.college-achiever.com

TRAFFORD

Ireland   United Kingdom   Canada   United States of America

Be a College Achiever™: The Complete Guide to Academic Stardom
James Duban, Ph.D.

Publishing information

This book was published in cooperation with:
Trafford Publishing
a division of Trafford Holdings, Ltd.
Suite 6E - 2333 Government St.
Victoria, BC, Canada V8T. 4P4
Toll-free 1-866-232-4444 (Canada and U.S.)
E-mail: info@trafford.com
Website: www.trafford.com
Trafford Catalogue #04-2554

First printing: 2005
Printed in Victoria, Canada.

National Library of Canada Cataloguing in Publication Data

A cataloguing record for this book that includes the U.S. Library of Congress Classification number, the Library of Congress Call number and the Dewey Decimal cataloguing code is available from the National Library of Canada. The complete cataloguing record can be obtained from the National Library of Canada's online database at:
www.nlc-bnc.ca/amicus/index-e.html.

ISBN 1-4120-4746-3

10 9   8   7   6   5   4   3   2   1

Trademarks

This book is part of the Be a College Achiever™ publication series and seminar services offered by James Duban Consulting, LLC. Be a College Achiever™ is a trademark of James Duban Consulting, LLC.

Trademarks appear throughout this book. Rather than put a trademark symbol in every occurrence of a trademarked name, we state that we are using the names in an editorial fashion only and to the benefit of the trademark owners and with no intention of infringement of the trademarks.

Purchasing information

Books, ebooks, and other publications can be purchased online from the Be a College Achiever™ website (www.college-achiever.com) or by mail (see the order form at the back of this book). You can also purchase this book on Trafford Publishing's website (www.trafford.com/robots/04-2554.html).

Attention colleges and universities, corporations, bookstores, and student, teacher, and counselor organizations

Quantity discounts are available on bulk purchases of this book for educational training purposes, fund-raising, or gift giving. Special books, booklets, or book excerpts can also be created to fit your specific needs. For information, contact James Duban Consulting, LLC, P. O. Box 270922, Flower Mound, Texas, 75027-0922, or e-mail info@college-achiever.com.

Disclaimer

The purpose of this book is to educate and entertain by providing general information about college life and academic success. It is sold with the understanding that the publisher and author are not engaged in rendering legal, accounting, or other professional services. If legal or other assistance is required, the services of a competent professional should be sought.

This book offers general advice based on the author's experience and personal perspective, and does not guarantee or promise any particular outcome. Also, this book does not, and cannot, take account of the rules and regulations existing on thousands of college campuses. Once you know the university at which you'll enroll, seek out the university's officials and designated offices responsible for helping you to meet all of your educational requirements. You'll want to obtain specific advice on such matters as financial aid, career planning, graduation requirements for particular majors and minors, course-hour requirements, individual course expectations, and graduate school admission policies. In cases where a conflict exists between the general advice offered in this book and the expectations of your university or professors, give priority to the latter.

It is not the purpose of this book to reprint all the information that is otherwise available to college students, but instead to complement and supplement other texts. You are urged to read all available material, learn as much about college life and academics as you can, and tailor the information to your needs. For more information, see the many resources at the end of this book.

Although every care was taken in the preparation of this book, the publisher and author assume no responsibility for errors, omissions or typographical mistakes. Neither is any liability assumed for damages resulting from the use of information contained herein. The book contains information that is up-to-date as of the printing date. Due to the changing nature of the subject matter, certain information herein may be outdated even at the time of publication.

Acknowledgments

Family, friends, colleagues, and former students have offered support and feedback. My wife, Karen Duban, encouraged me to consolidate the lessons of years of college-level teaching and mentoring into a practical manual for college-bound students. Friend and colleague Dr. Alan Gribben provided invaluable editorial advice, while others were highly supportive as well. Dr. Manus Donohue, who for many years was assistant dean and director of academic programs for the Texas Academy of Mathematics and Science, was among the first to confirm the need for such a book, as did my University of North Texas colleague (and long-time chair of the Department of Physics) Dr. Sam Matteson. Both shared ideas and perspectives about the ideal college education. Their dialogue proved immensely helpful.

I am appreciative, too, of many colleagues with whom I have conducted mock interviews for students competing for nationally competitive scholarships. My chapter on interview comportment has benefited from the spectrum of advice I have heard professors offer students for the past twenty years.

Then there are friends Roger Jahnel and Ruth Keefer, whose enthusiasm proved inspirational. Mr. Bill Wells, of Day-Timer®, Inc., was likewise supportive of my initiative. So, too, were a number of Barry M. Goldwater Scholarship winners, who have distinguished themselves in mathematics and science: Stephen Chen, Patrick Goodwill, Haley Hagg, Shawn Stuart, and Emily Witten offered invaluable advice relative to note-taking and test-taking in the areas of math and science. Harry S. Truman Scholar Shanna Whitley, in turn, offered regular encouragement and stands as a model for students seeking to achieve an ideal education. Related thanks go to Rotary Ambassadorial Scholars Devon Wootten and Jared Crebs, who kindly agreed to allow me to reference their stellar accomplishments.

I am grateful, as well, for the meticulous proofreading and helpful feedback of Yieu Chyan and Solomon Sallfors.

Books by James Duban

Melville's Major Fiction

The Nature of True Virtue

Be a College Achiever™: The Complete Guide to Academic Stardom

for my sons,

Edmund, Seth, and Nathaniel

Contents

Section 6 :: Reaping the Benefits of the Ideal College Education

Section 7 :: The Scholarship Application Process

Section 8 :: College Resources

Section 1 :: Introduction

Chapter One

About the Author

In large part, this book has evolved from nearly four decades of personal success in higher education (including my earning a Ph.D. at the tender age of twenty-five). However, I can still recall quite vividly the many difficulties I experienced as a college freshman. After getting my academic career off to a particularly rocky start, I then had to figure out—pretty much on my own—the road to college distinction. I did make it. Now, with this book, I take pleasure in giving my readers a significant head start on their career and life paths, enabling them to benefit from my hard-won discoveries.

My own freshman year

Here are just a few of the problems I faced as a college freshman: I came from a single-parent family and grew up in a major urban housing project, complete with a concrete playground and chain-link fences. Within this environment, I hadn't managed to distinguish myself academically before entering college. As a college freshman, I suddenly had to compete against students who had been raised with the expectation of becoming college stars. I had to learn how to excel.

The old engineering-calculus trap: Near disaster

I did eventually adopt workable strategies for academic success, but not without falling prey to a few pitfalls at the beginning. In my first semester, for example, I took engineering calculus without having had solid training in algebra; to make matters worse I also enrolled in general chemistry with insufficient mathematical skills to do well. Faced with catastrophic test results (despite eight-hour study days), I switched majors—from biology to English—and changed career paths. Although this was a step in the right direction, I did not understand, even then, the mission of a college-level essay, let alone how to research, structure, and compose one. (Take this as a hint that a good part of this book is devoted to these vital skills!)

On the rebound

But I was a quick study. Although I ended my first semester with only a 2.1 Grade Point Average (GPA), I progressed to a 3.7 in my second semester of college, and for the remainder of my undergraduate career scored nothing less than an A in every one of my classes. Along the way, I won "best essay awards" in my sophomore, junior, and senior years of study. I also established relationships with professors who were willing to mentor me (beyond the classroom), and I sought out study-abroad opportunities and scholarships to broaden my horizons. By the time I entered my senior year of study, I had become a semifinalist for a Rhodes Scholarship, had spent a summer in England studying at Oxford University, and was poised either to enter the workforce or to move on to graduate school.

Next stop: Graduate school

Because, as an undergraduate, I had done all the "right" things—and for all the right reasons relative to personal growth and development—I received a scholarship to attend Cornell University, where I earned my master's degree and my Ph.D. in English and American literature. During my four years as a graduate student there, I wrote my dissertation on American author Herman Melville, published scholarly articles in journals of high repute, and established the credentials to be hired as an assistant professor of English at a major state university. Attending graduate school at Cornell University was one of the most thrilling and intellectually rewarding episodes of my life. A fine undergraduate experience had prepared me well for advanced research in my field of study, early American literature. All my hard work in college had paid off.

Workable strategies + Inner burn = Grand Success

From the outset of my college experience, I learned that energy, commitment, and determination dictate success, even when one's competition appears to have had all the "breaks." To this day, I remain convinced that it's the drive with which you commit yourself to time-proven strategies for excelling in—and beyond—the classroom that brings about academic achievement.

Many voices of guidance = Leg up for you

Admittedly, mine was a roundabout road to academic stardom. With better planning, yours can be more direct, with far less uncertainty and anguish during your first year of college. The pages in this book detail proven strategies that will guide you towards college distinction. I have combined my own recipes for success with those of award-winning students and generous colleagues (many in math and science) who have shared their study habits and educational outlooks with me. In this book you'll find a number of voices combined to offer a comprehensive approach to college stardom. Students who implement these suggestions will have an unbelievable advantage in achieving their goals in college.

Setting standards of distinction

Much of my advice also comes from two other sources. I've been a professor of English for almost thirty years and—for the last twelve years—have served as director of my university's Office for Nationally Competitive Scholarships. Indeed, this book draws upon both of those contexts to offer a goal-oriented philosophy of education. My suggestions for college stardom are basically grounded in the standards of attainment demanded in numerous national and international scholarship competitions. Indeed, this is the first comprehensive college "how-to" book structured around the criteria for national scholarship competition.

And the winners are ...

The strategies I describe have frequently been used by the students whom I have personally taught or coached, and who have won the following prestigious national scholarships or the following placements:

- Rhodes Scholarships
- Marshall Scholarships
- Harry S. Truman Scholarships
- Fulbright Scholarships
- Andrew W. Mellon Fellowships in Humanistic Studies
- Atlantic Fellowships in Public Policy
- Morris K. Udall Scholarships
- Jacob K. Javits Fellowships
- Barry M. Goldwater Scholarships
- Rotary Ambassadorial Scholarships
- Ford Foundation Scholarships
- National Science Foundation Research Fellowships
- Intel Science Talent Search Scholarships
- Gates Millennium Scholarships

- James Madison Fellowships
- American Political Science Association Minority Fellowships
- American Psychological Association Minority Fellowships
- Jewish Federation Scholarships
- Hispanic Scholarship Fund Awards
- Law School Admissions and Law School Fellowships
- Medical School Admissions
- Graduate School Admissions and Graduate School Fellowships

Altogether, the students I've worked with have obtained well over a million dollars in nationally competitive scholarships. My coaching and mentoring achievements have been recognized by the Harry S. Truman Scholarship Foundation, by members of Rotary International, and by the Ronald E. McNair Post-Baccalaureate Achievement Program.

Teaching College 101

My advice, and part of the inspiration for this book, emerges from an introduction-to-college seminar that I have taught for National Merit Scholars and University Honors students. In that class we have explored perspectives presented in Richard J. Light's *Making the Most of College: Students Speak Their Minds*. We have also benefited from lectures by eminent professors and university advisors who encourage undergraduate research, community involvement, and study abroad. This class prepares college freshmen for the rigors of college and leaves them knowledgeable about what college success means *beyond excellent grades*. (See the Resources chapter for other helpful books, articles, and websites pertaining to college success.)

This advice is for everyone

Finally, my outlook is also influenced by my close work with the Ronald E. McNair Post-Baccalaureate Achievement Program. These students are the first in their immediate families to have the chance to earn a bachelor's degree. Exemplary students, they are hand-selected for their potential to conduct undergraduate research in advanced curricula leading to post-graduate placement and Ph.D. programs. I lecture to McNair students about admission essays for graduate school and guide them through the intricacies of national scholarship competition. In an era when superior grades are just a starting point for academic and professional success, I teach *all* students how to go the extra ten miles.

My basic advice: Aim high for an ideal college education

Not every student will compete for—or win—a nationally competitive scholarship. But since most scholarship foundations share common expectations about undergraduate excellence, you ought to organize a program of study, as early as your first year of college, that anticipates their standards of assessment and envisions an "ideal" education. The results will be impressive. Win or lose, you end up with a valuable education and more options for employment or "paid-for" postgraduate study.

National associations

I am a founding board member of the National Association of Fellowships Advisors. That organization urges university campuses to identify their finest students and advise them about the expectations and intricacies of national scholarship and fellowship competition. At NAFA meetings I regularly converse with representatives of many of the world's leading scholarship foundations about their methods of evaluation and their views concerning an ideal education. Readers of this book will benefit from those discussions.

Teaching experience

I have taught at the college level for over twenty-five years. During that time, I have administered an honors program in English, directed an intensive expository writing summer institute, been Chair of an English Department, and overseen a highly successful Office for Nationally Competitive Scholarships. A specialist in American intellectual and literary history, I have taught a wide range of courses to undergraduates, honors students, National Merit Scholars, and graduate students. Those classes have included freshman composition, writing across the disciplines, and expository writing.

Publications

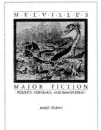

I have authored two scholarly books. One is about the major novels of Herman Melville. The other book traces the philosophical and theological backgrounds of the Henry James family. I've also published numerous articles in such leading journals as *The Harvard Library Bulletin*, *Nineteenth-Century Fiction*, *American Literature*,

Philological Quarterly, *The New England Quarterly*, and *The Papers of the Bibliographical Society of America*, among others.

Education

I earned my B.A. degree from the University of Massachusetts Amherst, and received my M.A. and Ph.D. degrees from Cornell University.

Conclusion

From these achievements and experiences I have distilled precise strategies for college stardom that can elevate your ambitions and invigorate your campus years. Read on, and become all that you are capable of being as a student and a college graduate.

The Nature of True Virtue

Theology, Psychology, and Politics in the Writings of Henry James, Sr., Henry James, Jr., and William James

James Duban

Chapter Two

This Book Is for Traditional and Non-Traditional Students

If you are new to college or if you're a high-school student heading to college, this book is especially for you. If you're supporting a new college student (financially or otherwise), you'll also benefit from reading this book, whether you're a parent, guidance counselor, or teacher.

If you're already deep into your college experience or you're a graduate student, you'll still find plenty of helpful advice in this book. In fact, much of what I talk about in these pages I didn't learn until I was in graduate school (or even later).

Although I anticipate that most new college students fall into the "traditional" category (18 to 19 years old, freshmen, recent graduates of high school), many of you will be "non-traditional."

The new "older college student"

Indeed, I have either known, taught, or counseled many non-traditional students who benefited from the advice now gathered in this book. Nearly all of these students were significantly older than their undergraduate peers and came from all walks of life. Some were seeking credentials for new jobs and careers; others were parents who enrolled in college after raising a family; still others were veterans of the armed services. To a person, these non-traditional students have been among the most devoted and energetic students.

In fact, several of these students worked under my supervision to become recipients of prestigious national and international scholarships. Two, for example, became Harry S. Truman Scholars; two became James Madison Memorial Fellowship recipients; another became a National Science Foundation Fellowship winner, one won a Rotary Ambassadorial Scholarship; and one became an Atlantic Fellowship in Public Policy award winner.

The benefits of being non-traditional

These non-traditonal students discovered that their age—far from being a liability—opened doors. After all, they had a wealth of experience, perspective, commitment, and public service. I taught these students how to apply many of the strategies featured in this book to win nationally competitive scholarships. In the course of competing for those awards, these students also refined their study skills, interview techniques, and writing acumen. They benefited in the same ways that traditional students have when taking to heart the advice collected in the following chapters. Many of these non-traditional students have moved on to earn master's degrees and Ph.D.s.

So take heart if you are a non-traditional student. View your age as an advantage—not a liability—when encountering the advice in this book.

One for all

Ultimately, this book seeks to help you, the college student, have the most rewarding college education. I offer suggestions to help you plan for success and achievement in the near and far future—in the classroom and beyond the campus. I aim to have you think of your college experience as the beginning of your *career* and urge you to set goals that will leave you with enticing options once you finish your undergraduate work.

The key is to identify strategies that will help you succeed in college—and then to put those strategies into practice. This book is a great start for exactly that process; so let's get to it.

Chapter Three

How Universities Are Organized and What that Means for You

First, let's cover some basics about college for those who are new to the concept. We'll review terminology, and sketch out who's who in the university scheme of things. It's always nice to know the essentials about an organization before you try to be a big success in it.

You may have wondered, for instance, if there's a difference between a "college" and a "university." As you know, these two terms are often interchangeable in casual conversation. There is a slight difference, but that will likely erode even more over time. For now, I'll introduce you to the traditional definitions.

University

A university is an organization for learning beyond high school. You'll often hear that a university is an "institution of higher learning." It almost always has a physical campus with many buildings for teaching and research (not to mention buildings for administration, student living, theaters, activity centers, etc.). A university awards degrees (certificates confirming that students have completed certain academic requirements) for both undergraduate and graduate study.

Sometimes a university has only one campus (the physical location of the buildings), and in other cases has several campuses.

Undergraduate

"Undergraduate" generally refers to the first four (or so) years of study at a university. The degree given for undergraduate work is called a bachelor's degree. Different kinds of bachelor's degrees exist—for example, a Bachelor of Science or a Bachelor of Fine Arts.

11

In order to earn your bachelor's degree at a university, you'll take a certain number of courses (for which you'll receive specified credit hours—usually three per class) in various subjects, meeting the academic expectations of your professors and the university.

Graduate

The other part of a university is the graduate division. The term "graduate students" refers to students enrolled in a graduate program at a university. Graduate students have already completed their "undergraduate" work and are now working either on a "master's" or a "doctorate" degree.

(The "doctorate" degree is often abbreviated as "Ph.D."—which means Doctor of Philosophy. People may earn the Doctor of Philosophy in any number of fields of study. Students can earn a master's (M.A., M.B.A., M.F.A., or M.S.) degree in anywhere from one to three years. The Ph.D. takes longer to earn—often two-to-five years beyond the master's degree. You must usually complete a master's degree in order to study for a doctorate degree.)

By the way, that's why many professors prefer to be called "Dr. So-n-so"—since they worked hard to earn a "doctorate" degree in graduate school. In class, you'll generally address your professors as "Dr. So-n-so" (if they have earned a Ph.D.) or "Professor So-n-so."

Professional schools

Professional schools comprise the other part of the graduate division of a university. These would include, for instance, law schools or medical schools (law degrees and medical degrees are technically doctorates as well—that is, doctorates of medicine and doctorates of jurisprudence). Other professional schools can award the equivalent of a doctorate for students who do extensive work and research.

College: Multiple meanings

By now you're wondering, "OK, so where does the word 'college' fit into all of this?" Well, "college" can mean a couple of different things. Generally, "college" refers to an organization that offers mostly bachelor's degrees. However, "college" can also refer to an organization that exists within a university.

Here are some examples of those organizations within a university:

- College of Science
- College of Liberal Arts

- College of Communication
- College of Arts and Sciences
- College of Education

An independent college

Bowdoin College is an independent institution located in Brunswick, Maine. It would generally be considered an undergraduate institution—that is, a college. Bowdoin offers, for instance, bachelor's degrees in Art History, Chemistry, Classics, and Computer Science. Bowdoin College offers several master's degrees but doesn't have a doctoral program.

A college that's part of a university

The College of Arts and Sciences is part of the University of North Texas. This college offers many different bachelor's degrees, including degrees in Women's Studies, Physics, and Journalism.

Other colleges

This might get a little confusing, but you should also know that some colleges offer two-year degrees rather than four-year bachelor's degrees. What used to be called "junior colleges" are now often called "community colleges," and they sponsor degrees that take about two years (if you're going full-time) to complete. Students who take classes at a community college often transfer most, if not all, of their course work to a four-year college, where they then earn a bachelor's degree.

So what do I mean when I say "college"?

This all leads me to the fact that, when I refer to "college," I'm talking specifically about either a four-year college that exists within a university or operates as a self-sustaining institution. However, when I talk about "the college experience" or "the college life," I'm referring to the undergraduate experience of students seeking a bachelor's degree.

Further divisions of undergraduate study

Different universities and colleges are organized in a variety of ways, so again I'll be talking in broad generalities here.

At a large university, the undergraduate program has components called "colleges," "divisions," or "schools." Each of those units is then further divided into "departments."

For example, the University of California, Los Angeles, has the following divisions that offer bachelor's degrees:

- Division of Honors and Undergraduate Programs
- Division of Humanities
- Division of Life Sciences
- Division of Physical Sciences
- Division of Social Sciences

Each of the above divisions will have multiple departments. Within the UCLA Division of Life Sciences, for instance, you'll find the following departments:

- Microbiology, Immunology, and Molecular Genetics
- Molecular, Cell, and Developmental Biology
- Organismic Biology, Ecology, and Evolution
- Physiological Science
- Psychology

A university "school" can also have multiple departments. UCLA's School of the Arts and Architecture has six departments:

- Architecture and Urban Design
- Art
- Design—Media Arts
- Ethnomusicology
- Music
- World Arts and Cultures

In sum, then, large universities are divided into colleges, divisions, and schools that are themselves divided into departments.

A note about special programs within a college or school

At some institutions you'll find within a college or school a special program that's not exactly a department but that nevertheless offers a major or a minor for a bachelor's degree. (We'll talk more about majors and minors later.) Generally, these kinds of programs require students to take a certain number of courses sponsored by various departments. You'll often hear the phrase, "interdisciplinary program." These kinds of programs typically have the word "studies" in the name, such as the Asian Studies program at Southern Methodist University.

Special programs depend, for their lifeblood, upon the good will of academic departments that allow their faculty to fulfill part or all of their teaching within the special program. Those programs often do not possess quite the status of the long-established "departments," but they are both more focused and yet more inclusive than the older disciplines. Compare, for instance, the innovative American Studies programs at many campuses with the better recognized but more rigid History departments.

Divisions within graduate schools

This gets more complicated; but suffice it to say that many, though not all, of the same departments offering bachelor's degrees will also be authorized to offer graduate degrees through the university's graduate school.

The Graduate School at Cornell University, for example, confers various master's and doctoral degrees. Through this school, you can earn, for instance, a Master of Arts in English, a Master of Science in Chemistry, or a Doctor of Philosophy in History.

Who reports to whom

OK, we've covered the basic academic divisions within a university. Now let's talk about who's who in the university scheme of things. Different universities will have different hierarchies, but I'll offer a general description so you'll at least be familiar with the fundamentals. Once you attend a particular university or college, you should familiarize yourself with your particular list of who's who. On the following page, take a brief look at the organization of the academic side of a university.

As you can see in Illustration 3.1 (on the following page), universities are basically organized around a hierarchy that begins with the student and ends with a board of regents or trustees. (In the case of state universities, the hierarchy would continue beyond the board or regents and extend to the state legislature and governor.) Looking at the illustration on the next page, let's start from the bottom and work our way upward.

Faculty within a department

For your purposes, the most important persons in this chain of hierarchy are the professors who teach you and who may end up supervising your research and writing your letters of recommendation when you graduate.

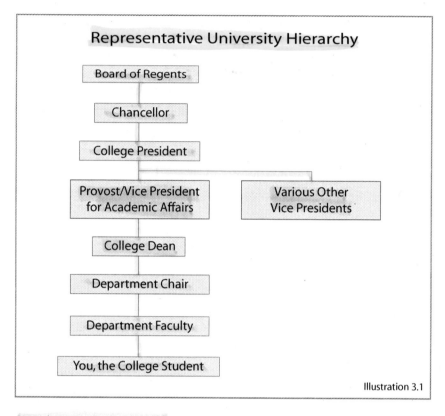

Representative University Hierarchy

Board of Regents

Chancellor

College President

Provost/Vice President for Academic Affairs

Various Other Vice Presidents

College Dean

Department Chair

Department Faculty

You, the College Student

Illustration 3.1

A note about tenure

Now's a good time to talk about what "tenure" means. Most universities award tenure to professors who are hired on a tenure-track appointment. They are reviewed annually and are then voted up or down for tenure (that is, for permanent job security) following their sixth year of service. Tenure implies that a professor has made significant contributions to his or her field of study and is generally a good teacher. Tenure, in theory, allows the professor freedom of expression.

Different kinds of faculty

There are basically six ranks of faculty:

1. Teaching assistants

These are graduate students who are earning their stripes. Most are working towards a master's degree or a Ph.D. They often teach the initial, introductory courses. You'll likely end up taking several of your early classes from teaching assistants.

2. **Lecturers**

   These are generally persons who have already earned their Ph.D. but who are not on tenure-track employment. They work from year to year, according to the needs of the department.

3. **Adjuncts**

   Adjuncts are very much like lecturers. They are hired from semester to semester, according to the needs of the department.

4. **Assistant professors**

   Assistant professors are usually hired directly out of graduate school and arrive to commence their six-year period of professional initiation, with the goal of obtaining tenure. You will often find assistant professors busily working on their first book, or on the several article-length manuscripts they must publish to earn tenure in a given department. Wanting to do everything "right," they are often among the finest and most energetic teachers in a department.

5. **Associate professors**

   After assistant professors gain tenure, they are usually promoted to the rank of associate professor. The expectation is that they will continue to be productive faculty members and work their way up to the next academic rank—usually five to eight years following their promotion to associate professor.

6. **Professors**

   "Full professors" have already passed through the rank of assistant and associate professor. They have presumably done so on the basis of a distinguished publishing record that connotes significant contributions to their field of study. They are often the leading professors in their fields of study and frequently have the most influence in the department.

The department chair

All faculty are hired by a department that exists within a college or school. (As I mentioned before, every college or school contains multiple departments, each specializing in a particular subject.) At the head of a department you have either a department "head" or a department chairman (often referred to as a "chair"). The department chair is appointed by, and reports to, the dean of the college or school.

The dean

Each college or school will be headed by a dean. The dean of the college or school is usually assisted by various associate and assistant deans. Much of the policy and procedures of the individual departments is set and enforced by this mid-level administrator, the dean.

The provost

Deans often report to a person who has the "double" title of "Provost and Vice President for Academic Affairs." The Office of the Provost exists within an arena known as the "central administration"—that is, the upper management division of a university.

The president and beyond

The provost usually reports to the college president. The college president of a private university reports to a governing board, often called the Board of Regents or the Board of Trustees.

The president of a state university reports to a board of regents; or, if the university is part of a "system" of universities (major state universities often have campuses in several cities), then the several university presidents answer to the system chancellor, who oversees all the universities within the system.

A chancellor is then accountable to a board of regents appointed by the governor of the state.

Who's who in the graduate school

At the head of the graduate school is a dean appointed by the Provost and Vice President for Academic Affairs. A number of associate and assistant deans then help coordinate the operation of the graduate school. Fundamentally, though, graduate schools are composed of the "graduate faculty" within various departments. Those faculty members offer advanced graduate courses for graduate students and are thus referred to as the "graduate faculty." In most universities, faculty members will likely teach a combination of undergraduate and graduate-level courses.

Conclusion

Don't be surprised if your particular university is organized somewhat differently. But the terms and concepts will be the same, and you'll have a "heads up" on who's who on your campus by grasping this hierarchical structure.

Section 2 :: The Ideal College Education

Chapter Four

Looking at the Big Picture: What Are You Aiming For?

This book is about planning for college success and achievement. The fact is, you should really plan for achievement long before you step foot on campus. Or even if you've already begun your college experience, now's the time to look down the road and think about where you're going and how you want to get there.

Of course, many opinions exist about what college achievement is, and later on we'll talk more about different viewpoints. My own perspective is primarily goal-oriented. I value goals in *any* endeavor—and especially in endeavors that require a commitment of four years of work and tens of thousands of dollars.

Here's my viewpoint: the ideal college experience significantly expands your curiosity and intellectual horizons, sharpens your analytical skills, encourages you to keep learning throughout your life, and leaves you poised to apply to a graduate (or professional) school, with the realistic hope that those graduate schools or professional programs will not only admit you but also pay you to be there. That financial assistance may take the form of scholarships, fellowships, or teaching assistantships. The scholarship or fellowship might also originate from an independent foundation or government agency.

On the horizon: Graduate school

You may be surprised to hear me say, so early in a book about *undergraduate* college success, that you should have a graduate or professional program in mind from the outset. But you most certainly should. The point is that graduate-school scholarships essentially reward only ideal undergraduate educations. And what if you choose *not* to attend graduate school? No problem: the successful college experience that prepares you for graduate-school applications also leaves you positioned to begin a rewarding career, with the potential for growth and advancement.

Your goals

So what should you be aiming for? What do you want to have "in your pocket" (besides a diploma) as you leave the graduation ceremony? If you examine what graduate schools or scholarship foundations seek from their applicants, you'll get a close-up view of what makes for an optimal college experience. Later in this book, we'll examine common questions you'll find in scholarship applications, but for now we'll focus on general accomplishments.

My own experience as a student, teacher, administrator, and advisor suggests that you should want to be able to boast of the following accomplishments and abilities by the time you graduate:

1. High grades

You ought to aim for a GPA of 3.8 to 4.0, especially in your major field of study. Some of you may deem high grades your only goal. *Wrong!* Good grades are but the first of several qualifications you want to accumulate.

2. Passionate competency

It is vital to achieve better-than-basic competency in a certain aspect of your curriculum. Indeed, you should demonstrate both an intellectual and emotional passion for your major field of study. By the time you're a college senior applying to graduate programs, your academic record, admission essays, and interview statements should imply that you've immersed yourself in this major because you find it fascinating to live and breathe that specific subject matter. Be prepared to talk about your field with expertise, fascination, and passion. That passion should reflect your determination to make a difference in either the theoretical or vocational dimensions of your area of study.

3. Contribution to a field of study

Strive, during your undergraduate career, to make a unique contribution to your field of study (through individual or team research), or to have a public "showing" of either research or creative endeavors (perhaps via poster-board presentations). Such contributions emerge from senior-honors theses, music recitals, fine-arts exhibits, entrepreneurial adventures, or participation in groundbreaking research teams.

4. **Capacity for innovation, exploration, and creativity**

   Develop techniques for conducting research and making discoveries in unexplored areas of your field of study. Your work should reflect your capacity for innovation and the joy you take in the play of ideas relating to your area of research or academic discipline in general.

5. **Taking responsibility for self-learning**

   Exhibit a propensity for self-learning. This involves taking initiative and accepting responsibility for your personal education. Identify leading books in your field and read them—whether or not a professor assigns those in any of your courses. Also, read articles in your field's top three or four academic journals. Know the current controversies and debates.

6. **Experience in the field**

   While you attend college, work a reasonable number of hours in your field of study, though not necessarily for pay. Even internships and participation on college research teams will demonstrate that you can complete projects, handle responsibility, communicate with peers and professors, and put your knowledge to real-world use. Employers and graduate admissions officers like to see outstanding students who have had some impressive hands-on work experience.

7. **Beginnings of professional networking**

   Establish professional relationships—both on and off campus—with leaders in the field. By the time you have finished your junior year of study, you should be able to approach at least three professors and realistically expect a *detailed*, positive letter of recommendation from them. That will require your establishing contact with them outside of the classroom. By that, I don't mean that you should invite them out for a beer; rather, you should initiate independent-study courses and research projects that entail ongoing dialogue well after you complete a course.

8. **Target specific jobs for postgraduate employment**

   It's not enough just to plan to work in a field of interest. You should plan to work in a *particular job* within a *particular field* (such as a patent lawyer, computer engineer, Methodist minister, cardiologist, or a political campaign director), as soon as possible. Better yet, have three particular jobs in mind following your senior year, or after graduate school; then think of one job that you'd like to have ten more years down the road. Knowing what you're aiming for will help you plan your degree program and seek part-time employment or internships opportunities early enough in your college career to help you reach your goals. You may, of course, end up changing your mind before your college career is over. That's fine. Just keep envisioning possible jobs, even if you're inclined to be flexible about the vocational outcome of your college education.

9. Campus participation/community service

Contribute in some way to the college or local community. This could be as simple as sitting on committees, participating in honors societies, or serving in student governance. You don't want your service to be so time-consuming as to compromise your grades. On the other hand, you can bolster your credentials if your service dovetails with your career goals and if you have exhibited *leadership*. When assessing the "service" dimensions of your college career, many national scholarship agencies distinguish between mere "membership" and genuine "leadership."

10. Leadership

Whether on campus, in the local community, or in your field of study, organize a constructive and helpful activity that would not have happened without you. If that leadership activity relates to your field of study, all the better. (Example: You, an English major, invite a local author to speak on campus about her most recent novel and then recruit several professors to participate in a follow-up panel discussion about narrative technique. Other examples would include organizing a student panel at a professional conference in any of the social sciences, or starting an annual juried art show if you're majoring in art.)

11. Communication skills

Develop excellent writing and verbal skills for a variety of situations. Try to have at least one publication, even if it's an opinion piece in the campus newspaper. Cultivate public-speaking opportunities, if only at local "Toastmasters" clubs. Learn to converse with professionals in your field (and adults in general) on an equal-to-equal basis.

12. Time-management skills

Develop work and study habits conducive to meeting deadlines and overseeing big projects. (Graduating from college with distinction is itself a big project!) Elsewhere I mention a DayTimer® approach to college life. Buy a DayTimer®; use it religiously.

13. Risk-taking and competitive spirit

Demonstrate a willingness to experiment, to take chances, to go out on a limb. Show that you enjoy a challenge. Do so through research endeavors or by entering student contests, such as writing competitions or art shows. Many professional organizations have awards for student work, including prizes for computer animation, film, or website design. Most academic departments have a number of competitive scholarships that they award for "best essay" or "best student." Find out what those are and then apply.

14. Expanding horizons

Develop interests that make you a well-rounded human being, especially if your exposure to the fine arts has previously been limited. Attend symphonies, art exhibits, and dance performances. If you're already a fine-arts major, consider taking an interest in, say, archeology or baseball. If there's an international center on campus, make an effort to chat and converse with students from abroad.

Whatever your outside interests, always have a fairly "highbrow" book you are reading for pleasure and that you are prepared to discuss. Students interviewing for scholarships often get questions about their current "fun" reading or favorite author (and you better have read more than one book by this "favorite" author!).

15. National and world citizenship

Be "up" on local, national, and international events. Have an opinion about hot topics and be ready to articulate your thoughts. Do so by regularly reading columns and editorials in your favorite newspaper, journal, or on a good website. Be open-minded in your opinions of current events, but always be ready to offer your principled, personal perspective. Being unopinionated and "wishy-washy" won't "wash" in interview situations. By extension, be capable of suggesting how your study, work, and talents will help make the world a better place.

Combining skills

Just in case you're thinking that all this seems too much, it's not. Many of these goals overlap, and some of your work and projects will accomplish more than one goal. For instance, consider this scenario:

You independently read about a current controversy in your field and then meet with a few professors to exchange views on the subject. You do extra reading to learn more about the subject and various points of view relating to the controversy. You incorporate your independent thoughts about the controversy into a paper. After professors offer feedback, you revise the paper several times and then present it at a student panel that you've organized, having also invited a few off-campus professionals to be panelists.

This one activity accomplished most of the goals detailed above. And think what you would have learned in the process. We each have our strong points, and you will end up emphasizing some goals more than others. Still, keep *all* of these goals on your list of "things I ought to do at college."

A real-life scenario

I've attached to this section two memos that you should look over and seriously ponder as you start your college career. These two documents are "real life" memos that I send to professors who are writing letters of recommendations for students applying for prestigious scholarships. I have also included a letter of recommendation that I wrote for a student whose range of accomplishments was formidable. Read over the memos and the letter and think to yourself: "Will I be able to ask three professors to talk about me in this way?" "Will these professors have lots of wonderful things to say about me?"

The rest of this book will help you answer these questions with a resounding "Yes!"

Conclusion

Structure a college education that will allow professors to write wonderful things about you, and specifically about your potential to make contributions to your area of study.

Letter to Faculty Endorsing Students for Rhodes, Marshall, or Mitchell Scholarships

You will best assist our nominating committee by writing a one-and-a-half to two-page single-spaced letter describing your impressions of this student. Might you consider responding, beyond whatever other categories you choose to cover, to the following questions when you construct your narrative?

Why does this student stand out? Please speak on the basis of direct observation. What is your basis of comparison, relative to the best students you have taught or observed?

Does the student have a lively intellect and **intellectual breadth**? Does the student demonstrate **curiosity**?

To what extent does the student have the ability to get things done? By extension, what is the student's intellectual promise for **advanced** achievement in his/her field of study?

If you are the student's **primary research** director, might you share a perspective that allows our committee to appreciate, relative to your field of study, the **nature and scope of the student's accomplishment**?

Has the student demonstrated the capacity to **work with others**? Please offer examples and specific outcomes.

Can you speak to the matter of whether the student is **compassionate**? Can you, by extension, comment on the student's **general character**?

Can you speak about the student's **leadership**, either in the local community or in the field of study? Most scholarship foundations look for leaders in a student's chosen discipline, and it would be helpful to have primary academic recommenders define what leadership is, relative to your discipline (in the lab and elsewhere), with respect to **intelligence, planning, and ability to communicate**. How does the student rank in these ways?

If the student is in the sciences, please assess, if possible, the student's **"community" interaction** in a lab setting, as well as the student's leadership in that setting. To what extent does the student's sense of community and leadership in the lab **foreshadow similar qualities associated with**

leadership in your discipline or profession? Might recommenders in the humanities and social sciences address this question as it might pertain to the "community" of scholars in their disciplines?

What are the student's prospects of making future contributions to the discipline? What, moreover, is the student's capacity to use his/her discipline or personal gifts to help change the world for the better?

Sincerely,

James Duban
Director
Office for Nationally Competitive Scholarships

Letter to Faculty Endorsing Students for
Barry M. Goldwater Scholarships in Math and Science

Thank you for taking time to write a comprehensive letter of endorsement for the student who presents this letter to you. This year's field of applicants is quite impressive. Letters of recommendation will, therefore, be especially vital when the campus nominating committee shortlists our maximum of four nominees. Allow me to mention several categories that would assist the committee in its deliberations.

Although with some variation, endorsement letters for previous Goldwater Scholars have:

a. been a least one and a half pages, single-spaced typing, with double-spacing between paragraphs. The research directors of Goldwater winners have typically written a two-page letter. The thoroughness of endorsement letters has significant weight at both the campus and foundation levels of deliberation;

b. typically opened with an assessment of this student's merit. Please offer, when possible, quantitative information and memorable examples of the student's scientific/mathematical acumen;

c. specified examples of mastery, accomplishment, and initiative to help the nominating committee assess relative merit;

d. typically concluded with an overall judgment about the **student's future as a research scientist**. Please avoid concluding sentences that urge the committee to contact you for further information.

If you have *supervised the student's research,* our committee wishes to hear about the student's potential to work on his/her own, or as a part of a research team. We would also appreciate your assessment of the student's claims, as recorded in the completed application, **about having made important contributions to the research project**. Stated otherwise, do the student's contributions **go beyond the mere following of directions**? (I am asking the student to present you with a completed copy of his/her application, with those claims highlighted in yellow.) **To what degree has the student made independent contributions through personal initiative**? Might you reiterate the nature of the research enterprise, comment on the **importance of the student's contribution** to your research project and to the profession, and predict what your student's current work signifies about his/her future an as independent researcher? The campus nominating committee is attentive, as is the Goldwater Foundation, to the student's aptitude for advanced research, and whether that aptitude is evidenced (when possible) by the student's having had a *pattern* of research experiences over several semesters in two or more locations. The information requested above will allow committee members to distinguish among good, better, and best, relative to the talent and prospects of our applicants.

If you have instructed the student in math, would you go into some detail about the substance of the course, the relative difficulty of the concepts that the student had to master, and the degree of sophistication shown by the student in both the syllabus-oriented coursework and **especially in any additional projects that you assigned to the student**? The latter information, when it exists, will be especially important information for our committee. If this student took the lead in a group project, our committee would want to know about that.

If you feel that the student's performance in math indicates **potential for success** in his/her field of specialty (in the event that the student is concentrating in something other than math), please feel free to offer your observations. If your status as a mathematician allows you to provide a unique perspective on the candidate's research project, here is the place to share those thoughts. On behalf of my colleagues on the nominating committee, thank you for creating time, amidst so many other responsibilities, to write a comprehensive letter of assessment.

Sincerely,

James Duban
Director
Office for Nationally Competitive Scholarships

Example Letter of Recommendation

I am pleased to recommend Daren Walters [pseudonym] for admission to your MFA program in Creative Writing. Daren was my student in two classes devoted to American literature, and in each class he demonstrated outstanding intellect and masterful writing. I would easily rank Daren among the top five undergraduates whom I have taught over the past 29 years at Cornell University, The University of Texas at Austin, and the University of North Texas. Daren has the intellect and discipline to excel in a rigorous graduate program. He also regards creative writing as something of a calling and has chosen to forego a career in the Foreign Service to pursue this passion. He will, I am confident, become a wonderful poet and professor (since he plans, as well, to earn a Ph.D.).

Daren's creative work usually takes the form of dense lyric poetry, eight-to-ten lines in length, featuring an intensity of image and diction that bespeaks artistic accomplishment and indicates immense potential for Daren's future as a poet. He aspires to become part of English literary tradition, and he appears to have the muse and passion to give it a shot. In a recent e-mail correspondence from Geneva, Daren remarked, "I have a very real sense of wanting to be part of the tradition of poetry. I feel that I have something to contribute creatively, and it seems wrong not to act on that belief." Although I've conversed with him about the poor academic job market for creative writers, he is still determined; his conviction is heartfelt.

Because Daren enrolled in two of my literature classes, I have more frequently dealt with his impressive literary analyses. Two of his papers readily come to mind. In the first, devoted to Faulkner's "A Rose for Emily," Daren argued that the narrator's pronoun choice (wavering between references either to "we" or "they") allows the narrator to veil his own complicity in the town's highly questionable response to Miss Emily. According to Daren, these verbal traces permit the narrator to distance himself from the town's collective guilt over the treatment of Miss Emily. The second of Daren's papers—about Ralph Ellison's *Invisible Man*—posits a narrator's sleight of hand to compensate for his inability to remain an unbiased witness of history. The result, Daren claims, is a "fiction within a fiction." In both essays, Daren elevates the reader's esteem for the aesthetic accomplishment of these diverse works of fiction, showing, as well, how the artistic achievement of each work relates to its social context and concerns.

Although Daren has not yet had time to undertake a complete search of secondary scholarship relating to each narrative, I am confident that his perspectives are innovative enough one day to be published. In any event, Daren's writing clearly illustrates that he understands the mission of scholarly prose—to take us beyond the status quo of knowledge and insight. He seeks to do the same through poetical utterance.

I recommend Daren, moreover, because he graduated with a perfect 4.0 GPA, because he is fluent in French and German, because he has won numerous academic scholarships, because he evidenced exquisite leadership as a Resident Assistant who supervised many undergraduates living in residence halls, and because he is now a Rotary Ambassadorial Scholar studying in Geneva, Switzerland. The $26,000 Rotary Ambassadorial Scholarship was one of only a few available in a 60-city district of North Texas. That scholarship honors somebody who is both academically accomplished and whose ambassadorial character and mannerism suggest that he will exquisitely represent America in distant parts of the globe. I know that Daren's year abroad will further inspire his creative insights and sensitivities.

Daren, in sum, is one of the most intelligent, genial, and talented undergraduates I have ever known. He will excel in an MFA program and certainly go on to earn a Ph.D. in creative writing.

Daren deserves a chance to have his individual talent become part of the poetic tradition. He has my enthusiastic recommendation.

Sincerely,

James Duban
Professor of English
Director, Office for Nationally Competitive Scholarships

Chapter Five

Anticipating Graduate or Professional School Early

Yes, this book is devoted to the "ideal" undergraduate experience and to offering students insights into the ingredients of that recipe. Still, my frequent references to graduate school should not confuse students or parents whose primary thought is, "I just want us to get through four years of an undergraduate degree, and then get a good job."

The point is this: graduate school may—just may—turn out to be the outcome of a model undergraduate experience; and if that experience is truly ideal, you may not have to pay a penny to go on to graduate school and earn either your master's degree or doctoral degree. Many of the best students *are paid* to do so (more on that below).

The professional schools

First, an ideal undergraduate education often leads to what are actually graduate programs in the fields of medicine and law. In other words, Law School and Medical School are simply two of many "graduate programs."

Because some students already know they want to be doctors, lawyers, veterinarians, etc., before they enter college, they are aware (early on) that college is only the first step towards their professional goal.

Graduate programs can sneak up on you

Other students, however, don't realize—until they are pretty far into their undergraduate program—that they should additionally plan on postgraduate study. Often one is expected to have more than a bachelor's degree to be qualified for a particular job. A master's degree or Ph.D. may well be the gatekeeper for higher salaries or initial opportunities at gainful employment. Think, for instance of grade-school, middle-school, or high-school teachers, whose salaries leap significantly with each new degree, or whose chances of climbing the administrative ladder increasingly grow dependent upon their having earned a master's degree or a Ph.D.

The M.B.A.

Then, of course, there is the Master of Business Administration (M.B.A.), and everything it implies to big companies about somebody's being qualified to assume administrative responsibility (think, for example, about President George W. Bush, who earned an M.B.A. at Harvard, and then went on to become an executive in the oil business, a big-league baseball owner, a Governor of Texas, and, of course, President of the United States).

You may come back to graduate school later in life

Nor is it the case that graduate school will necessarily follow directly upon the heels of the undergraduate experience. I have several friends who went back to school "years later" to earn their master's degrees—one in the field of education; another, in the area of business administration. Both found that their career paths and commitments eventually mandated a master's degree in order for them to qualify for the next stage of administrative advancement in their chosen professions.

The Ph.D., in turn, becomes a "must" for anybody who wishes eventually to teach at the college level, or to gain certification that will (as in a number of fields) solidify their credentials for higher-level administrative appointment, or to establish themselves as an authority in their area of interest.

Whether or not you choose to enter graduate school directly after earning your bachelor's degree, the ideal education ought to leave you entirely ready to do so. Moreover, as described elsewhere in this book, many graduate schools actually pay the best undergraduates to earn their combined master's and Ph.D. degrees—yet those offers seldom go to anybody other than students who have accomplished the ideal college experience.

Conclusion

Keep an open mind about entering graduate school, and about the undergraduate accomplishments that will help you gain admission should you eventually choose to pursue an M.A. or a Ph.D.

Chapter Six

Picking a Major and Identifying Specific Career Goals

Your major will be the primary academic area in which you choose to earn a college degree. After you select your major, you end up taking around eight or ten introductory (i.e., lower-division) and advanced (i.e., upper-division) courses in that one department (English, Mathematics, Biology, History, Business, for instance) in order to fulfill its degree-plan requirements. Below (and in general conversation) the term "major" is interchangeable with "field of study" or "discipline."

A "minor" field of study is one in which you traditionally take about four upper-division courses. Many universities require that you select a "minor" field of study in order to have you be that much better-rounded. I have seen students whose minors were whimsical as well as those who picked a minor because of its compatibility with the major field of study. I'll have more to say about that below.

Picking a major

There are three basic options for declaring a major:

1. **Early, with specific career goal**
   If you have a specific career goal, you can declare a suitable major early on.

2. **Early, with vague career goal**
   Even if you don't have a specific career goal, you can still declare a major early on, preferably in a field of study for which you have a strong interest and demonstrated aptitude. Indeed, the closer you come to your true "passion"—so much the better.

3. Later, after sampling around

You can spend time sampling various disciplines to see where your interests, aptitude, and talent actually reside before declaring a major midway through your college career. Quite a few professors and universities would urge the last approach to choosing a major. In fact, they defend "core" graduation requirements (those courses that everyone at the college must take regardless of their major) on just those grounds. Core requirements, most of which you will take in your freshman and sophomore years, introduce you to a variety of disciplines, allowing an opportunity to discover your true calling after an appropriate year or two of soul searching.

I was once a proponent of the "take-your-time-to-find-yourself" approach to declaring a major, but my perspective has changed somewhat. Let me tell you why.

The upside of declaring your major from the get-go

If you declare a major early on, and if you truly have the aptitude to excel in that field of study, you enhance your prospects of establishing yourself as a top student within the department in which you major. By declaring that major in either the second semester of your freshman year, or during your sophomore year, you'll have more opportunities to cultivate professional relationships with the department's faculty members. If you impress them enough, they might, as early as your sophomore year, take you on in a research capacity or otherwise find ways of encouraging you to succeed. While research opportunities might at first prove basic, those assignments can grow more complex and impressive by your junior year and position you for national scholarship competition and graduate-school applications (more about that below, too) by the time you are a second-semester junior or a first-semester senior. Students who "take their time" to declare a major often make their decision during their junior year of college and simply don't have sufficient time to cultivate research relationships with their professors.

By declaring a major early on, you'll also have more time to develop independent expertise in your field and then have a chance to take advanced courses in your major beyond those required for graduation. You'll likely participate in a departmental honors program (if that is available) and, I think, be more inclined to locate part-time employment or internships that relate to your field of study. All of these accomplishments are important aspects of my definition of the ideal college experience.

College career centers

You may ask yourself, "But how can I select a major when I don't really know what I want to 'do' with my life?" Many colleges have career centers where counselors will advise you about this issue. They even have tests designed to match your aptitude and personality with a given profession. Another idea is to seek interviews with professionals in the fields you are contemplating. Look into those possibilities. Once you've identified a prospective vocation, visit the academic department in which you'd most likely major in order to prepare for that career. Speak with the undergraduate advisor about a possible "game plan," including internships, for attaining a productive major (find out, moreover, if your university has a placement program).

Why you should chalk up accomplishments before your senior year

I'm emphasizing achievement *early on* in your college career since, if you intend to apply to graduate school (or to compete for a national scholarship), you'll usually begin writing your application essays at the end of your junior year and over the summer leading into your senior year. What will you have to talk about? What will your professors who write letters of recommendation for you be able to say? The answer is, "whatever you've done *up to that point*"—that is, during your freshman, sophomore, and junior years.

If you spend your freshman and sophomore years simply "sampling" among disciplines and not establishing inroads into a particular field, that leaves only your junior year for you to undertake all that needs to be done to establish yourself with distinction in a specific discipline.

In that sense, college is very much like high school. When you apply to college in your senior year of high school, you must be able to boast a record of accomplishment up to that point, regardless of presumably stellar "work in progress." The same holds true for college. You are therefore at an advantage if you are able to define your major early on and successfully immerse yourself in that field of study while also fulfilling the general "core" requirements demanded of all students.

If you follow this advice you'll be at an advantage when you begin applying for jobs during your senior year. Résumés should feature a "history" of achievement; they should illustrate a track record of performance to back up details about *current* initiatives and the more distant vocational goals.

The downsides of declaring a major early on

Not everyone will want to declare a major early on. Some students shouldn't. One downside to declaring a major too early occurs if the major doesn't work out. If you've taken four or five upper-division courses in your major and then decide to switch to another major, that change will likely extend your graduation by a year or more while you fulfill the requirements of the new major. That delay can cost you and your family anywhere from $10,000 to $30,000, depending on whether you're attending a public or private university.

Then there's the fact that some students just may not have a clue about what they're really suited for; a cafeteria-style approach to college in the first couple of years may be in their best interest until they are ready to settle down. For such a student, sampling would be better than committing oneself to a major too early and then making bad grades that permanently mar an academic record.

But even if you opt for the "sampling" approach to your freshman and sophomore years of college, start to build your leadership credentials as early as possible, and consider undertaking supplementary work in your various courses. By conducting an extra research assignment, you'd be learning more about the field and impressing some professor with your initiative. That commitment of above-and-beyond effort on your part might result in the sort of rapport with a professor that will lead to your majoring in that particular field of study.

Majoring after attending a two-year college

Numerous students attend a junior, community, or two-year college (I'll refer to all of these generally as a "community college") while fulfilling basic and core requirements that "transfer in" to the four-year university. Students who enroll at a community college sometimes do so for financial reasons (tuition is often cheaper and it's often possible to live at home) or because they're apprehensive about going to a "big university" before they're ready.

Community college is a place where many students learn a great deal, find professors who are very supportive, and complete numerous core requirements that often transfer to the four-year college. When these students finally enter a four-year university, they frequently know exactly what they want to do and precisely what their major will be. For the reasons discussed above, however, it's vital that transfer students hit the "big-university" road with all four wheels spinning. In particular, they need to go out of their way, by the end of their junior year of college, to engage in a summer research project (or some other similar endeavor) that brings them into closer contact with one of the professors at the four-year campus. If, because of the transfer scenario, they take a year longer to graduate, or to figure out exactly what to major in, *so be it*. Just make good use of the extra year and achieve as much as possible.

I might add that, when students achieve a very high GPA at a community college and then earn a very high GPA at their four-year college, that record of excellence works in their favor by demonstrating a continuity of achievement in two different academic settings. Conversely, when students do *not* do very well in community college but then do splendidly at a four-year university, that record of improvement speaks to their maturity in having finally "found themselves" once they settled upon a major and accomplished so much within it.

So, when do I pick a major?

There's no easy answer to this question. Economic realities, though, dictate against the "hell-if-I-know-or-care" attitude about majors so popular in several decades of the twentieth century.

Factors to consider when picking a major

While you may end up anguishing over a choice of majors, you can take several steps to make your initial choice a wise one and to enhance the probability that you won't switch any time soon. Keep the following advice in mind:

- **Know thyself**

  First, you should assess whether you have the necessary educational background, motivation, and credentials to undertake your major of choice. If you are uncertain, you should seek guidance to identify careers in which you'll most likely flourish. Students may wish to seek "career assessment" profiles, or to take advantage of campus counseling services designed to help them "find themselves."

- **Still, be open-minded**

  Sometimes, though, the "sample around" approach to college does work the way it's supposed to. Students *do* now and then take a required (core) course, become inspired by the professor and/or subject matter, and conclude, "This is it!" Just make sure that you possess the foundational skills necessary to prosper in this designated major or field of study. I believe that most stu-

39

dents lose interest in a major not from boredom, but from being academically unprepared to do well in advanced courses in that major. If mathematics has always been your weak point, why contemplate a major in accounting or physics?

- **Research your major**

  Undertake research about what's required in your projected major and be realistic about whether you have the aptitude and background to succeed there. In particular, make sure your math skills are up to speed for any math or science majors. If you're not well suited for a particular major, it's better to intuit that early on rather than bring your Grade Point Average (GPA) down in your freshman and sophomore years.

  As you move through college and beyond, so much hinges upon your cumulative GPA. You don't want consistently to be apologizing for a wretched freshman, sophomore, or junior year because "I didn't know what I was getting into."

  I urge you, therefore, to interview professors and undergraduate advisors to learn what's entailed in "the long run" before you travel the path of a particular major. If you choose a major wisely and then get involved productively in your department, you will feel a sense of accomplishment, fulfillment, professional identity, and positive reinforcement that will likely encourage you to remain in that field of study. While many other students will just be beginning to get their bearings within a "new" major, you will be well on the road to a research endeavor or internship that will serve as the foundation for your future distinction as an undergraduate, graduate student, or working "professional" in your discipline.

- **Looking way down the road: Job prospects**

  Similarly, I'd urge you to investigate graduate-school placement and job-placement statistics for graduating seniors within your prospective department. (If department advisors are evasive, be wary.) News organizations periodically review "average starting salaries" for college graduates having different majors. You ought to know that information. (See the Resources section for websites that will help you compare prospective job salaries.)

- **The "liberal arts" exception**

  Often, your major in college leads to a professional or graduate-school program that seems remote from traditional job prospects for a given "major." For instance, to prepare for law school, many students build their analytical skills by majoring in English, History, or Political Science. These students probably are not too concerned about the problematic job prospects for liberal arts students because they already plan to move on to law school. Still, because you can't "bank" on being accepted into a law (or other graduate) school, consider the long-range vocational benefits of your prospective "major" before making that commitment.

Double majors and double minors

The most ambitious students often have double majors and double minors. In effect, these students enroll in double-degree programs and literally complete the equivalent of two separate degrees in nearly the same time that it takes most students to complete a single degree. I can think of one student, for instance, who had an interest in international law. Accordingly, she majored in German and Political Science, while minoring in Mathematics and Business. (A "minor" usually consists of four upper-division courses in a field other than your major.) She argued that all of the thinking processes and skills entailed in these majors and minors were ultimately compatible—relative to logic, legal reasoning, problem-solving, and international law. She made a good case and never earned anything less than an A in any of her courses.

Still, don't even think of doing a double degree unless you are an extraordinarily strong student who is capable of earning mostly As under stressful circumstances—and unless you genuinely thrive on such challenges. It's challenging enough to be impressive with one major and one minor.

The balancing act

In that same vein, having a "minor" field of study can have a tremendous impact upon your future employment prospects. If, for instance, you major in computer science and minor in Business or Management, you are likely to open up possibilities for administrative placement that would be closed to the straight "Computer Science" major. Similarly, if you major in Music, but minor in Business, you are setting yourself up to be your own booking agent and accountant some day.

If you are able to "double-major" in two related disciplines (without undertaking a double degree, which would entail enrolling in two separate minors, as well), the combination of knowledge and talent can have an immense impact upon your future. Picture, for example, a student who "double majors" in Political Science and Spanish, with the aim of eventually practicing law. Such a student significantly enhances his or her client base. But even these double-majors should be reserved for students who customarily earn all, or mostly all, As. In other words, having As in a *single* major is far better than earning Bs and Cs in a *double* major.

Conclusion

The decision about a major will remain difficult and may require a bit of soul searching and sampling before you resolve the issue to your satisfaction. Even if you *do* select a major early on but then find that you've made the wrong choice, don't feel that you're forever "locked in" to an unwanted major. The average student, it is said, changes his or her major three times; so one or two changes of mind on your part will not be out of the ordinary.

At every stage, give the decision as much forethought and research as possible before you make the plunge. And, as I explained before, the earlier you can "find yourself" the greater the odds that you'll accomplish what it takes to have the ideal college education.

Section 3 ::
Excelling in the Classroom

Chapter Seven

The Successful Freshman Year: An Overview

Be academically prepared

You should believe that, with enough hard work, you can and will succeed in college. Still, being prepared for the challenges of college makes a difference. If you are not adequately *prepared*, your hard work might prove futile. So let's talk about the preparation that leads to a successful freshman year.

Writing skills

Before you arrive at college, know the ins and outs of writing a well-structured, grammatically correct, and stylistically impressive essay. Students sometimes have so many problems with their writing that even the best effort in freshman English may yield little more than a C—not to mention poor grades in "writing component" courses across various disciplines, including the sciences (just think of your first detailed lab report).

If you are still in high school

Thus, if you are a *high-school senior*, I recommend that you begin college *before you arrive at college*. Do so by enrolling in a freshman English class at a community college near your home town or city. You may or may not receive transfer credit for that course when you enroll in your four-year college. Still, that summer course would be an excellent investment in your future. Work diligently to gain control of your writing before the beginning of your "real" first semester.

After completing that junior-college summer course, take freshman English when you enroll in your college of choice in the fall. If, however, a community college is your college of choice, then enroll in freshman English there during the summer before your first "long" semester. Also, never place out of freshman English, even if you have the "credit" or course equivalency to do so. (For the reasons why, see the chapter "Which Courses You Should *Not* Place Out Of.")

If you've already started college or are a returning student

If, however, you have *already started college*, then make writing courses a priority. Enroll—beyond freshman English—in intermediate or advanced expository writing classes taught by professors who are known to be great teachers of writing.

If you are among the many students nationwide who earned a decent grade in freshman English, but who still cannot write well, seek out further instruction from a professor who will teach you how to write with distinction by providing intensive editorial feedback. Here's an idea: Approach a senior professor with the proposition that you will submit a page-and-a-half essay (double-spaced) once a week. Let the professor know that the paper will have a thesis paragraph, two supporting paragraphs, and a conclusion. Simply ask the professor to offer feedback on your form, style, and argument and then to inspect the paper again, after you've addressed his or her original comments. Despite the brevity of the assignment, professors will still utilize 100 percent of the editorial acumen that they would expend on a longer paper. The brevity of the assignment, however, will dispose them to offer comprehensive feedback—perhaps far more than they would be inclined to offer had you submitted a ten-page essay featuring the same problems on every page. (I have, in fact, taught many writing classes this way.)

If you're not comfortable with writing college-level prose, the sooner you address this problem the better: ignoring it will neither resolve the situation nor prepare you for writing "beyond the academy." Just as you need to have mastered algebra before moving on to trigonometry, so you must master the craft of persuasive writing prior to enrolling in advanced courses in most major fields of study.

An added benefit: Getting to know your professor

There is, moreover, an added advantage to seeking out writing instruction above and beyond what your college requires: you will form a bond with professors who offer this instruction, and they will likely be inclined to write a wonderful letter of recommendation for you after you graduate. Can you imagine the delight with which most employers or graduate schools would read a recommendation describing how you took the initiative to improve your writing on a weekly basis through extra work spanning one or more semesters?

Finally, when seeking out professors who are willing to offer feedback on your writing, don't necessarily limit yourself to English professors. Just about all professors live in a world of "publish or perish," and nearly all are in a position to comment instructively on your writing. I have worked on committees featuring exquisite stylists from such departments as chemistry, physics, music, political science, and history. Since those professors are usually preoccupied with responsibilities somewhat distant from the teaching of composition, they might be all the more willing to take on the occasional student who seeks out their guidance about writing.

Preferably, approach professors in whose class you are currently enrolled and tailor your essays to topics relating to their class. I think you'll be pleasantly surprised by their willingness to assist. Think of the benefit you'll accrue from having your professor think of you as the student who wants to go the extra mile.

Making sure your math foundations are secure (sequence your courses optimally)

Conduct research into the ideal sequencing of math courses, relative to what you need to know in one course in order to succeed in the next. Make sure that you have your foundations down solid. I can remember how difficult I found a freshman course in engineering calculus when I had had problems with high-school algebra.

I also know an accomplished engineer who earned a B in a college math course, but who took the course again because he didn't feel that he had enough mastery of the material to proceed to the next course in the sequence. (He made an A the next time around and now is president of an engineering firm.)

Recently, moreover, I conversed with another successful engineer who said that, if he had the opportunity to "do it all over again," he would have taken far more math and physics courses to prepare for his career in engineering. His self-assessment spoke to the issue of a *foundational* approach to majoring in a given subject (this person, by the way, ranked ninth in the country in a major high-school math and science competition).

So sequencing is vital to mastery—whether it occurs when you're moving from high school to college, or from one course in college to another, or from an undergraduate degree plan to a graduate degree plan. Do not, however, try to compensate for deficiencies in mathematics by enrolling in *summer* math courses. Many of my colleagues in math and science believe that you can't reasonably expect to master mathematical concepts in six or eight weeks that usually take four months to grasp.

The difference between memorization and thinking: Putting on your thinking cap

In high school, many students prosper through memorization but without seriously contemplating what they've memorized. When they arrive at college, they are surprised to learn that memorization is not enough. College professors expect you to comment in detail about the facts you've memorized. In the humanities and social sciences, for instance, memorization is simply an outline that begs to be filled in with analytical detail. At issue is the difference between quantitative and qualitative thinking, the difference between rote learning and insightful analysis.

In that vein, I once had a student complain about the difficulty of my examination. "In high school," he said, "I just had to answer the list of questions at the back of each chapter." "At college," I responded, "life is more complex." The earlier you realize that, the better.

Learn to read critically

Don't just read material (or listen to lectures, for that matter) passively. Of course, your first goal is to understand what you are reading; but you are not a coffee cup to be filled with someone else's educational brew. You have the ability to learn material while generating critical (by which I mean either genuinely "critical" or genuinely "evaluative") insights about the material under consideration. In college, you are expected to improve this ability, which I will call critical reading.

When reading classroom material, frequently stop and think: "What is this author's perspective? What are the assumptions behind these assertions? Where is this author 'going' with this evidence?"

Remember that, in most disciplines, various "schools of thought" exist, and the author may very well be advocating a particular school without coming right out and saying so. (For this reason, never skip the introductory section of a book—where the author often discusses his work's governing principles.)

Don't think that, just because a professor has assigned an author's work, you are supposed to accept the author's conclusions—hook, line, and sinker. In fact, the professor may have assigned the material precisely to see whether or not you are a critical reader.

I, for one, value students who question what they read. That shows they assess and evaluate rather than merely regurgitate. Nor do I mind if students question my own outlook in classroom discussion. I appreciate their doing so courteously and conversationally. Such challenges keep things lively and cause other students to join in.

Here are some additional questions you can ask yourself as you read critically:

- Does the author recognize possible objections to his position, and does he do anything to anticipate and disarm those?
- What kind of evidence does the author bring to your attention to support conclusions?
- How else might this evidence be interpreted?
- What are the broader implications of the conclusions?
- Does the author have a vested interest in his point of view?

Even if you are reading literature, keep your "critical reading" hat on. For instance, here are some sample questions you could ask yourself as you read passages in a novel:

- In what ways does the *tone* (attitude) of this passage pertain to its meaning or impact? Can I accept the words at face value, or is the narrator or author being ironic?
- In what ways does this passage reflect a mindset representative of the era depicted in the novel?
- In what ways might the passage violate or challenge the thinking of the age in which it appears?
- Am I dealing with an original thought, or is there a history of ideas from which this thought derives?
- What is the vested interest of the author or the author's narrator or literary persona?

Always recall that the best critical reading occurs on a second or third reading. It's usually at that point that you know enough about the work at hand to begin to ask the right questions.

Critical reading, then, is far from a passive experience; it is, rather, investigative and evaluative. It's of the same order of inquiry that we find in an excellent book review. Rather than simply summarizing the events in a book, a fine book review seeks to articulate the author's perspective and achievements and then to enter into constructive critical dialogue regarding the assumptions and assertions of the book.

When reading critically, prepare two or three observations for classroom dialogue

While reviewing your classroom material, take notes that will allow you to participate in classroom discussion. There's nothing as impressive as undergraduates who willingly engage in intelligent dialogue by referencing a passage they've marked in advance and about which they have formulated a critical opinion. If you don't want to appear to be showing off, simply make one of your points into a general question to pose to the professor or to the class. The professor will appreciate your interest in the material and the way your question encourages classroom discussion. A timely question is just as impressive as a great observation.

Sometimes students keep a reading journal, entering seminal quotations and offering their responses to those passages. William James, the noted psychologist and philosopher, did just that. Today scholars consult his reading notebooks at the Houghton Library of Harvard University. Mark Twain's wry notebooks and journals are housed in the Bancroft Library at the University of California at Berkeley.

Go to all classes

Some students, unaccustomed to the new freedom offered by college, don't attend all classes. More students do this than you might expect. The consequences are dire, since most professors formulate midterm examination questions around information offered in lectures. You will also make a bad impression on professors by missing classes and forego opportunities to regard this professor as a mentor who may agree to supervise one of your external research projects. The first and second class meetings are especially important.

In math courses, do all homework problems (even the optional ones)

Practice makes perfect. If a professor assigns optional problems, be sure to complete those, even if you do not receive extra credit. Those concepts will likely reappear in an examination and later be vital for understanding the next problem sets that come your way.

Realize the responsibility implied by a syllabus

Just about every professor will present you with an exhaustive outline (generally called a syllabus) of what you will cover during every class session of the semester. Always come to class having already read the material listed on the syllabus for that particular class session—even if the professor is lecturing a few days (or even a week or more) behind. We professors have ways of "catching up" on short notice, and you don't want to be left in the dust when we do.

Look down the road and read ahead

Moreover, look ahead on your syllabi to see if there are any longer reading assignments (for example, a 500-page novel) two or three weeks (or months) down the road. If so, get started early and read twenty pages a night of those longer works, in addition to whatever you review to prepare for the next class. That way you won't be in the position of having to read a very long work in only a day or two.

Don't overload yourself in your freshman year

Assuming that it is an option at your university, consider taking a maximum of four courses in your first semester of college (especially if, to help make ends meet, you are working an outside job). Be careful, though, not to drop below "full-time student" status if your doing so ends up compromising your enrollment status or nullifying your financial package. Be aware, also, that national scholarship competitions usually expect the applicants to have "full-time" student status.

Live in a dormitory, if you can afford to do so

Life in a dormitory, if you are able to finance that arrangement, will leave you centrally located on campus and allow you to participate in a meal plan. That translates into several hours each day that you don't have to drive to campus, find a parking space, shop for food, or wash dishes. By the way, use those saved hours *to study.*

Also, if you live in a dormitory, you may apply, in your sophomore year, to be a resident assistant. That may mean free room and board for three years of college. This is equivalent to a scholarship with a value of up to $21,000 over your last three years of college. I have known a number of students who did just that—to their and their parents' delight.

Do not let a negligent roommate get the better of you

If you live in a college dorm, you will likely have no say, in your freshman year, about choosing your roommate. Many roommate relationships are positive. Occasionally, though, a roommate turns out to be a slacker. If he/she wastes time and consistently plays loud music or ceaselessly entertains friends in your room, simply find a study lounge in the dorm or go to a nearby library. Roommates eventually change; bad grades do not.

Attend Freshman Orientation

Most universities go out of their way to arrange for every major campus program to peddle their wares at Freshman Orientation. The information—ranging from lectures about the campus libraries, to honors programs, to study-abroad programs, to national scholarships—is invaluable. Attend *all* of these sessions. Take good notes. Follow through.

Study groups

Get involved in study groups, but always come prepared. Moreover, join study groups in which each member is expected to pull his/her own weight in order to justify the benefits of shared learning. You don't want to be in a study group in which a few people do all the work.

Take a library tour

All campuses offer library tours in which you learn about the different libraries on campus (many campuses have several libraries devoted to different collections). Those tours also teach you about online catalogues, database searches, the locations of journals, microfilm locations, and interlibrary loan facilities, as well as about how to gain access to library catalogues from your home computer. Knowledge is power. Knowledge of library resources is magnified power.

If possible, purchase your own portable photocopy machine

Throughout your college years, you will likely photocopy thousands of pages of material. For $300 or less, you can now purchase a good portable photocopy machine. Save hours of time—and money—by being able to photocopy in the comfort of your own room. Or, if you need to photocopy something at the library, carry in your own portable machine rather than wait in line to spend ten or fifteen cents per page at copiers where you usually waste thirty cents just figuring out how to center the item you wish to copy. (The downside is the cost of ink cartridges, but I think the convenience is worth it.)

Have a personal computer and printer in your dorm room

Whereas foresighted students once brought typewriters to campus, you currently need your own personal computer and printer to complete projects and avoid long lines at "general access labs" on or near campus.

You can often purchase used or refurbished computers at half price or less. And always keep back-up discs or devices for the moment when your hard drive fails. I've seen a number of students lose weeks and months of work when their computers crashed.

Be sociable

Join at least one campus club in which you have a hobby-like interest; or else get involved in the campus denomination of your faith. Many students feel alienated at large universities and can grow dejected through basic loneliness. If you live in a residence hall, that can solve part of the problem. But by joining a campus club, or by participating in a religious organization, you can head off personal problems associated with loneliness. It is difficult to leave behind one's family and friends. Expect to feel somewhat disoriented and stranded for the first year or two.

Most student government organizations have booklets that list all university-related organizations and provide phone numbers of club officers. Take advantage of those booklets. Once you join a club, you can gradually assume a leadership role, perhaps working your way up to the presidency. Social enjoyment then becomes a leadership credential.

Do not cheat

One constantly reads about students who cheat—by buying their papers from Internet vendors or combining their own prose with sentences "borrowed" from Internet sources. This is the road to intellectual perdition. College is about developing your powers of research, your skill at dialogue and argumentation, and your sense of "the life worth living." Don't sell yourself or your family short by doing anything unethical—even if others are doing so. Just put in the extra five hours of study. And remember, professors aren't stupid; we can usually tell the difference between *your* writing and that of somebody twenty years your senior, and we can use computer search engines to track down even the smallest suspicious phrases in a questionable term paper. Leaning on other people—or other sources—becomes a regrettable habit that will let you down at the worst possible moment. Trust your own abilities to learn and grow intellectually.

Manage your money wisely

Many students, on their own for the first time, mismanage their money and quickly succumb to credit-card debt. This often results in their having to gain further outside employment, and that endeavor cuts down on their powers of concentration and academic dedication. Have a financial game plan, even if it involves student loans. Then live within your means. Try to resist the enticements of the credit-card vendors who set up tables on many campuses. They have led countless students into debt and despair. "Minimum" payments take decades to pay off!

There are many ways to save money while you are a student. Are you aware, for example, that you can purchase many of your textbooks, which range in price from $5.00 to $200.00 (in the sciences), for half price or less on such search engines as www.bookfinder.com? All you need to do is research the books you'll be using "next semester" and order them "used" online. Note that the more you order from a single online dealer, the fewer dollars you'll pay in shipping expenses. (Do, however, order used books on the Internet only if those have ISBN numbers identical to those that identify books required by your professors. You don't want to purchase outdated editions.) Another idea: recycled clothing stores, often located nearby, offer surprisingly current fashions at greatly reduced prices. I shop at those myself.

Take note of "drop-without-penalty-or-record" deadlines

Just about all universities have deadlines by which you may drop a course without having it appear as a W (withdrawn) on your transcript. Know those deadlines and, if you're having overwhelming problems, drop the course. You can always enroll in a summer-session offering of the course. Even after that deadline passes, a W is always preferable to a poor grade. Too many Ws look bad on a transcript, but an F or D takes away the grade points from those hard-earned As.

Before dropping any course, be sure that you will not compromise your status as a full-time student, relative to university requirements pertaining to your financial aid package or national scholarship prospects.

Conclusion

Having a successful freshman year is vital; it sets the tone for the rest of your college experience and may very well define choices you have later in life. For instance, the grades you make as a freshman affect your GPA just as much as the grades you make as a senior. Many students have spent the last three years of their college experience trying to bring up a low GPA after a disastrous freshman year. Other students reluctantly abandon career goals after doing poorly in difficult courses—such as calculus or chemistry—for which they were ill-prepared as freshmen. This doesn't need to happen; you can have a great first-year experience in college if you plan properly and follow the common-sense guidelines in this chapter.

Chapter Eight

Which Courses *Not* to Place Out Of

Many professors and guidance counselors would disagree with me, but I don't think you should try to place out of freshman English.

Freshman English

Before I explain why, let me back up a bit. For several years, at the University of Texas at Austin, I taught a course designed for incoming students who had placed out of the first semester of freshman English. In all that time, I met only two or three students who actually had writing skills impressive enough to have justified their exemption from the entering course in freshman composition. Those undergraduates who "placed out" lost a valuable opportunity to have an additional semester of hard-core writing instruction before entering their upper-division classes.

For eight years, moreover, I taught a summer course in "Advanced Expository Writing" for entering Plan II Honors Students at the University of Texas at Austin. Plan II is a highly elite, university-wide honors program at that flagship state university. My course was innovative because Plan II invited high-school seniors (those who had been admitted to Plan II for the fall semester) to devote the first six weeks of their summer vacation to a "get ready" course in expository writing. That was the only course they took during their six-week summer visit. They all improved vastly and, after returning to the university for their first fall semester, went on to achieve a high number of all-A or nearly all-A grade point averages in their freshman year and beyond.

Be mindful that my advice and experience run counter to the opinion, harbored by many students and professors, that the time to take your most serious writing courses is towards the beginning of your junior year of college, when (as they like to believe) you "really have something to say." Although a number of very eminent professors harbor this opinion,

I believe that they are mistaken. If you've waited until your junior year to learn how to write, you are so far behind that you may never catch up.

The point is this: Take advantage of freshman English to get your writing skills up to speed before tackling upper-division coursework.

What about mathematics?

I would offer similar advice for math courses. You need a solid foundation in trigonometry and algebra before you take engineering calculus or advanced chemistry. It is not usually the "science" component of science that keeps students from completing a pre-med curriculum, or from becoming biologists; it is the math courses that do so, for those preliminary disciplines are the "gatekeepers" of the physical sciences.

If you are weak in either trigonometry or algebra, enroll in whatever basic review course your university may offer. Conversely, if you qualify to "place out" of an introductory math course, *do not* do that if you plan to major in the sciences. Just earn an A in your introductory math course, even if you end up reviewing material with which you already feel comfortable. Practice makes perfect; success breeds confidence and further success. Once you begin earning As, you'll likely continue to do so. But it's very difficult to recover from an early D or a scattering of Cs.

Also, if you plan to enter a field such as engineering, or even biology or chemistry, take all pertinent physics and math classes as early as possible—and in whatever sequence makes most sense. In those math classes, you will master concepts that you need to know for other fields of science, while sharpening your general problem-solving acumen. You will also be able to avoid a delay in moving on with your major field of study for lack of prerequisite math or physics courses. It is very inconvenient to have to "catch up" on math courses you should have registered for early in your college career.

Your major field of study

By the same token, do not "place out" of any course related to your major field of study—even if you have sufficient Advanced Placement credit to do so. College professors teach from different perspectives and have a wealth of knowledge from which you can benefit—even in introductory courses. You don't know *everything* simply because you "placed out" on the basis of a test that may vary considerably from a professor's personal syllabus. Still, if you decide to "place out" of a course *outside* of your projected major field of study, do so only if you receive an equivalency grade of A. Bs and Cs will have an enduring negative impact on your overall

GPA, diminishing, as well, your ability to compete for prestigious national scholarships in your sophomore through senior years of study.

Which kind of writing class should you take?

Learning to write is foundational, with one level building upon another. The learning process for this is not as clear as that for mathematics, but writing education should roughly follow the pattern below. Students should learn to do the following:

1. **Use English properly**

   This phase covers spelling, grammar, punctuation, correct word choice, extended vocabulary, and an understanding of basic sentence components. Most students end up enhancing these skills not only by reviewing grammar books, but also by reading really good authors and seeing these strengths in action.

2. **Express thoughts coherently in writing**

   At this level, you should focus on sorting multiple ideas into separate paragraphs, constructing sentences, condensing and combining those, avoiding redundancy, and distinguishing among explanation, description, and persuasion (see later chapters for the art of generating persuasive prose).

3. **Understand basic logical arguments and citation conventions**

   You learn to advance an argument in the context of existing scholarship, properly documenting both primary and secondary sources. The point here is to understand that college-level essays are, in theory, part of an ongoing "conversation" with scholars who have previously written about your subject in books and journals.

4. **Organize persuasive or analytical prose**

   Here you learn to develop a thesis into a multi-paged essay having a title, introduction, paragraphs that logically cohere, and a conclusion. This would occur in a first- and/or second-semester English course, depending on the course material.

5. **Convey independently researched information in an engaging, persuasive, and sophisticated style**

   In a second-semester English course or in an advanced expository writing class, you will build upon freshman English, bringing together all the earlier phases of the writing experience.

6. Develop the flexibility to use different writing styles for different audiences or occasions

Know how to illustrate or support points both verbally and with graphic illustrations. Learn how to modify expository prose in varied situations—from grant proposals, to law briefs, to board-room presentations, to articles for academic journals, to newspaper editorials. This kind of class would most likely be an advanced expository writing class, or perhaps one that focuses on a particular writing style (such as business or technical writing).

If you are weak in the earlier phases of learning to write, get training in those areas before moving on to the later phases. Once you've progressed to the last phase, you're about ready to write an honors thesis.

Ask questions before enrolling

Before enrolling in a writing course, check the catalogue description and chat with the professor to make sure that the class will meet your needs. You will likely benefit more from a professor who offers abundant feedback than from one who takes a "hands-off" approach.

Avoid peer-editing classes

Be cautious of classes that emphasize peer editing. Peer editing works well in highly advanced classes, where students who critique your writing are already competent stylists themselves. Even then, they do not have the consistency or established pedagogy of a seasoned teacher of writing. Enroll in classes where you'll get abundant advice from a professor; then benefit from whatever peer feedback is available. Ask the professor in advance what percentage of personal vs. peer feedback the course offers.

Creative writing classes

Taking a creative or technical writing class will help your writing and inspire your imagination; but you should first focus on basic and intermediate expository writing to develop skills that will help you excel in all your classes (including creative writing classes) and in your later professional life.

Conclusion

Don't place out of freshman composition or out of foundational math courses that are gatekeepers to the physical sciences. Don't place out of courses in your major field of study; instead, earn As in those courses. Enhance your expository writing as early as possible.

Chapter Nine

Selecting Courses and Professors

Don't settle for less

Never forget that you are a paying customer of the university and deserve the fine education you've been promised. Still, you may need to do some of your own investigating to get the highest quality education. In my opinion, the single most important factor is the quality of the professors under whom you study. Take the time to find out about them; learn whom you want to study with in your various courses (especially when it comes to professors in your major).

You wouldn't buy a car or a home without first shopping around, right? Isn't your college education just as important as a car or house?

Challenge the computer

When several "sections" of the same course are taught by different professors, you should try to learn in advance who the various teachers are for those sections. Learn something about the teaching record of the various 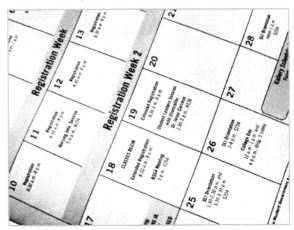 professors and then, if possible, switch into the section of your professor of choice.

In other words, don't let the computer arbitrarily make the final decision for you (any more than you would allow a computer arbitrarily to pick any other feature of your life). Despite what front-desk personnel might say, computers are not the final arbiters. In many cases, students *do* have a choice.

Add/Drop: Your chance to get whom you want

If it turns out that you're enrolled in a class with a professor with whom you'd rather not study, don't give up hope. If you have a valid reason for wishing to be in another section of that course (providing the option exists), try switching into the other class during the Add/Drop period. Add/Drop usually occurs during the first week of class. A professor whose class is full on Monday may have two or more openings by Monday afternoon—after students drop the course or don't show up for any number of reasons. You may then be able to add a different section of the same course, taught by your professor of choice.

Note: If you're trying to switch into a particular class, I would advise you to attend the *first* meeting of that class even if you aren't sure yet whether you'll be able to gain admission. Neither should you miss the first session of the class you're trying to leave, since you don't know yet whether you'll be able to switch. No need to start off the semester already behind the other students.

Finding out about your professors

So, how do you find out about how well professors teach? One way is to consult public teaching evaluations. Most universities have students fill out professor evaluations at the end of the semester.

At some universities, the numerical results of student evaluations are available at specified locations, such as the main library. In those evaluations, students grade their professors in anywhere from five to thirty (or more) categories. The bottom line, however, often features two key categories: "Overall Course Evaluation" and "Overall Teacher Evaluation." Scored on a 4.0 scale, anything from 3.5–3.7 is quite good; 3.8–4.0 is exceptional. These are usually fairly good guides to the responses of most students who took the course. You'll likely be happier in a class taught by a 3.5–4.0 teacher. Ask around campus to determine how to gain access to student evaluations and where those are available.

Also be aware of private websites, such as www.pickaprof.com or www.ratemyprofessors.com. Through open-records petitions, or through the solicitation of student comments, a number of private initiatives inform students about data ranging from a professor's grade distribution in various classes to student comments about that professor's course. This information may be free or available for a fee.

A word of caution about teaching evaluations

Don't allow teacher-evaluation statistics to be your exclusive guide. Some professors who are quite brilliant but very demanding may score lower than they should because they have very high standards and grade rigorously. Although many of your 3.5–4.0 teachers are just as demanding, beware of using student evaluations by themselves to determine your choice of a professor. Seek out at least two other indices, such as the advice of the department's undergraduate advisor and the professor's reputation in his or her field of study.

Undergraduate advisors

Undergraduate advisors within different departments can usually identify the best teachers. Visit the undergraduate advisor, show the advisor the list of professors who are teaching the course(s) you'd like to take (you can easily get this information from the online course bulletins), and ask whom they would recommend, based upon their knowledge of the professors' teaching styles. So as not to sound prejudicial, say, "I assume that all these professors are quite qualified, and that each has something special to offer—but have any of these professors been recognized for their teaching in the past?" Then promise to keep the information confidential, and definitely do so.

The professor's scholarly reputation

Learn about a potential professor's scholarly reputation—that is, his or her record of publication and/or creative endeavors. Since you will eventually be seeking letters of recommendation, you stand to benefit from studying with a professor whose work has been recognized either nationally or internationally. The undergraduate advisor will often know who these professors are and may be able to pair you with someone who is known to be both a great scholar/researcher and a fine teacher. You can also log on to the department's website and look up the publishing records of various faculty members. As a last resort try typing their names into an Internet search engine (such as Google.com) and see what turns up.

But even if distinguished professors don't have a reputation for being teaching stars, be brave enough to enroll in their classes, and simply be determined to learn all you can and to impress those people well enough to garner letters of recommendation down the road. Such professors often look for "the right stuff" in a student; when they find it, they will form a bond that can last throughout your undergraduate career—and beyond.

The inspiration factor

At the same time don't sell professors short if they are known more for their excellence as teachers and mentors than for their scholarly reputation. I have seen great teachers such as these imbue their students with a passion for learning, creativity, and critical thinking. Those professors often sponsor extensive office hours and are willing to meet individual students, or groups of students, off-campus to continue "the discussion." They, too, take time to write comprehensive, highly supportive letters of recommendation.

In my freshman year of college, I studied with a foreign language professor known primarily for his excellence as a teacher. He guided me towards a degree in the humanities. While I went on to study with other wonderful professors, known nationally and internationally for their scholarly reputations, I still value the personal concern that this caring educator showed me (especially when all was not going smoothly) during my first semester of college. To this day, I feel privileged to have studied with him.

When your professor is not really a professor

All too often, introductory courses at the freshman and sophomore level are taught by graduate students. Don't sell them short—they are young professionals learning their way in the world of teaching, and they often have an enthusiasm as impressive as their grasp of the material. Still, they are required to undergo student evaluation, and you would be wise to check out the results of their evaluation statistics, just as you would those for a full professor.

Do not worry about this person's as-yet-fledgling publication record. You will seldom ask graduate students for letters of recommendation attesting to your performance in freshman or sophomore courses. Just get the best graduate student—to the extent you can determine that from published data, or by visiting the graduate advisor and asking who among the graduate students is well known as a successful teacher.

In cases involving multi-section courses at the freshman and sophomore levels of study, faculty and graduate-student assignments often occur at the last minute, making it impossible, at first glance, to be able to research student evaluations. Not so. Most graduate students teach the same course semester-after-semester. Thus, you may go to the department sponsoring the course and ask for a list of graduate students and faculty who have recently taught the course you plan to take and who are likely to do so again. You may then conduct your research on that basis and—during the first week of class—try to switch into their sections of your class if you are not satisfied with your arbitrary placement.

Another word of caution when choosing professors: Politics

Academic freedom, as it is usually conceived, mandates that faculty members may teach a course from whatever perspective they deem appropriate. To the minds of some faculty members, however, "everything is political," so they teach their courses by injecting political perspectives. They argue, as well, that any effort to remain neutral simply perpetuates the status quo and is therefore supportive of the prevailing political consensus (in other words, even teaching English becomes political). I personally don't agree with this "everything is political" attitude, but I think you should know before you go to college that some professors hold this view. What amounts to political indoctrination—with no other views mentioned—can show up in disciplines seemingly far removed from contemporary politics.

So how will you know before the class starts whether the professor teaches a subject with an unfairly rigid political slant? Well, you could approach the professor in advance of enrolling in the course and ask whether his or her method of teaching reflects a particular political orientation or outlook. Whatever their response, they have a right to it—but you also have a right to determine if that is the "angle" from which you wish to study the subject matter, especially if you feel that politics ought to have hardly anything to do with the class. You can also pick up clues in course descriptions and by talking to other students who have taken a class with the professor.

Know where your professor stands in the field of study

In a related vein, different professors will teach from different perspectives outside of the spectrum of politics. It is your right to inquire whether there is a governing approach, and to compare the responses of several professors teaching the same course. If there's just one professor teaching the course you need, then simply take the course and understand that the perspective you're receiving is probably just one of several possible outlooks. No one professor has a monopoly on ways to approach the material. They all, however, hold serious perspectives. Understand the perspective, earn your A in the course, but keep an open mind.

Conclusion

Don't let a university computer determine your professors. Take advantage of Add/Drop to make changes in your schedule as needed. Conduct research and enroll in classes taught by the best teachers, especially if they are known for their research or ability to inspire their students.

Chapter Ten

Getting to Know Your Professors

Those crucial letters of recommendation

When you apply for national scholarships, graduate schools, or study-abroad programs—or when you seek an entry-level job into your chosen profession—you'll need letters of recommendations from three to five professors. Start thinking about that at the *beginning*—rather than at the *end*—of your college experience.

Before your senior year, you should get to know at least three professors (preferably in your major field of study) well enough so that you are comfortable asking them for letters of recommendation. They, in turn, should feel enthusiastic about writing a *comprehensive* letter of recommendation for you. (The ideal letter ought to be a minimum of one-to-two pages in length, single spaced, with double spacing between paragraphs.)

I've seen so many students who, after three or four years of college, tell me that there's still no professor who really knows them well enough to write a comprehensive letter of endorsement. That dilemma is difficult, if not impossible, to resolve when a student is about to graduate without ever having established a rapport with any faculty members.

A short letter of recommendation may get you nothing

A supportive but short letter of recommendation may not be much help. Professors who are in a position to write little more than a one-paragraph courtesy letter (detailing only the student's grade and industry) seldom do the student a favor. The dutiful one-paragraph letter of recommendation occurs when students have failed to develop a mentor relationship with a professor. The student shows up out of the blue and says, "I made an A in your class two years ago; and, oh, by-the-way will you write me a letter of recommendation?"

One-paragraph letters are the kiss of death in national scholarship competitions, but the fault is less the professor's than it is the student's. The obliging professor may churn out a reference that says almost nothing at all.

How to get to know your professors

For comprehensive letters of recommendation, approach only professors who know you well. And, to write the kind of letter that persuades someone to grant you a scholarship or a job, those professors need to have something substantial to talk about.

What do professors generally mention in worthwhile letters of recommendation? Typically they write about how you've demonstrated your intellectual and creative skills: classroom participation, essays, examinations, publications, projects, research, and/or organizational skills. They'll also specify the positive aspects of your personality, particularly as those relate to your ability to work efficiently. Are you, for instance, a self-starter? Do you take initiative? Are you a self-learner? Do you have enthusiasm? Are you a team player? All of these questions relate to facets of your professional identity that you should develop in college.

Generally speaking, you'll seek a letter of recommendation from professors with whom you've had a "mentoring relationship." You should aim to have a mentoring relationship with at least three professors, all of them, if possible, in your major field of study. When you are researching the scholarly credentials of professors with whom you wish to study, put stars next to the ones you think you would like to get to know the most. But even if you don't get your professor of choice, work extra hard to impress every professor with whom you study.

Here are some ideas for developing a mentoring relationship with several professors you hope will someday recommend you for scholarships, admission to graduate school, or employment in your field:

1. Stand out in the classroom

Sit towards the front of the class and always come prepared with at least three points to make that day. Keep your points brief, and space your observations so as not to give the impression that you're monopolizing classroom discussion. A good point is often one that facilitates further discussion, so it doesn't hurt to ask a question that demonstrates your attentiveness and encourages other students to respond. By participating sporadically, without monopolizing the class, you will stand out as somebody who finds the material engaging.

2. Office visits

Get to know your professors by visiting them during their scheduled office hours—perhaps once or twice a month to talk about a point of interest. Come prepared with your reflections on a certain issue—reflections that go beyond the range of what the professor covered in class. Chat about fifteen minutes and then realize that the professor has other students to see and other obligations. That sort of visit will provide the professor with a pleasant break from students who visit mainly to discuss problems with their grades or because those students don't understand the material. And it will help him keep your name and face in mind.

3. Timing matters

You will also stand out as one of the few students who understands that—appearances to the contrary—many professors do not enjoy having students come up after class to pursue a point of discussion for the next ten minutes or during a walk back to the professor's office. Between classes, professors may wish to take a breather before they begin teaching their next class, or they may need to work on their research or committee assignments. Quite a few professors don't relish unexpected student conversations. The best time to approach the professor for follow-up discussion is during an office visit.

4. Discuss your thesis for an upcoming paper with the professor

As suggested elsewhere in this book, you should visit a professor several weeks before a paper is due to display the index-card outline of the thesis you plan to develop and the scope of your supporting argument. Few students ever do this. The professor will think highly of your planning and initiative (and you might get some great feedback before you submit your paper, thus upping your grade and improving your relationship with the professor).

5. Turn in well-written papers

Make sure that your essays are well researched and well written. Even if a professor thinks highly of your initiative and intelligence, the professor will not be wholeheartedly supportive if you lack the communication skills to impress colleagues in graduate school or professional school. On the other hand, a student who both thinks well and writes well is assured of superior recommendations.

6. **Print if you have sloppy handwriting**

   When you take essay examinations, print if your handwriting is a challenge. Sloppy handwriting rubs professors the wrong way when they have thirty or more bluebooks to correct. (Bluebooks are small pamphlets with blue covers and ruled pages. Bring them to class if the instructor requests this.) Don't have your handwriting suggest that you're not intelligent or that you have a sloppy attitude towards the course.

7. **Take at least two courses taught by the same professor**

   If you take a course offered by a very good professor and you anticipate asking him for a letter of recommendation, take another course from that same person. When professors write letters of recommendation, they can speak so much better about you if they are able to draw upon their impression of you from at least two courses. In each of those courses, keep a list of the innovative points that you raised during classroom discussion, noting especially when you politely challenged the prevailing view. You can eventually ask the professor if he would like to review those "journal" entries to refresh his memories about your classroom participation. (If the answer is "yes," type out the best five of those instances, and present those, on one page, to the professor.) Moreover, save your papers, quizzes, and exams to present to professors at such time as you request a letter of recommendation. Those items will likewise remind your professors of your excellence, and of the words of praise they may have entered on your work.

Independent research

Before the end of your junior year of study, do an independent research project with at least one professor. Here's where you will go significantly beyond the realm of classroom instruction and show how capable you are of *taking initiative and conducting advanced and independent research*. This is the *strongest* thing a professor can say about a student. Be aware, however, that professors will be reluctant to allow you to conduct research under their supervision if you have not first proven yourself in one or two classes with them. For that same reason, you should attend office hours with some regularity in order to demonstrate your genuine engagement with the subject matter.

Science research teams

Students in the sciences most often exhibit independent research skills while working on a professor's *team* in the professor's lab. Such a project has numerous components, and the professor frequently divides up assignments among his graduate students and a few undergraduates. You should follow instructions flawlessly and prove worthy of being entrusted with part of an experiment where you are expected to undertake your own innovative investigation of a vital component of the team's endeavor.

Of the twenty-nine Goldwater Scholars whom I've coached, nearly all had earned a trusted position on a professor's research team, and each could make a claim to having contributed something significant to a research project.

How did they obtain these opportunities? By knocking on doors, by chatting with the professor and displaying an eagerness to conduct research, by being willing to undertake any assignment and do it enthusiastically until a more glamorous task came along, by persevering politely until the professor finally invited them into the lab, and by not screwing up once the professor invited them to be part of the team. In the sciences, lab directors are very much like orchestra leaders: they expect superb teamwork, intermixed with virtuoso solo performances.

Other opportunities for research

Research assignments in other departments or fields take different forms—often internships or on-location "hands-on" experience. I think, for instance, of journalism students who have earned summer internships on prestigious newspapers; or of sociology majors who have worked for child-protective agencies or for organizations that provide assistance to unwed mothers; or of pre-law students who have worked part-time for attorneys. These are all expanded forms of "research" that lead to solid letters of recommendation. In the humanities or fine arts, a research endeavor often takes the form of a prolonged research paper, or of an extra, time-consuming creative endeavor. As an undergraduate, I took that route, creating bonds with my professors that have lasted a lifetime. At some schools, moreover, it is possible to find part-time employment as an editorial assistant for a scholarly journal. Ask around.

Another resource: Faculty advisors

I have also seen stellar letters of recommendation emerge from professors who have been the "faculty sponsors" of an organization, and who have praised the efforts of the student president of that organization for having been highly innovative in making the organization function optimally.

Don't forget the thank-you note

Finally, write thank-you letters to any professor who composes a letter of recommendation for you. So few students ever do that. When you get accepted to some school, or when you obtain a job, send another note that again thanks the professor and mentions how important his or her recommendation was. Consider copying the letter to the professor's department chairman and to the dean of the college. But if you do that, make sure that the letter is grammatically flawless and has no spelling errors. The presence of such infelicities could actually prove embarrassing to the professor. Thereafter, keep in touch with this professor, who stands to become a lifelong friend and who one day might even become your colleague.

Conclusion

Get to know your professors by going the extra mile. Stand out in ways that provide professors with documentary evidence that they can later use to praise you.

Chapter Eleven

Structuring Your Time

Much of your success in college will hinge upon your ability to structure your day fruitfully, making the best use of your time. Many students *intend* to structure their day optimally, but they somehow fall short of doing so. A well-structured day does not occur spontaneously; you've got to work at it. It takes discipline—discipline that spans the entire day and most of the evening.

Creating a schedule to live by

First, purchase a Day-Timer® (or a similar personal organizer and time management product). A Day-Timer usually divides every hour of the day into 15-minute slots. Use the Day-Timer to plan what you will be doing for each coming week, anticipating, as well, the time you will devote each day to major projects due weeks or months "down the road." Schedule each day of the week, starting at 8:00 a.m. and finishing with 9:00 p.m. Schedule every 15-minute block of time.

Of course, you'll first want to block off all of your classes for that week and enough time to get to the class. If you must work an external job to help make ends meet, put those hours in. Then begin filling in the remaining blocks of time with other required activities. Schedule how much time you'll spend for lunch and dinner. Schedule anticipated social or physical exercise activities. Even schedule a short mid-afternoon nap if that will help you study through the evening. The most productive students use Day-Timers and even color-code various entries to remind themselves what's "coming up."

In other words, create a routine—and live by it.

Scheduling study time

Don't let time between classes be wasted time. Fill in Day-Timers so that you study subjects between classes. In fact, you should devote a minimum of 90 minutes per day (outside of class) to each of your classes.

During those ninety minutes, review notes, keep up with assigned homework and/or reading, and begin term papers. If you have to read a 500-page novel, for instance, use part of your ninety minutes to read twenty pages per day. By budgeting your time wisely, you avoid last-minute crises and can complete extensive projects with minimum pain. The same goes for term papers.

If your official homework requires only thirty to forty-five minutes, use the rest of those ninety minutes for long-term assignments in that class: review for midterm and final examinations, work on term papers, or attend the office hours of teaching assistants or professors.

Elsewhere in this book, I have urged you to conduct research in your field at the earliest possible time. Schedule that activity into your Day-Timer, as well.

Take it with you everywhere

The most successful students I have known have their Day-Timers with them at all times and stick to their schedules meticulously.

Spread out your classes

If possible, break up your classes between Monday/Wednesday (or Monday/Wednesday/Friday) and Tuesday/Thursday. Granted, some students *must* take all of their classes on TTh or on MW because of work schedules. If you are working part-time, then break up your classes between MW and TTh. Otherwise, spread your courses over the entire week.

I urge you to spread your classes over four days and avoid having to take four or five back-to-back classes just two days of the week. That is a painful way to attend college and leaves you exhausted by the end of the day—too exhausted to study productively in the evening. By spreading your classes over a four-day period, you build in more time to study between classes and allow yourself the psychological benefit of digesting the contents of each course after it meets.

Be an early bird

Take early-morning classes, if possible. Fewer students enroll in 8:00 a.m. classes, and some professors like to teach at that hour so that they will end up grading fewer papers. By signing up for early-bird classes, you often get more attention from the professor and a head start on the day. By starting earlier, you are also able to allot more time to preparing for your courses and other college-related activities.

Saving time in a residence hall

Finances permitting, live in a campus residence hall. As mentioned above, this will also help you budget your time better. You won't have to spend two hours or more commuting to campus and searching for a parking space. Moreover, if your dorm has a meal plan, you won't have to shop for food, prepare it, and clean dishes. Spend those saved hours in the library or in the lab.

Ditch the TV and computer games

Leave your television and computer games at home. Both will rob you of valuable time better spent studying or reading. Achieving an excellent record in college is serious business. Now is the time to leave the bad habits of youth behind you.

Beware of cell phones and incessant e-mailing

Freshmen who are lonely or homesick will often spend hours in cell-phone conversations or e-mailing/instant-messaging their friends. I have known undergraduates who participate in late-night four-hour sessions to respond to accumulated e-mail messages. *Don't*: be covetous of your time; keep these exchanges to a minimum.

As for wasting time on cell phones—well, that can occur all day long, but especially during free off-peak dialing hours, when students might otherwise be studying productively. Cell phones now make students accessible even when they are at the library. I frequently see undergraduates *outside* the library, engaging in prolonged, sometimes passionate, cell-phone conversations.

The temptation to call somebody is pervasive. When, during one of my classes, somebody's cell phone rang, I allowed the student to silence the ringer without incident. Still, the event roused my curiosity. Before proceeding with the lecture, I asked, "How many of you are carrying cell phones?" Eighty percent of the class raised their hands. One of the students then asked the question that had not occurred to me: "How many of you have received calls (on vibrating ringers) *during this class*?" Half of the students with cell phones—yes, half—said that they *had*. Little wonder that so many students are now speaking on cell phones as they walk from class to class, as they eat their lunches, or as they postpone or ignore study obligations throughout the day and night.

Learn to carry a cell phone strictly for emergency purposes. Also, master the art of brief e-mails, followed by such words as "I'll catch up with you Thanksgiving/Christmas/this summer."

Gambling

Poker—whether in back rooms or, worse yet, online—has become an obsession of many college students. Although cable television glamorizes and valorizes this "sport," you have neither the time to waste nor, most likely, the money to lose (whatever your high-school bravado, you'll always find someone at college who can, and will, take you to the cleaners).

Getting into a scheduled routine actually makes life easier

Don't imagine that the preceding advice is too much for you to handle. You're eighteen (or so) only once, and you have the energy to devote yourself to college with fervor and conviction. If you don't think so, consider one student whom I know and respect. He worked forty hours per week to support himself and his family; he has alternately been a part-time and full-time student over the last several years while earning and maintaining a perfect 4.0 GPA. If he can do it, so can you.

Conclusion

Structure your day meticulously and honor your commitments. Use a Day-Timer to plan ahead and avoid activities that needlessly rob you of precious minutes (that quickly become lost hours).

Chapter Twelve

Taking Notes and Studying for Exams

Because taking notes and studying for exams is an integrated process, I'll cover these two related topics in one chapter. Success in both endeavors demands that you attend every class and listen attentively to the professor's lecture and to classroom discussion.

You should take notes and study those systematically *every day*. Doing so will prepare you for midterm and final exams in the best manner, allowing you to avoid the usually ineffective last-minute "cramming" study sessions for which college students are so infamous.

Listening carefully for the main points in lectures

Taking notes *effectively* involves more than just writing down everything the professor (or anyone else in the classroom) says during the class. You've got to learn to distinguish—on the spot—the main points from those that are less important or even irrelevant.

Which are the main points? The ones your professor will expect you to know when you take your midterm and/or final examinations. Yes, lofty intellectual stimulation is valuable; but superior grades are keys to success, and you earn those by mastering what you must know for exams. No matter how entertaining or affable the professor is when lecturing, always take notes with an eye towards his or her examinations.

Note-taking during lectures

First, don't assume that everything a professor says has equal weight. When professors lecture, they have in mind a pre-set number of facts and perspectives for which they'll hold you responsible on midterm examinations and comprehensive final examinations. Because lecturing is a form of performance that requires rhythm, flow, and continuity, professors often interject less vital information between main points. This in-between material may be explanation, extrapolation, or just plain filler.

Note-taking becomes especially difficult when you're dealing with professors who have delivered a lecture so many times that they virtually know it by heart and, in the course of their performance, blend vital points with off-the-cuff observations that are never likely to appear on an examination. When taking notes, distinguish between what's vital and what's not.

Don't get sidetracked by classroom discussion

While classroom "participation" is often very constructive, it can distort your sense of the main points for which a professor will be holding you responsible on an examination. When taking notes during a discussion between professor and student(s), focus on the professor's *response* to the points raised by the student(s). The professor conceivably might incorporate elements of classroom discussion into a midterm or final exam, but you have to be able to gauge the relative importance that the professor attributes to such dialogue.

Getting feedback if it's hard to tell the vital from the non-vital

Because it's *your* responsibility to be able to understand the main points of a professor's lecture, it's in your interest to fill in blank spots. Just raise your hand and politely ask for clarification.

If, on the other hand, you've followed the lecture with general understanding, but you're afraid that you still don't quite understand where it has all been heading, seek clarification towards the end of the lecture (but at least five minutes before the class is scheduled to adjourn). When doing that, try not to make the professor feel as if he has been an ineffective lecturer. Rather, formulate a question that demonstrates your understanding of the issues up to that point in the lecture; then ask if that pretty much sums up the entirety of the issues under discussion. If you have missed a vital point, the professor will likely tell you.

The challenge here is to convey the impression that you're engaging in a conversation rather than simply asking the professor to repeat what he has already said. Suggest, in tone, how exciting it is to talk about the material, implying at the same time that you're not sure if you have an accurate sense of "the big picture." Or consider saying that you found point "X" vital, but you'd appreciate some elaboration upon its significance to the overall lecture. When you seek clarification in this way, you help to facilitate dialogue without making professors appear to be poor communicators (especially when they may feel that they've just given a brilliant lecture).

Seeking clarification outside of the classroom

If the class has teaching assistants, approach them later and feel free to be quite *blunt* in seeking confirmation of the main points, especially since the professor's ego is no longer "on the line" in front of the entire class. The teaching assistants probably have helped to grade the professor's examinations in the past, and they are likely aware of the main points for which you'll be held responsible.

Or, if you visit a professor in office hours, you can then be as frank as you want about not quite grasping a few points in a lecture. When speaking to a professor, any confession that "I'm lost" is far better made in the office than in front of the entire class.

Looking for "outside" clues to find the main points of a lecture

You should also be able to gauge what's vital in a lecture from the syllabus, from required reading, from homework exercises, from classroom handouts, and from whatever the professor writes on a chalkboard. The key is to learn to distinguish between the distracting entertainment dimensions of a class and the basic substance for which you'll be held accountable on examinations.

Yes, you're entitled to your opinion

I don't mean to suggest that you're not entitled to your own perspective on the assigned reading material or the subject of the lectures; it's just that professors are more likely than not to create examination questions from the points that *they* emphasize in class, and for which they hold everybody accountable. So you can be creative in offering your own perspectives, but be scrupulous in articulating the professor's knowledge and points relative to lectures and reading assignments.

Keeping up with the reading material

Even when professors wander from the assigned topic, or when they fall behind in covering the assigned reading, always assume that you will nonetheless be responsible for the content of the assigned reading. Professors wouldn't have assigned that material if they hadn't wanted you to learn from it. In literature classes, for instance, the lectures usually concern the literary works themselves, and you're not likely to get much out of the lectures if you haven't done the reading.

Also—just as you take notes in class, so you should make outline notes of the materials you read. (Otherwise they tend to run together in your mind.) Keep those notes just as organized as you do your lecture notes. The main points of the lectures will often correspond directly to the content of the readings. Sometimes, however, this won't be the case, and you'll need to clarify with the professor the degree to which an examination is likely to be based upon classroom lecture or the assigned reading.

Lecture vs. reading material on the exams

It's permissible to seek clarification, either in class or in office hours, about how much emphasis the professor might place, in an examination, on lectures vs. reading material. It's best to ask this sort of question in an office hour, though, given the delicacy of the situation. You don't, after all, want to sound like you're trying to get out of reading the assigned material. This would be an automatic turn-off for the professor. Remember, your goal is not simply to earn an A but also to be in a position eventually to ask the professor for a letter of recommendation.

So, to get an idea of where to focus your effort when studying for an exam, raise that question only after you've discussed several points about the reading materials with the professor. This lets the professor know that you were responsible enough to complete the assigned reading. You thereby earn the right to ask the professor to explain what the relative proportions might be on a typical examination between the points raised in class and those in reading assignments not covered in lectures.

Stated otherwise, engage a professor in dialogue about the material rather than convey the impression that you are a "grade grubber." Of course you have a right to want to earn the highest possible grade, but diplomacy is important when making inquiries about the probable content of examinations.

Read what a professor has published on the subject

If your professor has published books or articles on the course subject matter, read some of those chapters or articles. You'll then have more insight into the lectures and be better poised to seek information during an office visit. The professor will be flattered that you've taken this initiative to supplement your own learning. (Your initiative also provides more evidence for a future letter of recommendation.)

How to write down your notes

When you take classroom notes, double-space your writing in your notebook. Why double space? Because this allows you to add supplementary definitions and illustrations in the in-between space. That additional information may come from the class reading material or from further explanations that emerge later on.

Another strategy is to write on only one side of the page, leaving a wide margin for further writing, comments, or clarification during review sessions. Use different colored pens when clarifying issues. This technique especially facilitates an office visit, during which you can seek amplification about a certain blank place in your notes; you'll have a ready-made space to enter new ideas raised by the professor in response to your questions.

Computers in the classroom

Finally, some students now find it convenient to take notes with a laptop computer. If you're a great touch-typist, go for it. You can then triple space your hard copy of your notes and later make additions.

A note on handheld computer devices (such as the palmOne™ or a BlackBerry): Most students do not use these for note-taking. If you choose to take notes on a handheld computer device, let your professor know in advance that you're doing so, lest he erroneously think that you're sending e-mails during his lecture or working on some other project.

Ask if you can tape-record the lectures for a second listening

Ask professors if they'd have any objection to your tape-recording their lectures. Let them know that you'll review the tape immediately and then tape over the lecture when you next return to class. If a professor agrees to allow you to do this, you can listen to the lecture again and fill in blank lines with points that, in retrospect, you now deem significant. Or, just as importantly, you can cross out non-essential points that earlier seemed so vital.

Focusing closely during the lecture, getting feedback during or shortly after the lecture, and then listening to the lecture a second time on tape virtually guarantees your ability to transcribe nearly all of the essential points.

After reviewing your notes, ask for clarification again

If you've reviewed the notes a second or third time and you're still not clear about what some of the main points were, don't hesitate to get further elaboration. Visit the teaching assistant. If the teaching assistant is unable to help, confer with the professor during office hours. You're paying for that course; the professor is obliged to offer help. Just ask politely and respectfully. The professor will typically admire your dedication.

Highlighting the key words and phrases after identifying the main points in a lecture

You'll want to repeat this "main points clarification" process for each lecture (the "main points" are the ones you're presumably going to be held responsible for in midterm and final examinations). However, before you start the notes for one lecture, highlight in yellow (or your favorite highlighter color; my wife likes green or pink) the *key* points of the previous day's lecture. Highlight only key words or phrases that evoke a much larger point.

This process of highlighting the key words and phrases of the *previous* lecture before clarifying the main points of the *current lecture* will help to provide a transition from one lecture to the next.

The integrated note-taking and studying process

The "integrated approach" means that taking notes (and then reviewing and filtering them) is part of a semester-long, nightly process of studying. Through that repetitive process, the ideas and concepts become so fixed in your mind that, during a final exam, you'll easily recall information from the very beginning of the semester.

Here's the basic process:

1. Attend class and takes notes during the lecture. Emphasize in your notes the main points of the lecture. Read all outside material assigned by the professor.

2. Seek clarification on the lecture's main points from teaching assistants, the professor, and the reading material. Listen to the lecture a second time on tape, if possible. Add to your notes accordingly. (We'll call this process the clarification process.)

3. Highlight the key words and phrases in the clarified lecture notes.

4. Go to the next lecture and take notes for main points. Do the required reading. Start the clarification process.

5. Before you review the current lecture notes (to complete this clarification process), review all the previous lecture notes, pausing over the highlighted key words or phrases. If you have not yet highlighted key words and phrases in the previous day's lecture notes, do so before moving on to the current notes.

6. Finish the clarification process before you attend the next lecture.

7. On days you haven't had a lecture, take the opportunity to review all the previous lecture notes and highlighted key words and phrasing.

8. Repeat this cycle during the entire semester.

It all adds up

By the time you review notes for class number ten, you will have studied your first day's notes ten times; your second day's notes, nine times; your third day's notes, eight times, and so on. By the end of the semester, you will have reviewed your highlighted notes several hundred times (if you were to add all of those numbers together). You will find, moreover, that, by the eighth class meeting, for example, you're virtually skimming through the notes for classes one through six—because you've reviewed those note pages so many times.

This process of note-taking entails major commitment, part of the ninety minutes per day that you should be allotting for *each* of your four to five classes. *Believe* me, by your junior and senior years this investment of time will be paying tremendous dividends in the form of higher grades and exclusive memberships in honor societies and academic organizations.

Getting ready for an exam

Here's how you can get ready for an examination in the humanities or the social sciences. About three weeks before a midterm or a final examination, review each work or major concept that you've covered in class. On an index card, enter five to ten key ideas (summarized in no more than five words apiece) for each of the works or concepts that will likely appear on the examination.

If, for example, you're studying the Protestant Reformation of the sixteenth century, you'll likely have to recall the so-called "Five Points of Calvinism." You could roughly summarize them as follows:

1. Man totally depraved

2. Grace is unconditional and unmerited

3. Not everybody saved—limited atonement

4. Grace is irresistible when offered

5. The saved persevere—can't fall away

Since you've reviewed your highlighted notes every night, those three or four words can evoke several sentences that readily come to mind. Study those points over and over, so that you will be able to enter the examination with a mental list of things to say about each important concept.

Create an acronym

Perhaps a week before the exam, try to take the five ideas on each index card and create an acronym, each letter of which evokes one of the main points about that concept.

One of the most famous acronyms in Western culture is the word "TULIP." Any student who commits that word to memory can give a lecture on the "five points of Calvinism":

Total depravity

Unconditional election

Limited atonement

Irresistible grace

Perseverance of the saints

The acronym allows the student to recall the five points, and each point lends itself to a paragraph-length discussion during a blue-book examination. Acronyms are memory devices that open up a wealth of recollections waiting to be harvested from the serious study and nightly review of one's notes and reading.

While the concepts you prepare in acronym form may not exactly match the questions posed by the professor, they often will; and that will give you an organized outline for responding to most essay-format test questions that emerge from the professor's lecture or from assigned reading.

Study groups

As suggested earlier, study groups are a useful way of supplementing private study—especially in mathematics and the physical sciences (though I have seen successful study groups in the humanities as well). If that works for you, organize study groups and incorporate the results of those conversations into the main points on your index cards. Most campus libraries have rooms set aside for meetings of these discussion groups.

The pyramid of exam preparation

Here's an illustration of the integrated process of note-taking and exam preparation. You can see how this integrated approach offers the best chance of making As on exams:

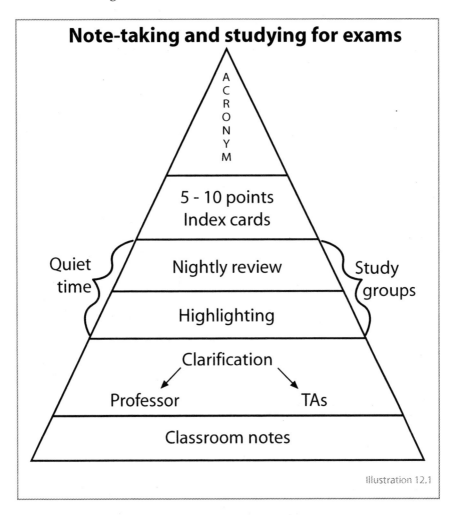

I used this technique from my sophomore year onward. During those years, I scored an A in every one of my undergraduate courses. I also used this method to prepare for every graduate-school exam I took at Cornell University, as well as for the comprehensive oral examinations that I passed before beginning my doctoral dissertation work.

Extra tips for mathematics and science students

Since I'm not a science professor, I polled several very successful math/ science students to find out about their note-taking and studying techniques, which I'll share with you here.

Note-taking if the professor hands out an outline

Math and science teachers often distribute outlines and handouts corresponding to the substance of each lecture. Take notes right on those outlines to avoid having to recopy material. Annotate the notes with key points from the lecture that clarify the notes. If you must take notes from scratch, focus on keeping up, since copying verbatim is nearly impossible. Copy the important diagrams, and jot down a few words about each critical concept. You can always go back and fill in the gaps. That's a lot better than forgetting to note a crucial concept and then being unable to go back to fill in your knowledge about it.

One idea: Taking notes in a small notebook

A former Goldwater Scholar, who was also an Intel Science Talent Search Finalist (ranking in the top ten students nationwide) let me know that, lacking pre-printed notes, he usually took notes in a small notebook to force himself, from the outset, to distinguish between what was vital and what was not. (This advice, solely for math and science, differs from the note-taking advice offered above relative to the humanities and social sciences.)

Doing the reading helps with note-taking and vice-versa

When taking notes in math and the sciences, be sure that you're "up" on all assigned reading. The assigned reading serves as a mental road map that allows you more comfortably to locate—literally to "note"— the main topics in a professor's lecture. Even better, *read ahead*. The very best students do so in order to get the most out of lectures, enabling them to ask intelligent questions and thereby turn book knowledge into usable understanding.

Some people learn best by listening to a lecture; others, by reading the assigned chapter. If you read comprehensively and attend all classes, you will likely understand both the lecture and the book chapters. The psychologist William James claimed that people learn the most by approaching the same body of knowledge through different senses. Hence the combination of reading and listening noted here would prove an optimal strategy for study—especially if you have permission to tape your professor's lecture and replay it in order to refine your notes.

Repetition is the key to understanding

In math and science courses, review, review, review. Repetition is the key to long-term retention and useful application of what you memorize. When memorizing not-too-exciting lists of technical material, try to employ different senses—that is, memorize a list of words; listen to that list of words on a tape-recorder; then consult visual illustrations of the list.

In other science courses requiring a great deal of memorization, a nightly drill will facilitate memorization and eventually allow you to begin to apply what you've memorized. The bottom line in preparing for math and science exams is to study in such a manner as to facilitate both recall and total comprehension by the time of the examination.

Connecting the dots

Highly successful students often rewrite their notes, refining them in the process, in order to let the information "sink in." The key here is *not* to rewrite the notes verbatim, but to distill everything in such manner as to reason your way through the diverse topics. If you are unable to do that, visit a teaching assistant or the professor and seek an explanation that will allow you to recopy your notes with greater clarity.

If possible, make note of connections between ideas, since the professor may not stop to do so during a lecture. Stated otherwise, revamp your notes so as to articulate those links explicitly. The more connections you are able to draw, the better you will have mastered "the big picture," tracing the broad direction of a lecture.

Outlining notes

Successful students in mathematics and the sciences also make outlines of their notes, along with all topics covered in external reading. They then use these sheets as prompts, to recall as many details as possible. This method mimics the "acronym" technique for test-taking in the humanities. Even here, the emphasis is equally divided between memorization and understanding. Without understanding, memorization will fall short of the mark, and true comprehension only occurs over months and weeks of review, and with several steps in digesting one's notes. True understanding seldom comes from crash studying. Start early and distill your notes often.

Be wary of relying entirely on "past examinations"

Some science professors post their past examinations on the Internet and encourage students to study those in order to prepare for upcoming exams. Definitely make use of posted examinations, but realize that most professors refine those every year. Ultimately, you must master every significant point covered in the assigned reading and in your lecture notes. Don't let access to past examinations lull you into false sense of security.

Get help when you need it

Here's an innovative study technique used by one of my Goldwater Scholars who transferred to Stanford University. The professor's teaching assistants held office hours in a rather large room. The student would bring her homework to that room during the teaching assistants' office hours and complete her homework there. That way, whenever she reached a brick wall, she was able to ask questions, get immediate feedback, and move on rather than waste time with misguided approaches. In essence, she had three tutors for the price of her tuition alone. Pretty slick. However you acquire help, get it as soon as you need it in math and the sciences. You can otherwise lose control of the material very quickly.

Find out, as well, what free tutoring programs the department or school offers. Take advantage of those.

Study groups for math/science students

As suggested elsewhere in this book, join study groups. Nightly sessions lasting two to three hours allow students to complete their homework with greater understanding, since somebody is bound to have superior insight into various points under discussion. (Be sure that completing homework within a study group is agreeable to your professor—otherwise use the study group only to review material.)

Last-minute cramming doesn't work for math/science students, either

Even the best students in math and the sciences find that it often takes more time to study with comprehension than they originally estimated it would; they therefore learn to study consistently and comprehensively every night. The best students do not cram, since last-minute desperation does not allow students to master underlying principles and concepts.

Work the problems

When studying math, you should work on practice problems every night, until you have a firm grasp of the underlying concept in advance of the examination. If you have problems with the practice problems, seek out a teaching assistant's, a tutor's, or the professor's help—long before the examination. One particularly successful math student I interviewed said that he re-did all of his math homework problems when getting ready for exams. What better preparation?

Conclusion

Realize that you can either go into an examination as well prepared as possible—or wing it, hoping that the key points miraculously come to mind. Which do you think will work better?

Chapter Thirteen

Tips for Taking Tests

Let me stress, first and foremost: there is no magic tip for test-taking that can take the place of solid, consistent *preparation*. The best tip for test-taking, therefore, is for you to review the previous chapters on note-taking and studying. As you know, I believe that if you have properly prepared for an exam you will be able to anticipate—and be ready to elaborate upon—the exam questions in humanities and social sciences courses.

Similarly, if you've done the requisite memorization for science courses, and if you've tirelessly worked and reworked representative "practice problems" in math—to the point where you understand the underlying principle of the problem—then you ought to do well in any exam.

That said, there are still a number of things you can do—while you are actually in the process of taking the test—to enhance your prospects for earning a good or excellent grade.

Test formats

Examinations come in a variety of formats: essay, short answer, multiple choice, fill-in-the-blank, problem-solving, or outright demonstration (for instance, accomplishing a task on the computer in a computer class). The exam often combines several of the formats listed here. Most exams take place in the classroom or an exam room, although professors sometimes allow "take home" exams. Most of the advice I offer below relates to the conventional "timed" exams, for which all or a large part of the exam grade pertains to essay questions.

The "essay" exam

In the humanities and social sciences, the "essay" examination is the most common format, especially for midterm and final examinations. Other parts of the exam may be short answer or multiple choice. In mathematics and the sciences you will, of course, have problems to solve and scientific facts for which you'll be held responsible.

Unless you take a multiple-choice Scantron exam, or your professor passes out worksheets containing problems for you to solve (with allotted space for each problem), you'll take most of your college essay exams in "blue books." These are sheets of lined paper bound in the shape of a thin booklet, and having blue paper covers. They cost less than a dollar and are available at your local campus store, or in area bookstores. Always bring an extra blue book with you to each exam. Occasionally you will run out of space for your answers, and you want to be prepared.

Penmanship does count

If you're taking an essay exam, write neatly. You'd be surprised how many students have sloppy handwriting. That's a real turn-off for the professor, who then has to work extra hard merely to see *what* you're saying. If your handwriting is atrocious, *print* your responses.

We professors have to make our way through countless blue books, usually over weekends and holidays. So why not have your bluebook be one of those about which we say, "Ah, neat handwriting; this will be a pleasure to read!" That can't hurt, and it may even help in instances when there's a close call as to whether the response merits a B+ or an A-. What will certainly help is the professor's ability to read each of your words and comprehend all of your sentences.

I can recall a number of blue books containing such messy handwriting that I couldn't make out key words in a sentence and had to guess about those from the larger context of the sentence.

Pen vs. pencil

Also, for essay exams write in *pen*, not in pencil. Pencil does not convey a professional image, and a dull pencil becomes so faint, at times, as to make for a difficult "read." If you need the security of being able to erase, then invest in erasable pens. Those cost about $1.25. Generally, however, professors will not mind crossed-out words and phrases.

In math and science courses, on the other hand, you may be expected to do computations in pencil, so as to be able to erase. However, good handwriting will be an asset there as well, especially in exams requiring sentence-length explanations.

Timing matters, too

Second, bring a watch to each and every exam, just in case the room does not have a working clock on the wall. At least one-third of my students fail to do that. To figure out how many minutes to allot to each question, divide all the minutes at your disposal by the total number of test questions. Determine a schedule and then stick to it.

I have seen students spend so much time on the initial question that they either didn't have time to finish the entire exam or ended up spending little time on the remaining questions. Failing to answer a question will lower your exam grade immensely, even if the answers you *do* have time to offer are brilliant. Pacing is the key.

Here's a basic example. Assume that you have to answer four questions in eighty minutes (in a typical Tuesday/Thursday class): accordingly block out twenty minutes for each essay. Draw on your store of knowledge to answer each question (if you've prepared properly, you'll have plenty to say). When the amount of time you've set aside for each question is over, move on to the next question. Stick to your schedule.

Of course, this is a very simple example. If your exam consists of a variety of formats with different weights for the overall grade, then divide the time you have according to the weight of the section. For instance, if the short-answer section of an exam counts for ten percent of the grade, then spend only ten percent of your time on those questions.

Here's a tip for adding material later in the exam period. You may remember something you could have said in an earlier essay, or perhaps you'll have a few minutes left at the end of the exam period to review what you've written. If you think that you have more to say in an essay, you'll need room to add those additional thoughts. So, when you finish an essay, always try to leave at least three-fourths of the last page *blank*. Use this space for "afterthoughts"; your professor will have no way of knowing that you added these sentences later.

Don't be the first one out the door

Along that same vein, do not be spooked when some student turns in a blue book after only forty-five minutes. In general, the first person to leave hasn't studied for the exam and has little to say. My best students are usually those who take advantage of every single minute to search their mental outlines and memories for every possible point they might retrieve.

There are usually five to seven students still writing when everybody else has left. Most of those who remain are the A students.

Outline each essay answer before answering

Most importantly, for courses in the humanities or social sciences, sketch a brief *outline* at the beginning of each essay question. You have already learned how to study with index cards and acronyms. Before you begin to compose any essay question, expand those acronyms and other memory devices into a rough outline of the points you plan to raise. In fact, if you have twenty minutes to devote to a particular essay question, spend up to four or five of those minutes jotting down your outline.

Why an outline? Because professors usually judge you, relative to the rest of the class, on the number of key points you raise. In fact, in order to grade equitably, we usually look for certain points that we have stressed and therefore grade according to our internal checklist of appropriate responses. If you adequately touch on each of those points in your essay, you're likely to get full credit for that question. But if you raise only three out of the possible six points on the professor's "checklist," then you will probably earn only half credit for that answer. Thus, if you outline your answers before you begin to write, and if you stick to your outline, you are more likely to anticipate most of the professor's checklist. You are also less apt to get sidetracked or fail to answer the question thoroughly.

Again, by creating an outline based on consistent study throughout the semester, you guarantee that you will touch upon most or all of the points for which the professor is looking. Students who do not use outlines often latch onto one or two very good points and discuss those at length for three or four pages. They're then surprised to find that they've received a C or a D for that response. Your grade for an essay will not usually depend on the number of pages you write—it will, rather, be tied to how many of the points on the professor's checklist you manage to address.

Outlines also steer you from point to point in a logical order. When you start with an outline, even a crude one, the resulting essay is more coherent and less likely to look like random thoughts littering a blue book.

After you finish the essay, simply go back to the outline and place a large X through it—to demonstrate that you don't expect the professor to grade the outline. Still, the professor will get to *see* the outline and will know immediately that you have a comprehensive and organized understanding of the material. If, therefore, one of your points is somewhat vague, the professor may be more inclined to give you the benefit of the doubt, since obviously you "know your stuff."

I have found that students excel when they preface blue-book essays with substantial outlines. For many years, I have encouraged students to use this technique and have consistently observed positive results.

What to do when you can't finish the last essay

You may find yourself only part way through the last essay question and suddenly hear the professor announce "OK—two minutes left." Don't panic. In those two minutes, do not try to elaborate upon everything else that was in your original outline for the last essay. Finish the essay by composing a key-word outline for the points you would have raised in detail. Time permitting, place a dash after each point and add a few words to show the direction that you might have taken with that concept.

Professors who see such an outline at the end of an incomplete essay are inclined to infer that you had mastered the remaining points and would have elaborated upon those intelligently, given the time. You may get a far better grade on that last question if you use this method for completing your response than if you simply write another sentence or two with no explanation of what else you had wanted to say.

Writing flattery at the end of a final exam won't help your grade

At the end of the final essay in your exam, *do not* write compliments to the professor on the inspiring nature of the course. One or two students in every class do this at the end of the final exam, and the compliment usually strikes the instructor as disingenuous. Regular classroom participation is where genuine enthusiasm emerges. If you want the professor to be positively inclined towards you, demonstrate your enthusiasm throughout the semester, not on the last page of your final exam.

Conclusion

Outline your answer before composing it. Pace yourself. After completing a response, leave three-fourths of a page blank—for afterthoughts. If you run out of time on your last response, include elements from your outline—to show how you would have completed the answer.

Chapter Fourteen

Preventing and Handling Academic Problems

Students commonly experience academic problems, especially during the first semester of college. If a problem arises, don't be afraid to take action. In fact, you should take immediate action—before things get out of control and you find yourself in a dean's office begging for a "late" withdrawal from your courses.

Preventing academic problems

The preferred strategy for dealing with problems is pre-emptive. This preventive advice can be summed up in two words: Be prepared.

Math and science

Make sure you are academically prepared for the courses you plan to take. Many problems occur when students take courses for which they are not yet prepared—especially in the sciences. Before enrolling in Engineering Calculus, for example, speak to a professor about your current background in math. See if you are better suited to an entry-level math class. The same holds true for Organic Chemistry and other science classes. Make sure you have the skills that are prerequisite for success in that class. If you don't, first enroll in a course that prepares you for the more difficult class—which you can then take the next semester. Don't worry about "falling behind"; you can always catch up.

Communication skills

Make sure your written and verbal communication skills are up to speed.

Almost all college classes have a writing component, and you'll want to be an impressive writer. (In fact, written communication is so vital that I've devoted an entire section in this book to preparation for college-level writing.) But verbal skills are also important, and you should seriously consider enrolling in a speech class, or even in an elective drama class (students who can "act" are effective speakers).

Nor would it hurt to read vocabulary-building books, especially if you haven't been an active reader before college. Joining social clubs that require you to interact with other people will also help develop your verbal skills. So will your local "Toastmasters Club," which gives people practice in speaking publicly.

Learn about your professors before you enroll in their courses

Earlier, I advised researching your professors to learn if you wish to study with them. You may learn that a professor's personality and teaching style are inconsistent with your ability to learn or to make a high grade. For instance, I know someone who avoided a professor who prided himself on awarding just one A per class, per semester. That policy struck the student as unfair, so he took control of the situation by enrolling in an alternate section of the same course. His was a smart decision, as far as I'm concerned.

I would, though, offer two caveats: (1) don't make enrollment decisions on the basis of rumors or off-hand remarks from unreliable sources, and (2) don't shy away from "tough" professors just because they are considered demanding; these professors are often the best because they have high standards for their students. They might write the best letters of recommendation, as well, for students whom they consider up to snuff.

Take advantage of the Add/Drop period if a course gets off to a bad start. If, after the first several classes, you have good reason to believe that you should not stay in that class, then either drop the course or try switching to another section of the class taught by a different professor.

Don't overload yourself

If it is a legitimate option at your university, consider taking no more than four classes (twelve hours) in your first semester. Although a five-class, fifteen-hour load (on a semester system) is considered conventional, it can prove overwhelming for some freshmen. Better to start out with a quite reasonable class load than to have everything collapse in on you.

Also, be careful not to drop below "full-time student" designation, as that could compromise your enrollment status or nullify your financial aid package. You'll find, as well, that national scholarship competitions usually demand "full-time student" status.

Also, endeavor not to schedule two very difficult classes back-to-back. You may not be able to absorb as much in the second class.

Come to college emotionally prepared

This may seem obvious, but students do sometimes get into trouble academically because they won't or can't take care of themselves. Some behavioral patterns are incompatible with a highly successful college education. Drug or alcohol use, compulsive gambling, unstable and/or abusive relationships, depression, living in a party-like atmosphere—any one of these or some combination of them can destroy a successful college career.

Avoid these problems—and try not to get emotionally involved with people who already have them. If you are experiencing one or more of these entanglements, make the necessary changes before you get to college. If you can't do that on your own, take a step in the right direction and seek professional help. College, in and of itself, will never cure such difficulties. Its pressures will only compound them. Live the sort of life that allows you to stay focused on your academics—just as you would do with a full-time job at which you wanted to distinguish yourself.

Handling academic problems

Stuff happens, even on college campuses. Below are some of the more common issues that can arise for college students. Whatever the problem, get administrative or professional help at the earliest possible time.

Getting additional clarification

If you don't understand the lectures or written material in a course, take full advantage of a professor's office hours to get more information. Better yet, if the professor has teaching assistants, visit them first, and then follow up with the professor to clarify any issues that remain unclear. Most teaching assistants and professors offer up to five or six office hours a week, yet relatively few students ever visit. Don't feel as if either the professor or the teaching assistants are doing you a favor by taking time to work with you. That's why they are there.

When you attend an office hour, however, *come prepared*. Don't expect the professor simply to review everything he or she has already covered in class. Have a precise list of items for which you need clarification; be able to specify what you understand and what you don't. That helps professors help you.

Hire tutors when necessary

You may find yourself needing a tutor at some point in college, especially in your freshman year. Don't be embarrassed to ask for one. Many colleges offer tutoring services for free or at a discounted rate. If you can't get adequate tutoring from your college, or if you're dissatisfied with whomever they assign you, swallow your pride and hire a better tutor. This is especially important in foreign-language, math, or math-based courses.

Professors likely know the best tutors, since their graduate students always need extra money and are more than willing to take on this sort of assignment. Otherwise, you might seek an undergraduate tutor—let's say a senior math major known for his or her mathematical prowess. Often the Learning Centers on campus keep lists of advanced students willing to tutor for a fee. One way or the other, you *can* locate a qualified tutor.

If you are being tutored in math or math-based courses, have the tutor sit beside you while you complete your homework, and have him interrupt you whenever you make a mistake. Pay the tutor to make you work out the problem correctly—so that you will understand the principles behind the correct answer and be prepared to complete a problem like this on your own. Part of the tutor's job is to get you to the point where you no longer need a tutor. (And, by the way, this describes the way I hired a tutor when, as a freshman in college, I had difficulty in my Engineering Calculus class.)

Be aware of drop deadlines

Nearly all universities allow you to drop a course without any permanent record of that transaction on your transcript—but only if you do this within the first few weeks of a class. There is no disgrace in dropping a course that is overwhelming. If you've tried working with the professor, but still seem to be in over your head, opt out while that is still an option. Make plans to take that course later—after you're better prepared. Always keep track of the "drop-without-record" deadline.

Before dropping any course, however, find out if your doing so will cause you to surrender "full-time student" status and thereby nullify your undergraduate standing or financial aid package. In such cases, discuss your problem immediately with appropriate university officials.

Following that "drop without record" period, universities generally allow students to receive a grade of W (Withdrawn) or W-P or W-F (Withdrawn-Passing; Withdrawn-Failing). It's better to have a W-P than a D or an F. (It happens to the best of us—I myself took a W in an astronomy class my freshman year!) Learn the deadlines for this procedure, but be aware that too many Ws can compromise your transcript and prospects.

Be aware of retroactive withdrawals

Most students never realize that, in dire circumstances, a student can receive a withdrawal from a course either after the official drop-with-out-penalty deadline or, in rare cases, even after the semester has ended. Assistant or associate deans within the colleges that sponsor the course often have the authority to authorize a retroactive W. These grades are limited to distress cases involving students who should have withdrawn from courses (but who failed to do so) for reasons relating to personal health, divorce, or bereavement. Don't, however, seek one of these Ws for flimsy reasons; you'll just end up embarrassing yourself.

Personal problems

Campuses typically offer a variety of services to assist you with personal matters—such as health or legal problems. For instance, if you are having trouble with a landlord, you may be able to get legal advice from the university legal office sponsored by Student Services (as opposed to university counsel, which represents the university's interests).

You may also wish to consult with designated chaplains of your religious denomination. They often have a building close to campus. Give them a chance to counsel you. They've likely seen your problem before and can offer advice. Psychological counseling is often available at the campus Counseling Center, if you suffer from depression. Under normal circumstances, of course, your parents and family should be your first resource whenever troubles arise.

For financial problems, the financial-aid office always has counselors. Many students have told me that they quickly accumulated credit-card debt in the early years of college and that they then had to work extra hours to pay that debt. Those extra hours negatively affected their academic performance. Work with the financial-aid office whenever money becomes a problem.

Be cautious of an "Animal House" fraternity life

Be wary of zealously committing yourself to a fraternity in your freshman year. In the long-run, that affiliation could be invaluable and rewarding (the social skills you develop there, relative to getting along with others and practicing leadership, can be especially vital in the world of business). But, in the short run, hazing, drinking, and carousing can derail your college experience. It's far easier to go out for three-to-four-hour pizza runs than to hunker down for organized nightly study. *Animal House* is a great movie to watch, not to *live*.

Students with disabilities

Nearly all universities now have an "Office of Disability Accommodation." If you have a physical disability that affects your academic performance, register with this office and take advantage of the variety of services that can make your stay on campus more productive.

Personal-interaction problems with professors

It is uncommon for students to have personal-interaction problems with professors, since most professors are professional and courteous. If, however, a serious difficulty occurs, but falls short of personal intimidation, then you ought to visit the professor to see if there's a way to resolve the situation expeditiously.

If, on the other hand, the problem relates to personal intimidation (and that will be rare, but it does sometimes happen), then you should visit the department's undergraduate advisor to explain the matter and to request either to be withdrawn from the course or switched into another section of the same course. The undergraduate advisor, in turn, may then choose to talk to the department chair about the professor to decide how best to address the problem.

Stated otherwise, a chain of appeal exists that usually goes from the professor to the undergraduate advisor, to the associate chair (if one exists), to the chair, to the dean, to offices of equity and diversity, and higher. Simply determine the correct protocol within that department and take it from there. On such occasions, you may choose to have a parent accompany you. In cases where the student has a legitimate complaint about a professor's decorum, a parent's presence can have a dramatic impact upon the chain of command responsible for remedying the situation sooner rather than later.

Complaining about grades

If you feel that you've received an unfair grade on either a paper or an examination, use diplomacy when approaching the professor. First, be quite sure that your response on an examination or essay assignment actually met the specified criteria for a higher grade than you received. Professors customarily place remarks on your exams and essays that point out exactly why you earned the assigned grade.

If you feel that either the professor or a teaching assistant overlooked your achievement in that area, then visit the professor during an office hour and be polite and talkative. Demonstrate an awareness of the professor's (or teaching assistant's) criticism of your performance and—on those rare occasions when it's appropriate to proceed further—be prepared to point out passages where you believe that you met the criteria for a higher grade or score. If the verdict ends up being against you, you might inquire about the possibility of "extra credit" work. Finally, when making such appeals, project the attitude that you want to benefit by having a professor review your exam/paper and point out exactly what went wrong. Use that knowledge to your advantage in the next exam/paper.

In cases where you are dissatisfied with the professor's response to your visit, explore the departmental protocol for "grade appeals." Do, however, be aware that other professors will seldom overturn a colleague's grade. They assume that he or she best understands the purpose and standards of the assignment.

Extensions on papers, and missing exams for family/employment emergencies

Life is complex and unpredictable. Illness or family emergencies may cause you to seek an extension on an essay assignment or a midterm examination. In this case, visit the professor during an office hour (or telephone or e-mail if an office conference isn't feasible) and respectfully explain the situation and why you would like an extension. Be prepared to let the professor know by what date you could reasonably complete the assignment. Different professors will respond differently. Just give it your best shot. I, for one, sometimes grant brief extensions on essays, but I seldom allow students to postpone an examination for reasons other than bereavement or illness.

In general, however, earnestly avoid seeking a semester grade of "incomplete." Even if a professor is willing to award you an "I" rather than a conventional grade, you should resist that option. "I"s become a veritable albatross around your neck. It is a great mistake to be completing previous courses during a new semester or over the summer. That is when, instead, you should be moving on to new courses, new work, new achievements.

Leaving a class early because of a doctor's appointment or other obligation

At some point in your academic career, you will have to leave a class early for a legitimate reason. Try *not* to approach the professor before class begins to explain that at such and such hour, you'll have to leave for a doctor's appointment. He or she may understand why you're leaving, but the rest of the class will not, and you'll *appear* to be rude when you depart without apparent cause. To avoid that scenario, sit near an exit, wait until the professor is just about to begin the lecture, raise your hand, and say something like, "I've got to leave at 11:30 a.m. for a doctor's appointment. Please accept my apology in advance." The professor will appreciate your courtesy and *everybody* will then understand why you're leaving early.

Discipline Problems

Campuses have rules, just like other corporate entities. Those rules are usually stated in a student handbook. These may not always be what you might expect, so you should read through the handbook that sets out those rules. Times have changed in the last several years; in particular you should be aware of the expanding jurisdiction of speech codes. Moreover, the use of cellular telephones and cellular telephone cameras is now restricted in some classrooms. A student's Internet visits to inappropriate websites can be tracked. Become (and stay) familiar with what is allowed and disallowed. You do not want to have the momentum of your career disrupted by the necessity of disciplinary hearings and appeals.

Conclusion

To handle problems, take action before a situation gets out of control. Remember:

- You can prevent a good number of academic problems by honing your writing skills and by learning about professors before you enroll in their classes.

- Take whatever steps are necessary to clarify course material, and be aware of help options and "drop" deadlines.

- Avoid an "Animal House" lifestyle.

- Be diplomatic when asking professors to review a grade or grant an extension.

- Avoid inappropriate behavior.

Chapter Fifteen

Distance Learning

What is distance learning?

Many universities, including very prestigious ones, are now offering distance-learning courses. Such courses are sometimes called "distributed learning" because the professor's lecture is distributed electronically to as many people (sometimes in other parts of the country or world) as wish to sign up for that course. In some distance-learning scenarios, you may never be in the same room with the professor or with any of the other students in your class. Other "blended" distance-learning classes may require occasional visits to campus.

Within the next decade, most college students (whether they live on or off campus) may complete twenty percent or more of their college classes through distance learning. While distance learning can never take the place of the conventional college-classroom experience, computerized instruction is rapidly gaining ground in certain fields.

Technology makes it all possible ·

A distance-learning class can involve any or all of these Internet technologies:

- Desktop video or computer conferencing
- E-mail
- Chat rooms
- Message boards or discussion forums

Distance learning may also occur by other non-Internet means, such as surface mail, video, interactive or cable television, or satellite broadcast.

So, how does this work?

You'll probably see and hear the professor's lectures online, using some sort of software on your computer that allows for streaming video. (The university offering the distance learning course will make this software available for you to download.) Sometimes you'll be watching a live broadcast of your professor's lecture and sometimes you'll watch a pre-recorded lecture. Also, you may use your own computer at work or at home to view the lectures, or you may be able to use a computer that's available on campus.

You'll interact with your professor and other students through e-mail, chat rooms, or message boards. Some distance-learning courses allow for e-mail questions, to which a professor can respond directly and instantaneously. Still other distance-learning classes entail video conferencing that allows for at least some face-to-face (or image-to-image) interaction.

In writing courses, you'll probably get feedback on your writing through e-mail or through comments returned in your original document.

Who can benefit from a distance-learning course?

Distance-learning courses have become popular among students who feel quite at home at their computers. The same courses also provide university access to persons who would otherwise be unable to travel to a college campus to enroll in that particular course. People who have conventional 8:00 a.m. to 5:00 p.m. jobs find that they can participate in distance learning during evenings and on weekends. For these and other reasons, universities are actively encouraging their faculty to sponsor online courses, though most professors still prefer the classroom format where they can see and speak with their pupils.

The bottom line behind the hype

There is a bottom-line dollar incentive for university sponsorship of distance learning. Universities compete with one another to earn your tuition dollars and are just as happy to have your tuition coming to them via distance learning as through conventional classroom registration. There is, moreover, a nearly infinite market of revenue for distance-learning enrollment. Count on American universities to continue to compete aggressively for those dollars—and for many colleges to be offering more and more online classes even to students who live on campus.

Some of the downsides

As I think back on the most stimulating and inspiring courses I took as an undergraduate and as a graduate student, I cannot imagine duplicating those classroom experiences online. There is something that happens in face-to-face contact that's never going to occur when you look at a computer screen or read an e-mail. I wonder if students will get the same feedback and support, whether they will feel as connected to their campus and colleagues, and whether professors will in turn learn as much with less student interaction (yes, we learn from students, too!). And what about those crucial letters of recommendation? How can professors write as enthusiastically about someone they barely know except from the cool medium of Internet exchanges?

Some university classes also involve hands-on activities, such as lab work for a chemistry class. These hands-on activities will be exceedingly difficult to duplicate on a computer screen, not to mention the loss of camaraderie that often results from cooperative student work.

The jury is still out on distance learning, but there's no question that it will play a role in every university's future.

Should you take distance learning classes?

So where does this leave *you*, relative to these courses? First you should decide whether you have the discipline and steady work habits that could make those courses work *for you*. If you really need the structure and personal feedback of a traditional classroom setting, then distance learning shouldn't be your first choice.

Before enrolling in a distance-learning course, you ought to learn as much about your prospective professor as you would if you were researching professors with whom to study in conventional classes. Obviously, some distance-learning professors will be better than others. A distance-learning professor may or may not have the credentials or publishing experience you would desire. Contact the professor who is offering the course as well as students who have already taken the course to ask how the course material is presented. In other words, be an informed consumer. If the feedback you get from students is superb, then this may be the course for you (especially if taking it will help you avoid some unnecessary transportation costs).

Your writing and communication skills will be critical

Before enrolling in distance-learning classes, be sure your expository writing is up to speed. A huge difference exists between advancing an idea in speech and having to commit the same thought to prose that will be assessed by the professor and possibly by other students in the class. What can pass as intelligent conversation can come· across as less than impressive in writing. Before enrolling in a distance-education course, be aware of the extent to which your written utterance will determine your course grade—even in casual online "discussion" contexts.

Remember, part of your goal when you take any class is to make a very positive impression on the professor—so much so that the professor will be willing to oversee your future research or creative project. If you demonstrate through e-mail or chat-room writing that you're having a hard time expressing your thoughts coherently, you'll be less likely to develop a mentoring relationship with that professor. I would especially caution you to avoid many of the faddish writing conventions that crop up in e-mails and chat rooms and stick as much as possible to traditional English spelling and grammar.

Also, be careful not to put anything in writing that could be read as insulting or demeaning either to the professor or other students. It's easy to get carried away in a debate; what might sound OK with a certain tone of voice in classroom dialogue may appear harsh and offensive in writing.

What else will you need to do in a distance learning course to get the same benefits offered in a traditional classroom?

Do you have to do *more* than just take the course to get the identical benefits? In my opinion, yes. When you enroll in a distance-learning class, you should still seek out opportunities to visit the professor, and in such manner as to make an impression beyond that facilitated through e-mail exchange or in a computer chat room. Stated otherwise, have the professor come to know you personally, so as to be able to link a face with a name, and then to link that name to a committed person having a fine personality. You also want the professor to be able to recall several office visits characterized by intelligent dialogue.

Conclusion

Ask yourself whether distance learning is right for you. In sum, if you are living on or near your college campus, and if you are considering a distance-learning course in your major field of study, you want to take into account whether or not such enrollment would likely result in research or other mentoring opportunities with the professor who sponsors your distance-learning course. If you are already "set" on both a research assignment and on comprehensive letters of endorsement, then these concerns may weigh less heavily in your decision about enrolling in distance-education courses.

Section 4 :: Mastering Effective Communication

Chapter Sixteen

Why Communication Skills Are So Important

In college

Success in college requires advanced writing skills. You'll compose term papers, essay exams, scholarship or award applications, and e-mail communications with professors. Moreover, some online courses require your participation in chat rooms or online forums. Then there are certain majors quite literally *about* writing or communication: English, Technical Writing, Journalism, Marketing, Speech, Graphic Design—even Computer Programming.

In the real world

Even after you've graduated from college, you'll need advanced writing abilities. Many employers lament the failure of their employees to put words together coherently, especially since today's jobs require much more writing than most people might suspect.

Expectations are even higher in graduate programs, which require a constant stream of essays, essay examinations, and then a major thesis (for a master's degree) or a dissertation (for a Ph.D.). Even if you eventually become self-employed, you'll likely communicate in writing with clients, colleagues, or professional organizations.

There's no getting around it: excellent writing skills are a *must*—now and in the future.

Although undergraduates who made superior grades in high school consider themselves to be good writers, I have seen very few freshmen who possessed *excellent* writing skills when they entered college. I have, in fact, witnessed a decline in merely *competent* writing skills, even among the highest achievers. Television, the Internet, and computer games have clearly taken their toll.

Planning for future scholarship applications

Remember, too, that good writing assists immeasurably if you apply for nationally competitive scholarships. Your campus scholarship advisor will be able to offer far more comments pertaining to the substance of your scholarship essays if he or she does not have to spend excessive time urging you to correct multiple stylistic problems in different parts of your application.

Find a writing class appropriate for you

Beyond freshman composition, take one or more upper-division elective courses (such as expository writing, or advanced expository writing) to improve your persuasive writing skills. See the chapter "Which Courses *Not* to Place Out Of," for additional information about which courses you should take.

Reviewing some basic concepts for future study

Although we can't cram an entire writing course into a few pages, we should review some basics about college-level writing. The purpose of this section is to acquaint you with concepts that you'll want to develop in your college writing. You will be at an advantage if you understand these categories early in your college career.

We'll cover:

- The basics of writing the college-level essay.

- The index-card approach to structuring an essay.

- Learning to edit your own prose.

Chapter Seventeen

The Basics of the College-Level Essay

Why is the college essay so important? It's the most common way you'll communicate with your professors to show what you've learned, and to demonstrate that you can conduct research and develop ideas persuasively. College-level essays are not about regurgitating what you have read in a chapter or heard in the lecture hall. College essays demonstrate what you bring to the table of intellectual discussion in your area of study.

Note: Don't think to yourself, "But I'm only a freshman in college; what do I have to contribute?" As an individual, you have unique and intriguing perspectives to share with your colleagues. Indeed, you should start thinking of your professors and fellow students that way now. Every field needs new blood, new thoughts, new discoveries, and new life experiences. That's why you're in college.

How should you view yourself when you write the college essay?

First, you are now a scholar. That means that you aim to offer information or perspectives that would otherwise be unavailable to persons interested in your topic.

What are you writing about?

Second, you are analyzing a body of data critically—that is to say, analytically and persuasively. This body of data might be a poem, an art exhibit, a historical movement, a scientific experiment, a recent sociological trend, the works of a philosopher, or secondary criticism about a novel.

Who is your audience?

Third, you are writing to the informed reader. The informed reader is anybody who is already familiar with your data but who stands to gain a new perspective about it. For instance, if you are writing about an assigned novel, assume that your reader has already read the novel and its plot but hasn't considered the work from *your* perspective.

What's the goal of a persuasive essay?

The essay should advance a thesis addressed to the informed reader. This thesis should offer a new perspective on the data you are analyzing. The illustration below shows the relationship among you (the scholar), the informed reader, and the data under scrutiny.

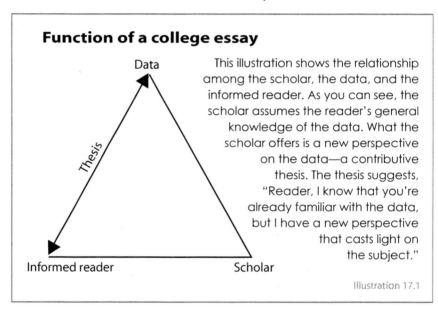

Function of a college essay

This illustration shows the relationship among the scholar, the data, and the informed reader. As you can see, the scholar assumes the reader's general knowledge of the data. What the scholar offers is a new perspective on the data—a contributive thesis. The thesis suggests, "Reader, I know that you're already familiar with the data, but I have a new perspective that casts light on the subject."

Illustration 17.1

Examples of arguments

In offering that new perspective, you advance an argument (also referred to as your thesis). An argument has all manner of variations. Here are a few—and only a few—common arguments that come to mind:

- New evidence suggests that a commonly held belief:
    a. can no longer be believed,
    b. should be modified, or
    c. should be viewed with more skepticism.

- One of two competing beliefs is more correct than the other, and for reasons not specified before.

- An effect or event has more causes then previously thought.

- An item or event can be seen from a different perspective, and thus new conclusions drawn about that item or event.

- A trend is not really a trend—or, conversely, that it is more of a trend than other scholars have realized.

- A research team has been wrong in their conclusions because of incorrect evidence, biased attitudes, or faulty logic.

- Two items or events are more similar than scholars have previously thought, and certain conclusions can be drawn from the similarity.

- On the surface something appears one way, but upon closer inspection it appears another.

- One element of a whole has been under- or over-valued.

- A well-known set of facts can, with additional evidence, be extended even farther.

Sound contributive

You should convey the sense that your clarification, or perspective, is a vital contribution to the field's dialogue about the data under consideration. In other words, as a scholar, you should take a stand, go out on a limb, come to a conclusion—that is, suggest something new. Even if you're not sure whether other scholars have already advanced your thesis (or a similar argument), learn to *sound* as if *you* are making a contribution to the field of study. When, during your academic career, you are actually poised to make new points, you will have become accustomed to this tone of contributive prose.

Remember, unless your professor instructs otherwise, your college essay should *not* be a mere summary of what you've read, seen, or heard.

The basic elements of the college essay

The college essay features these basic parts:

- Title
- Opening paragraph, which engages the reader, introduces the general topic, and states the thesis
- Series of logically connected paragraphs relating to and supporting a progressively unfolding thesis
- Concluding paragraph

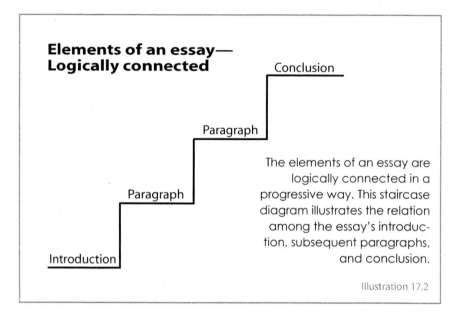

**Elements of an essay—
Logically connected**

Conclusion

Paragraph

Paragraph

Introduction

The elements of an essay are logically connected in a progressive way. This staircase diagram illustrates the relation among the essay's introduction, subsequent paragraphs, and conclusion.

Illustration 17.2

A real-world analogy

The above basic structure of the college essay appears in more than just essays. Consider how similar it is to a courtroom trial. First an attorney makes an "opening statement" (equivalent to an opening paragraph) so that the jury will have some idea of what's going on before seeing any evidence. In an opening statement, each attorney advises jurors what to believe (the thesis statement). The attorney then presents a series of witnesses in a logical order (like paragraphs in an essay); all this evidence will hopefully support the attorney's version of the truth. Then the attorney makes closing remarks, summarizing the evidence and explaining why the jury should come to certain conclusions (like the concluding paragraph does in your essay).

Analyzing an example

Now let's consider each of these parts. I'll illustrate my advice with segments from a brief essay about Nathaniel Hawthorne's short literary sketch concerning Benjamin Franklin's childhood. One of my sons—at the time, a high school sophomore—wrote this analysis, which I've "edited up" to college-level persuasive prose (you can see the full "before" and "after" essays at the end of this chapter).

Hawthorne's sketch depicts how young Ben had to learn not to justify a wrong by saying that he had committed it for the public good. In essence,

Ben steals a pile of stones (which were destined to help construct a house) in order to make a fishing wharf that can be enjoyed by many more people than the original owners of the stones. Ben's father teaches him the errors of his thinking. My own son's challenge was to generate an argument about the sketch that goes beyond what the average reader might have inferred simply from reading the story.

The title

The title should cover the range of your topic and hint at your thesis. The title shouldn't be too bland or too long. The "before" rather ho-hum title for my son's essay was "Hawthorne's Message." The "after" title ended up being:

Morality and Leadership:

The Subtext of Hawthorne's "Benjamin Franklin"

Note how that title implies, from the outset, that the writer sees something that most readers of the story would otherwise have missed. We now *want* to read on. The writer has us hooked.

The opening paragraph

The opening paragraph first offers an engaging overview of the general topic, by way of leading up to a thesis statement. The opening paragraph also anticipates several of the issues you'll develop persuasively in the body of the essay.

When you need to take account of secondary scholarship

If your professor expects you to consult secondary scholarship (that is, books or journal articles about your topic), the opening paragraph should promptly summarize the drift of those books or journal articles in a sentence or two—saving elaboration and formal citation for a footnote. Unless your essay poses a direct response to somebody else's conclusion, don't go overboard—prior to advancing your own argument—in reviewing secondary scholarship (save that exercise for graduate school!). Rather, say just enough to show that you've read a number of interesting studies, and that those leave room for a further perspective—*yours*. Unless otherwise stipulated by your professor, the undergraduate essay should convey, first and foremost, your own point of view.

When you don't need to take account of secondary scholarship

If your professor does not demand that you consult secondary scholarship, then consider advancing your thesis by challenging what you think to be the prevailing view of most readers. The example below takes just such a stance in claiming to clarify an otherwise evasive but vital point. The writer states that he has something new to add to what he imagines to be the response of most readers to Hawthorne's tale; in other words, the writer argues that the sketch holds more significance than initially meets the eye. It is here that the student establishes his claim to insight and authority, alerting the reader (as most students fail to do) to the fact that he's offering far more than a mere summary of the data. You simply must grow accustomed to using a contributive tone, one that suggests that your essay stands to enhance our knowledge.

When to advance the thesis in the opening paragraph

As illustrated below, the opening paragraph concludes by advancing a thesis. You should state your thesis in the last sentence of your opening paragraph unless you are writing a very long essay or honors thesis. Essays of that length may require a separate paragraph of chattiness before you arrive at a thesis paragraph. Usually, though, you should advance your thesis at the end of paragraph one, so that readers know exactly what you aim to demonstrate.

So here's the enhanced version of the opening paragraph composed by my son:

> As a diplomat, patriot, and delegate to the Continental Congress, the venerable Franklin possessed immense leadership capacities. Hawthorne's short sketch "Benjamin Franklin" suggests a link between those admirable qualities and an incident in Franklin's childhood. Hawthorne describes a youthful mishap for which Franklin was to blame: Ben and his friends justify the theft of a pile of stones (destined to build the foundation of somebody's house) for the construction of a fishing wharf. Ben rationalizes the theft through appeal to "the advantage of many persons." While young Benjamin comes to see the error of his ways, more is at stake than Ben's penitence for a single misdemeanor. Indeed, the sketch offers a far more complex insight, one that turns out to be pertinent to any

number of adult dilemmas: the end does not justify the means. We may infer, moreover, that this early childhood lesson stands intimately related to Ben's much later capacity to undertake public benefactions and to exercise fair and responsible leadership in an emerging democracy.

The "in between" paragraphs: Getting from one to the other

After the opening paragraph, there will be a series of paragraphs that advance your progressively unfolding thesis. Those paragraphs usually feature a separate thought, along with varied forms of evidence supporting that thought. Arrange these paragraphs so as to advance your thesis by building upon the preceding paragraph.

These paragraphs need to hold the reader's attention. At no point should your reader ever wonder, "Why am I reading this information? What does it have to do with this essay?"

Your new best friends: Transitions

Good writers help the reader along by linking the paragraphs (and the sentences within paragraphs) with verbal (and sometimes graphic) cues called *transitions*. You need effective transitions to help the reader follow your logically unfolding argument. Sometimes transitions are between paragraphs (inter-paragraph transitions), while other transitions link sentences within the same paragraph (intra-paragraph transitions). Significantly longer writing even features entire paragraphs devoted to transitional thoughts.

Intra-paragraph transitions can be as simple as one word, or quite a bit more complicated.

Here are some examples of simple transitions between sentences or bits of information:

- They went to the movie. **However**, Bill stayed home.
- I don't like cold weather. **Nonetheless**, I always look forward to building a snowman after the first winter storm.
- After lightning struck, Bonnie never could grow flowers in that part of the yard. **Still**, she tried year after year to get zinnias to grow there.

Transitions between paragraphs, on the other hand, can—and should—serve more than one function. Think of them as multi-purpose guideposts on a long road with potentially confusing twists and turns. Those transitions remind readers of where they've just been (the preceding paragraph), what the overall thesis continues to be, and where the essay is now going in this new paragraph. I call this technique the "three-fold transition" as illustrated below.

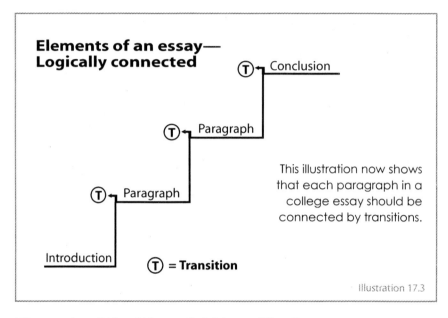

Elements of an essay— Logically connected

(T) Conclusion

(T) Paragraph

(T) Paragraph

Introduction

(T) = Transition

This illustration now shows that each paragraph in a college essay should be connected by transitions.

Illustration 17.3

Elements of the "three-fold transition"

A three-fold transition, which appears at the beginning of a new paragraph, accomplishes all of these goals:

> **Goal 1**: Refers back, ever so quickly, to the main point of the preceding paragraph.

> **Goal 2**: Loops back to remind readers of the essay's governing thesis.

> **Goal 3**: Introduces the subject of the new paragraph.

> **Goal 4**: (Bonus!) Accomplishes Goals 1 through 3 in such manner as to assume that you and the reader have arrived at a new and exciting phase of your progressively unfolding argument.

These three-fold transitions take a while to fashion. They often don't fully emerge until you're into the third or fourth draft of your essay, so you needn't panic if they don't come out just right in your first draft. When formulating these transitions, you'll likely see patterns in your thought process that you initially overlooked. Or, just as importantly, you'll be able to recognize gaps in logic that you need to remedy. Below is an illustration of how these goals of the three-fold transition work together.

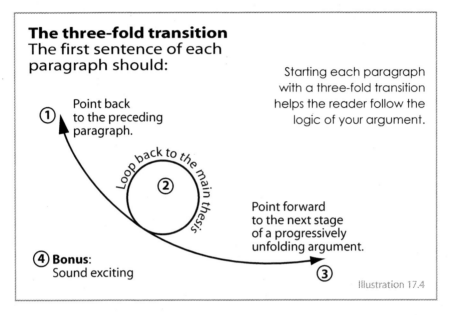

The three-fold transition
The first sentence of each paragraph should:

① Point back to the preceding paragraph.

Loop back to the main thesis ②

Point forward to the next stage of a progressively unfolding argument. ③

④ **Bonus**: Sound exciting

Starting each paragraph with a three-fold transition helps the reader follow the logic of your argument.

Illustration 17.4

Example of a three-fold transition

Let's go back to the essay about Ben Franklin's childhood. Below is an example of a three-fold transition that picks up on the essay's thesis statement (that Hawthorne's sketch arguably explores a youthful precedent for Ben Franklin's emerging sense of leadership). This transition comes from the third paragraph of my son's essay:

> This subtle emphasis on Ben's emerging capacity to lead relates, oddly, to his being pulled from school to assist in the family business of candle making.

Here's how this transition sentence fulfills the three elements of the three-fold transition (as well as the "bonus" point):

Goal 1: "This subtle emphasis" points back to the preceding paragraph.

Goal 2: "Ben's emerging capacity to lead" reiterates the essay's thesis.

Goal 3: "Being pulled from school to assist in the family business" points forward to the subject of the paragraph.

Goal 4: "Relates, oddly" provides a sense of drama that implies that we're at an interesting stage of the argument that the reader would have overlooked were it not for the insight of the writer.

Another example of the three-fold transition

The three-fold transition of the next paragraph takes us even farther:

> Nowhere, though, is Ben's introduction to the responsibilities of leadership more intense than in his misadventure involving the theft of personal property to build a public fishing pier.

Here's the analysis for this second example:

Goals 1 and 4: "Nowhere, however" implies that we're focusing on a new and exciting consideration that logically follows from the preceding paragraph.

Goal 2: "is Ben's introduction to the responsibilities of leadership" reiterates the essay's main thesis.

Goal 3: "than in his misadventure involving the theft of stones for a public fishing pier" informs readers exactly what the new subject matter of this paragraph will be, intimating that we've arrived at the exciting new consideration of private-versus-public rights in a democracy. Again, the implied tone is that readers would be at a loss were it not for the insight of the writer.

Taken together, the elements of this transition make readers feel comfortable and excited about where they've been and where they're going—and all in relation to a central argument that you haven't let them forget (you'd be surprised how many college students allow us to forget their main thesis by the time they've reached page three of an essay!). With practice and commitment, you can excel at effective transitions.

How to sound persuasive, rather than as if you are offering mere plot summary

Don't be afraid to sound judgmental. Doing so adds authority to your tone and makes us appreciate your contribution. Note, for instance, the sentence below. I have italicized the judgmental rhetoric that lends a tone of authority to the writer's utterance.

> Although Ben seeks to convince his father of the propriety of the theft—*with a lame reference to public benefit*—his father *aptly* remarks that the end does not justify the means, for evil breeds evil and can trample individual rights supportive of democracy: "'No act ... can possibly be for the benefit of the public generally which involves injustice to any individual.'"

In other words, when you write, steer the readers the way you want them to go. Moreover, before you get to a quotation, utter words (in this case "supportive of democracy") that make us interpret the quotation the way you wish us to do so. Don't leave the readers the option of interpreting a quotation in a manner that's inconsistent with your argument.

How to finish a paragraph (other than the essay's concluding paragraph)

Every paragraph should have a concluding sentence that summarizes the main point of the paragraph. Do so conclusively. Drive home the main point of that paragraph. The concluding sentence of the paragraph under consideration above (following directly after the quotation "No act ...") reads as follows:

> That lesson would have been vital for any person aspiring to leadership in a democratic republic averse to "old world" tyranny.

The last sentence of your paragraph should forcefully drive home the point of the paragraph, making the reader think, "Absolutely right! I've never heard it put better! I'm so pleased that I've read this paragraph and learned something new."

Here's another example of persuasive, contributive prose that takes us beyond plot summary to a well-crafted argument. The paragraph terminates in a powerful concluding sentence. The paragraph under consideration draws out the benefit of Ben's having been removed from school early to help support the family business of candle making:

> Far, though, from hindering Ben's education, that absence from school *actually had a positive effect* because of Ben's exposure to the political debates that occurred among the men who would gather in the candle shop during the day. Just by listening to his father's friends, Ben sharpened his powers of analysis and dialogue. That instruction *was likely more important than* anything Ben would have studied at school in his primer. *If knowledge is power, then Ben's time in his father's shop served as an enviable basis for future leadership.*

Why you generally should not conclude a paragraph by anticipating the point of your next paragraph

As you conclude one paragraph, do not try to anticipate the point of your next paragraph. Rather, save the thrust of the transition for the first sentence of your new paragraph. Students who place the transition in the last sentence of the preceding paragraph often end their paragraphs with an utterance that appears unconnected to anything we've just read. Readers must then wait until the middle of the *next* paragraph to figure out what's just happened above. "Oh, I get it," the reader thinks to himself, "they were anticipating the *new* paragraph in the last sentence of their preceding paragraph."

By that time, however, the reader is confused, frustrated, and (if he or she is grading thirty other essays) probably unforgiving. As you grow more adept at expository writing, you will occasionally end your paragraphs conclusively while anticipating the thrust of your next paragraph. But don't count on having that occur more than once every several pages.

The concluding paragraph

Readers should infer from the first sentence of the concluding paragraph that we've arrived at the end of the essay:

> To conclude, Hawthorne seems to suggest that Franklin's moral and political thinking greatly prospered from what might otherwise appear to have been transient and insignificant incidents dating to Ben's youth.

The paragraph should then expand on the theme and lead "outward" to further speculation and implications for the informed reader:

> The co-author of the Declaration of Independence could conceivably have benefited from these experiences, learning how part of the challenge of life is to turn disadvantage into advantage—but to do so in a way that best serves the public good through a fundamental respect for individual rights and reasoned discourse. Finally, then, Hawthorne's sketch implies that Benjamin Franklin might not have developed the *character* necessary for effective ambassadorship, statesmanship, and leadership had he not commenced his real education at such a tender, but marvelously impressionable age.

Note how the paragraph continues to convey the tone of *contribution and insight* that would have been unavailable even to the informed reader had the student/scholar not intervened with these splendidly contributive paragraphs—all concluding in this final reiteration of what's been said above, yet with a tone that itself sounds contributive, laying the ground for further discussion and dialogue beyond this essay.

The diagram below illustrate how you can avoid having your concluding paragraph sound like a dead end; instead, have it suggest that we

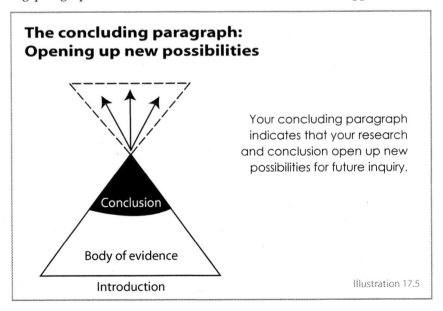

**The concluding paragraph:
Opening up new possibilities**

Your concluding paragraph indicates that your research and conclusion open up new possibilities for future inquiry.

Conclusion

Body of evidence

Introduction

Illustration 17.5

might use your insight as a point of departure into further inquiry—in this case, into the relation between ethics and leadership, or between political theory and political practice. The best essays in the humanities and social sciences seldom settle the issue once and for all; rather, they suggest that the thesis under consideration provides a constructive avenue for even further inquiry.

Conclusion

All essays ought to have a compelling title and opening paragraph. The basic structure and tone of subsequent paragraphs (no matter how many) should feature three-fold transitions, persuasive evidence and dialogue, and a cogent concluding sentence. Then, finally, should come the compelling conclusion for the entire essay. It little matters whether the essay is four pages or twenty-five pages; your mastery of these structural elements will help set your writing apart from less skilled efforts at a college-level essay. Review the "Before" and "After" essays following this chapter to see these guidelines in action.

But how do we organize the "raw materials," as it were, to construct these paragraphs? That question leads to the "index-card approach" to researching, structuring, and composing college essays, which we will cover in depth in the next section of this book.

"Before" Essay

Hawthorne's Message

Benjamin Franklin, a well-established figure in history, has contributed significantly to making the United States a great nation. Being a diplomat, delegate and playing a vital role in the American Revolution, Franklin most definitely possessed among his many skills immense leadership skills, even as a child. Nathaniel Hawthorne's sketch of adolescent Benjamin is an account of a certain mishap for which he is to blame. The sketch was thought to be a simple-minded tale intended for children, but a deeper more complex moral lies between the lines. But in the end Ben learns that the end does not justify the means. Yet this notion is a complicated idea that is understood and contemplated by adults. I propose, therefore, that in writing this account of young Franklin's education, Hawthorne perhaps illustrated an early lesson in Ben's life but to show how a person must learn and comprehend this concept before becoming an effective leader.

And so looking back upon Benjamin Franklin's outstanding achievements, one would think that he went through years of schooling, yet at age ten Ben was pulled from school to help with the family business. The incident did not hinder Ben's education, for in that time he missed school he was learning lessons in life skills, negotiation, and forming a basic consciousness of what is right and wrong. Ben's father was a very respected man throughout Boston, and many men of note would visit the Franklin household for the sake of speaking of colonial and political affairs. After making candles Ben would take advantage of the situation and sit in the corner to listen to his father give and discuss his opinion and try to make sense of what he heard. Benjamin was most definitely a keen lad to listen every day, and after hearing many conversations he was quickly learning.

Although Ben gained much knowledge from his father, Ben unknowingly made one of the greatest mistakes of his childhood, and also learned one of the greatest lessons of his life. One day Benjamin dashed to the bog where the tide would bring in all types of fish. He didn't know that he would soon do an evil deed by stealing a stack of stones that somebody had placed there to help build a house. Because there was no place that the boys could stand, when fishing, without getting muddy, Ben shouted, "Boys, I have thought of a scheme which will be greatly for our benefit, and the public benefit." And so, not realizing how they were being misled, the boys asked what could be done, and then Ben explained to them that they would build a jetty. His companions thought it to be a grand idea, including the suggestion that they steal the stones. Ben, trying to find rational reasoning with stealing, told the boys that when they were taking these stones they would be benefiting hundreds of people if the stones were used to make a jetty, whereas only one person would be able to benefit from the stones if they were to be used for a cellar. And in the night, under Ben's misleading and unlawful instruction, all of the stones were removed and a beautiful jetty was built. The next morning the builders noticed the stolen stones and quickly reported the theft to the authorities. Not taking long for the truth to come out about Benjamin leading the group, Ben was summoned before his father. After being asked why he would take property not belonging to him, Benjamin explained how he did it only for the public benefit. His father made haste in correcting Ben and explaining to him that the end under no circumstances justifies the means, and therefore evil can only breed evil. Ben's quick and bright mind realized his error and reflected upon his misguiding words that he used upon his friends to persuade them to steal the stones.

Ben, therefore, with his lesson learned, went on to make good decisions his whole life. And he did so because he based all his decisions upon principles that he lived by every day. Could this day perhaps have influenced Benjamin Franklin to propose the Declaration of Independence?

Revised "After" Essay

Morality and Leadership:

The Subtext of Hawthorne's "Benjamin Franklin"

As a diplomat, patriot, and delegate to the Continental Congress, the venerable Franklin possessed immense leadership capacities. Hawthorne's short sketch "Benjamin Franklin" suggests a link between those admirable qualities and an incident in Franklin's childhood. Hawthorne describes a youthful mishap for which Franklin was to blame: Ben and his friends justify the theft of a pile of stones (destined to build the foundation of somebody's house) for the construction of a fishing wharf. Ben rationalizes the theft through appeal to "the advantage of many persons."[1] While young Benjamin comes to see the error of his ways, more is a stake than Ben's penitence of a single misdemeanor. Indeed, the sketch offers a far more complex insight, one that turns out to be pertinent to any number of adult dilemmas: the end does not justify the means. We may infer, moreover, that this early childhood lesson stands intimately related to Ben's much later capacity to undertake public benefactions and to exercise fair and responsible leadership in an emerging democracy.

This subtle emphasis on Ben's emerging capacity to lead relates, oddly, to his being pulled from school to assist in the family business of candle making. Far, though, from hindering Ben's education, that absence from school actually had a positive effect because of Ben's exposure to the political debates that occurred among the men who would gather in the candle shop during the day. Just by listening to his father's friends, Ben sharpened his powers of analysis and dialogue. That instruction was likely more important than anything Ben would have studied at school in his primer. If knowledge is power, then Ben's time in his father's shop served as an enviable basis for future leadership.

Nowhere, though, is Ben's introduction to the responsibilities of leadership more intense than in his misadventure involving the theft of personal property to build a public fishing pier. Although Ben seeks to convince his father of the propriety of the theft—with a lame reference to public benefit—his father aptly notes that the end does not justify the means, for evil breeds evil and can trample individual rights supportive of democracy: "'No act ... can possibly be for the benefit of the public generally which involves injustice to any individual'" (199). That lesson would

127

have been vital for any person aspiring to leadership in a democratic republic averse to "old world" tyranny.

To conclude, Hawthorne seems to suggest that Franklin's moral and political thinking greatly prospered from what might otherwise appear to have been transient and insignificant incidents dating to Ben's youth. The co-author of the Declaration of Independence could conceivably have benefited from these experiences, learning how part of the challenge of life is to turn disadvantage into advantage—but to do so in a way that best serves the public good through a fundamental respect for individual rights and reasoned discourse. Finally, then, Hawthorne's sketch implies that Benjamin Franklin might not have developed the character necessary for effective ambassadorship, statesmanship, and leadership had he not commenced his real education at such a tender, but marvelously impressionable age.

1. All quotations are from "Benjamin Franklin," in George Parsons Lathrop, ed., *The Complete Works of Nathaniel Hawthorne*, 12 vols. (Boston: Houghton Mifflin, 1883), 12:199; cited henceforth parenthetically.

Chapter Eighteen

The Index-Card Approach to Structuring an Essay

Writers have different techniques for researching, composing, and editing essays. Having taught writing for close to thirty years, I've concluded that the index-card approach produces the best college-level essays. I have, moreover, personally used the method to help generate my own scholarly essays and book chapters.

What you're writing about

When composing college-level essays, you generally need to write about something other than personal experience. That "something" might include—among many other topics—a novel, a set of poems, one or more paintings, an historical event, archeological artifacts, the results of a scientific experiment, a building with architectural distinction, or statistical data in the fields of sociology, psychology, or political science.

Primary data (primary sources)

Your primary data—consisting of facts, quotations, or statistics derived from material you've researched—usually constitute the main subject of your essay. You must begin your research early enough to become very familiar with the primary data. So, to take an example, if your subjects are several poems by an author, you'll need to read those carefully. If your primary topic is a dance performance, you'll need to see the dance several times. Ditto the results of a survey, an advertising campaign, or any other subject matter about which you're expected to generate a persuasive argument.

Secondary sources

After you've become very familiar with your primary data, your professor may require that you know what professionals in the field have already said about your subject matter in books, journals, magazines, or in the published proceedings of conferences. You should be able to find that secondary source material at your university library. If you need help, a reference librarian will assist you in locating secondary sources.

Before you start the writing process, then, you need to read both primary and secondary data. But for the first go-round, read or study the subject for enjoyment and edification.

Reviewing primary sources and generating a thesis

Then ask yourself, "What is worth arguing?" "What point do I stand to clarify by writing a persuasive essay?" As for determining the merit of an argument, you should generally ask yourself, "Based on my encounter with the primary and secondary sources, how can I go beyond what the average reader or students would already know or infer about this topic? What might I argue that stands to clarify the topic in a way that leaves the reader feeling indebted to me for having expanded or clarified its significance?"

If you start the writing process early enough, you can generally *know* if your thesis is valid and worth the investment of time: simply visit your professor during an office hour and ask. If you do this well in advance of the deadline, your professor will have that much more respect for you. If you get the "nod" on your thesis, you no longer have to worry about its validity; rather, you have simply to gather enough data on index cards to support the argument.

Rereading your primary data

On the basis of your response, *reread*, review, or re-examine (called "reread," henceforth) your primary data to see if those data end up supporting, in different combinations of ways, the argument that you plan to advance.

Only after rereading your primary data, with an eye towards your thesis, are you truly able to gather quotations and statistics that support the structure of your argument. If, for instance, you formulate a thesis three-fourths of the way through a novel, how could you possibly have underlined pertinent passages on pages 3–50? The significance of those pages, relative to your thesis, will become evident only when you reread the primary data. Thus, to allow yourself sufficient time to formulate a thesis—and to reread multiple times in the course of gathering data to support your argument—make an effort to begin your assignment as soon as you can, preferably months in advance of your deadline.

Underlining and annotating

If you own "hard copy" of the primary data (such as a paperback book), underline and annotate whenever you come to a passage or section that validates your perspective or thesis. You annotate when, in the margin of the book, you pen a response to various passages while you're reading or rereading. The primary data will then contain both the quotation and some of your reflections about the significance of the quotation. Whenever I annotate, I usually do so with an eye to my thesis. I also enter observations that I'll later be able to transfer onto index cards and expand into two or three sentences of "argumentation," relative to the passage under consideration.

Whereas in high school you are sometimes told never to enter a mark in any of your books, in college you should make a practice of heavily annotating the books that you own.

However, it is vandalism to mark up library volumes. Instead, underline and annotate these secondary sources after you photocopy pertinent passages from them. If you are quoting or referring to a passage from a scholarly journal, for instance, photocopy those passages (along with the "Contents" page of the journal volume). Then underline and annotate to your heart's delight, especially when you see areas of an argument that you might challenge, or areas with which you agree, but which you are able to use as a point of departure in refining the point at issue in your own essay. If you need to quote a segment of a library book, keep a record of pages that you need to photocopy and *why* you need to photocopy that page. Photocopy the page (along with the book's title page and copyright page) and then annotate that page. This is all part of what is referred to as "primary" and "secondary" research.

(Be sure and retain your original photocopies, even after you transfer your thoughts and evidence to index cards. Before you submit your essay, you'll need to check all your quotations and paraphrases for accuracy. Having the original photocopies with the bibliographical data—author, title, city, publisher, date, and so on—will help in the finish-up and editing process.)

So when do index cards come into the picture?

Don't start transferring data onto index cards until you've finished your readings and annotations. While reading your data to validate your thesis, you'll underline and annotate far more passages or information than you can use in your essay. That's why it's vital not to enter anything onto index cards until you've completely finished underlining and annotating your primary and secondary data. Otherwise you'll spin your wheels with unnecessary labor. When you finally transfer information onto the index cards, you'll want to be selective about what you actually include in your essay.

Entering information onto the index cards

Next comes the process of transferring quotations and statistics onto index cards. To facilitate that process, purchase a stack of 500 8 x 5 non-ruled index cards at an office-supply store. Then program your computer and printer so that the screen has margins mimicking the 8 x 5 index card. Set your printer so that it will then reproduce the contents of the 8 x 5-like screen directly onto an index card.

Start by typing your underlined and annotated passages onto the computer screen. The passage should go at the top of the screen.

After you have finished typing the quotation onto your computer screen, ask yourself, "Why do I find this quotation or fact vital—and to what dimension of my argument is it relevant?" Beneath the quotation that you've just entered onto the screen, type the mathematical sign for "such that" (//) and elaborate in your own words about why this piece of data is pertinent or vital, drawing connections to central issues. You'll find that the marginal annotations that you made when reading your primary and secondary data will help you generate "such that" commentary on an index card. This commentary, in turn, gives you a head start after you arrive at the writing-process stage, during which you will transform the entries on your index cards into persuasive prose.

Create an index card for each piece of evidence, or for each reflection that you plan either to use word-for-word, or upon which you will elaborate, in your essay.

Example index card

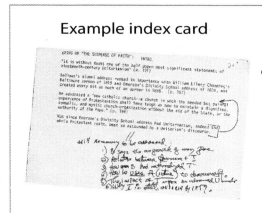

Here's an index card that I created to write a scholarly article. Notice that the quotes and research material are at the top of the card, while the hand-written commentary is at the bottom.

Illustration 18.1

Organizing the index cards

After you've entered all of your quotations, annotations, and related reflections onto index cards, spend several hours sorting the cards into separate stacks. Simply go to the library and find a very large table in a quiet area. Camp out there. Then take your stack of index cards and begin to sort them by concept.

Every time you arrive at a card that reflects a new concept, take a clean index card, hold it vertically, and create a half-inch fold at the bottom of the card. (Have the folded segment pointed toward you.) Then label the top of that index card with the pertinent concept, relative to the card you've just sorted. Each time you come to a card that pertains to that concept, slip the new card into that stack.

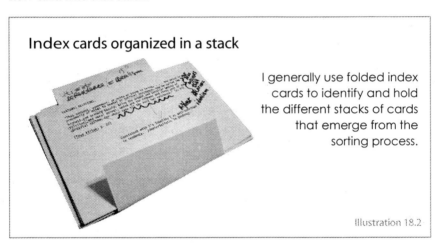

Index cards organized in a stack

I generally use folded index cards to identify and hold the different stacks of cards that emerge from the sorting process.

Illustration 18.2

Identifying the basic categories of your argument

When you arrive at any card that addresses a new idea, simply create a new vertical identification card, labeled at the top and folded at the bottom. You now have a category divider, into which you will place any and all cards relating to that dimension of your argument. If you've gathered around 100 index cards by culling quotations and annotations, you'll likely generate ten to twelve separate stacks of cards. Each stack will provide the data necessary to generate from one to two paragraphs of prose.

Categories for the introduction and the conclusion

Also, create stacks for the introductory and concluding paragraphs. The data for the introductory paragraph might emerge from primary texts or from your own reflections over several weeks or months. If, for example, you are walking across campus and think of a generally engaging point that would serve you well in an introductory paragraph, make note of that point and (later that same day) turn this note into an index-card entry destined for a group of cards devoted to your opening paragraph.

The same goes for observations that could enhance a concluding paragraph. When collecting data for the concluding paragraph, seek quotations that drive home the point of your overriding thesis, but which you can afford to save for the final paragraph. You then structure your own observational prose around a few provocative quotations in your concluding paragraph.

My second book (about Henry James) took me ten years to research and compose. When I wrote my introductory and concluding paragraphs, I found myself coming across index cards that I had created six years earlier for that very purpose. I never otherwise could have remembered to include those points in parts of my book.

Arranging stacks for the flow and logic of the essay

Before you begin to transform the information on your index cards into an engaging, persuasive essay, you should first arrange the stacks in a logical order—one that anticipates the flow and structure of your essay. Say to yourself, "If I'm going to argue such and such, then I need to introduce *this* stack of cards first; *that* stack, second; *this* stack, third—and so on, until you've arranged all your stacks in a logical order.

At this point, you still might choose to change the order of these stacks, concluding that "this" stack should actually come before or after "that" stack. Fine. It's far preferable to correct the structure of your essay before you begin to write than to have to do so after you have composed a major portion of your argument.

Arranging the cards within each stack for flow and logic

After you've placed your stacks of cards in the best order, you should similarly arrange the several cards *within* each stack. Take the first stack aside, spread all of its cards on a large table, and arrange each card in the best possible order within that particular grouping of cards. By doing this, you will create a blueprint for the order of each of your sentences within a given paragraph. Do this over several days—and for every stack of index cards. In effect, you will have constructed the genome, the double helix, that dictates the organic-like growth of your essay—from beginning to end.

By following the instructions above, you will also guarantee your ability to structure your essay in a progressively unfolding way, and then to implement three-fold transitions at the beginning of every paragraph (save the first and last). After all, you'll know what you just said and will be able to refer back to it (step 1); you'll always have your overall thesis in mind (step 2), and you'll be able to articulate the topic of the new paragraph (step 3). Having a tone of enthusiasm—that extra *oomph* in the three-fold transition—will follow of its own accord. (For a review of these three-fold transitions, see the preceding chapter on writing the college-level essay.)

Bonus points

At this point in the writing process, you will also be able to visit your professor, display your wonderfully arranged stacks of cards, and ask whether you've researched or anticipated all vital emphases. You can't imagine how impressive you will appear when approaching a professor this way, some three weeks before the paper is due. In a world where most students typically wait until the last possible minute to compose an essay, you will stand out as conscientious and devoted. The professor will likely make further suggestions—either to correct a current emphasis, or to suggest an additional one. You can't lose, either way.

The metamorphosis: Transforming index cards into persuasive prose

Picture yourself at a movie theater, waiting in a long line of people to purchase tickets. To control the flow of the crowd, the theater positions all of you along a row of velvet ropes, linked together by intermittent poles. This is an apt image for the process of writing with index cards: the poles

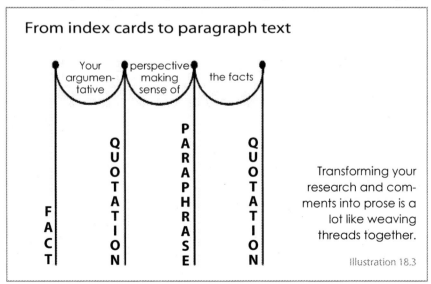

From index cards to paragraph text

Transforming your research and comments into prose is a lot like weaving threads together.

Illustration 18.3

represent facts that you've printed onto each index card; the velvet ropes linking the index cards represent—and this is absolutely vital—*your perspective*, the words that *argue* the significance of the assembled facts and their relationships.

The art of transforming index cards filled with facts and quotations into a well-argued essay involves the craft of envisioning, in persuasive rhetoric, your "take" on the facts and then shaping the reader's response to those facts *before* they even reach the quotation or data that you introduce to support your point. The more persuasive and judgmental your own prose, the more professional *authority* you bring to the tone and substance of your writing.

An example of a persuasive paragraph composed from index cards

To illustrate this process, let's review a paragraph I generated from my own research about Herman Melville's *Moby-Dick*, and specifically about a character named Starbuck in that novel. You may recall that Ahab is on a maniacal quest of vengeance against the White Whale, and that Starbuck, the first mate, is the only character who understands how evil Ahab's actions really are. But rather than stopping Ahab, Starbuck keeps assisting him, though with remorse.

An examination of secondary scholarship about *Moby-Dick* reveals that Melville's novel contains, among many other emphases, an allegorical commentary on the Mexican War of 1846–1848, waged by President James K. Polk. At the time of that war, the Democratic Party favored the campaign, whereas the opposing political party, the Whigs (later called the Republicans) deemed the war unjustified. Still, since the war was a "popular" war, and since the United States was assured of eventual victory, the Whigs grudgingly funded the war in Congress.

I'm going to draw upon some of my own past scholarship to argue that, in the person of Starbuck, Melville dramatized the tepid nature of the Whig Party's resistance to President Polk's war of aggression against Mexico. Because previous studies already argued that the novel references the Mexican war, I used that existing scholarship as a point of departure to concentrate on a specific character to whom political significance had never before been assigned. Granted, you will never likely write about this specific topic, and the nature of such research is extremely advanced. But you need to understand the advantage of arranging research on index cards, and then turning those into flowing and persuasive prose.

That infallible method of composition will allow you to slide through any college-level essay assignment, however complex.

Card reproductions

What follows are examples of information that I placed on separate index cards from primary and secondary sources. I gathered those quotations from a book *about* the Mexican War (that book being my secondary source) and from a nineteenth-century political monthly magazine, *The American Review: A Whig Journal* (along with Melville's novel, that journal was a primary source). Imagine me at the point in the writing process where I have arranged the cards in such order as to chart the flow of the paragraph and argument under construction.

Card 1

Starbuck "waxes brave but nevertheless obeys" (Herman Melville, *Moby-Dick, or the Whale*, ed. Harrison Hayford and Hershel Parker (New York: W.W. Norton & Co., 1967), p. 394. //

This sounds very much like failed Whig resistance to President Polk. Cite Alan Heimert's more general article about "*Moby Dick* and American Political Symbolism," *American Quarterly* 15 (1963): 498-543 to lend credibility to this perspective.

Illustration 18.4

Card 2

Starbuck engages in "tacit acquiescence" (p. 144) just a few pages away from Ahab's words about a "ratifying sun" (p. 146) for the mission of vengeance against the White Whale. //

Ahab's rhetoric is highly political and invites a political reading of the relationship between Starbuck and his crazed captain. Ahab's talk about "ratifying" will head off arguments against a political reading of the novel.

Illustration 18.5

Card 3

A Whig perspective on the war: "the great political and moral crime of the period."

But the Whigs fail to act: "the army must obey the government, right or wrong."

From: "Mr. Slidell's Mission to Mexico," *American Review*, April, 1847, p. 325 //

Precisely anticipates the hesitation that Melville dramatizes in Starbuck's fervent protest but ultimate inaction.

Illustration 18.6

Card 4

"the conservative majority of the Whigs...refused to translate their dissidence into a position of wholehearted opposition" (p. 82).

John L. Shroeder, *Mr. Polk's War: American Opposition and Dissent, 1846-48* (Madison: University of Wisconsin Press, 1973) //

Quote this to show that historians of the Mexican War support my general political point about ineffective Whig resistance to President Polk.

Illustration 18.7

Card 5

"'Pull, pull my boys,' said Starbuck, in the lowest possible but intensest concentrated whisper" (p. 192) //

Note how Melville has Starbuck ordering his men to row harder in their pursuit of the whale; but the "whisper" shows a reserve that may correspond to the political turmoil of Whigs who objected to the war while continuing to fund it.

Illustration 18.8

Turning the index cards into scholarly prose

Now let's turn these index cards into prose. Sit in front of your computer and generate a thesis-oriented transition. Then ponder the substance of each card, deciding what persuasive rhetoric to insert between quotations and facts in order to *take possession of the facts* by imposing your interpretation upon them and by avoiding anything like mere plot summary or a summary-like tone.

Again, your mission is to persuade, not to summarize. For purposes of illustration, I'll use **bold type** when I insert words emphasizing my scholarly perspective about the facts. In those passages, I'll aim to sound persuasive, politely suggesting that, were it not for me, readers would likely miss a vital point. When turning index cards into prose, try to have your own words shape the reader's response to the upcoming fact or quotation. Don't allow readers to draw their own conclusions when they arrive at a fact or quotation. After all, the thesis is *yours*, not *theirs*.

This is where the art of persuasive writing merges with the index-card approach in generating an essay. And notice how easily this can happen if you've previously arranged your key quotations and observations on index cards. Those cards now sit before you, waiting to be transformed into persuasive prose:

> **Even more suggestive of Starbuck's Whig-like temperament is his political posturing.** When "Starbuck waxes brave but nevertheless obeys," [1] **he resembles the Whigs who protested President Polk's war against Mexico (1846-48) but who still voted to fund it. Indeed, Starbuck's** "tacit acquiescence" and Ahab's **otherwise odd reference** to "'yon ratifying sun'" (pp. 144, 146) **may well echo Whig editorials that half-heartedly condemned President Polk's Mexican campaign. While the Whigs called the war** "the great political and moral crime of the period," **they just as readily claimed that** "the army must obey the government, right or wrong." [2] **That inconsistency seems to characterize Starbuck's conflicted way of encouraging his crew during a whale chase:** "'Pull, pull my boys,' said Starbuck, in the lowest possible but intensest concentrated whisper" (p. 192). **Here evoking the mixed emotions of American Whigs, Starbuck aids and abets, his resistance falling short of genuine indignation or open protest.**

1. Herman Melville, *Moby-Dick, or the Whale*, ed. Harrison Hayford and Hershel Parker (New York: W. W. Norton & Co., 1967), p. 394. Citations will henceforth appear in the text. For scholarship that links Melville's novel to the Mexican War in general, see Alan Heimert, "Moby-Dick and American Political Symbolism," *American Quarterly*, 15 (1963): 498-543.

2. "Mr. Slidell's Mission to Mexico," *American Review*, 1847, April, p. 325. See, for other Whig concessions to President Polk, "Our Army of Occupation," *American Review*, August 1846, p. 172; "Hon. Joseph Reed Ingersoll," *American Review*, July 1848, p. 102; "President's Message: the War," *American Review*, January 1847, p. 11. John H. Schroeder, in *Mr. Polk's War: American Opposition and Dissent, 1846-48* (Madison: University of Wisconsin Press, 1973), explains that "the conservative majority of the Whigs ... refused to translate their dissidence into a position of wholehearted opposition" (p. 82).

Notice how note 2 reveals that I had many more quotations than I chose to use in my final arrangement of index cards. Do not feel bad about cutting down on quotations that you've worked so hard to gather in the first place. It's far wiser to offer a concise and compelling paragraph than to bore your reader with quotation after quotation. And it's always better to cut back than to have a professor tell you that you've not mustered enough data to begin with.

Conclusion

This, then, is the art of writing with index cards. It forms the craft of research, followed by an architectural approach to structuring an essay before you actually compose it.

Don't join the majority of students who believe that they can simply sit at a computer for three consecutive nights and knock out six to eight pages per night, thereby completing a term paper. From nothing comes nothing; from research, underlining, annotation, and index cards emerges a tried-and-true method of delivering persuasive essays. Whereas others will stare at their computer and wonder *what* to say, you will already have arrived at the drift of your argument and nearly every fact that you plan to use as you transform quotations and facts into persuasive writing. Your challenge will not be to determine what to say, but rather how to allocate sufficient time to say it eloquently.

That eloquence, in turn, depends upon your ability to edit your own prose. Self-editing will therefore be the topic of the next chapter.

After you've used your index cards to transfer your information, evidence, and thoughts onto paper, you should have the basic elements of your essay down pat, including:

- An engaging opening paragraph that advances a thesis.
- Paragraphs that start with thesis-oriented transitions to keep readers on track.
- Paragraphs that end cogently, making readers feel that each paragraph was worth reading.
- Paragraphs that have data and brief quotations to validate your argument.
- A concluding paragraph that drives home your point, while underscoring the related issues that your thesis has clarified or stands to clarify.

At this stage, you've completed your first rough draft (a significant milestone!) and—to achieve a maximum degree of eloquence—you're ready to begin the editing process. We'll discuss that in the next chapter of this book.

Chapter Nineteen

Learning to Edit Your Own Writing

Few writers compose the perfect sentence, paragraph, or essay the first time around. Great prose more often evolves from rough drafts edited not once, not twice, but many times.

Getting started

The writing process generally falls into these four phases:

1. Undertaking research and generating ideas.
2. Organizing thoughts in a logical manner.
3. Writing the first draft.
4. Editing, editing, editing.

For the first three phases, I recommend the "index card" approach, which I discussed in the preceding chapter. Now we'll focus on writing and editing.

Writing vs. editing

When I think about myself as somebody who writes and edits, I see myself wearing different hats and following different rules for each enterprise. They are almost like separate occupations.

When you wear the "writing hat," let the words and ideas flow and try to maintain the momentum of writing. Don't start and stop. Backing up to perfect a phrase, or anguishing over grammar will corrupt the creative process. Your focus, when you wear the writing hat, should be to establish a logical train of ideas as you write. If you're using the index-card approach to research and write the first draft, you shouldn't have any problems with generating written material.

Only after you've written a significant part of your essay should you put on the "editing hat."

Editing is more than editing

When I refer to "editing," I'm talking about much more than proofreading. Real editing gets to the heart of the essay and brings out its structure, flow, and logic. At this stage, you're supposed to stop, ponder, and be critical and more demanding of yourself. Fuss over weak points and poor transitions. Make yourself sound more professional by substituting judgmental rhetoric for phrasing that is mere summarization. Endeavor to sound conclusive.

Editing is therefore as much a part of the writing process as composing the initial rough draft is.

A bit about my writing/editing style

Some writers edit as they go; others edit only after they've finished a rough draft. Which you choose to do depends on your time frame and the length of the piece you are writing.

In my own scholarly writing, I edit the previous day's work before moving to the next stage. For a longer piece, the editing process may very well occur over several weeks or months. Because I edit "from the beginning" at the start of every writing session, I may each day spend as much time revising as I do writing. After editing every page that I've written up to that point, I'll spend an hour or two composing a rough draft of the next several paragraphs. When I return to my writing the following day, I'll again edit *all* that I've written, including yesterday's paragraphs. I then begin the writing process anew by consulting another stack of index cards and turning the information on those into rough-draft prose.

I follow this procedure until I've completed the "first draft" of the entire essay. By that time, though, I've also edited (revised) parts of the essay dozens of times.

Editing after completion

Even after I've "completed" the essay in this manner, I'll continue to edit, often surprising myself with the upgrades. Deadlines permitting, I'll also place the essay aside for a week and return to it with fresh eyes, far more critical of my own writing than when I was immersed in the process of building the initial draft. That lapse of time provides me with additional perspective, allowing me to read my writing as others might—that is, as somebody who is "not on my side" might. I am then even more demanding than I was during the initial phases of composition.

The ultimate goal: Editing for clarity

Comprehensive editing *crystallizes* ideas. By encouraging succinctness, editing allows *writer and reader alike* to comprehend the full scope and implications of the writer's thoughts. In fact, editing fortifies the integrity of our ideas by helping us say exactly what we mean and clarifying those concepts for readers. Essayists cannot afford to be mystics, whose utterances stand to be interpreted differently by various readers.

(Indeed, when I criticize students' sometimes garbled prose, I'll ask them to show their sentence to ten different friends and to ask each of them what it means. If they get five identical answers, I add, then I'll reconsider my assertion that their prose is confusing. In close to thirty years, I have yet to have a student return with any positive results from that experiment.)

In brief, vigorous editing crystallizes our thoughts and allows writer and reader to understand a passage of prose in precisely the same way.

While no one can master the craft of editing overnight, I can provide you with a comprehensive and systematic approach to self-editing—an approach that takes the mystery out of the process and dispels the myth that people are *born* as either good or bad writers. With enough practice at editing, you can develop into a fine writer, thereby enhancing your prospects for success in college and beyond.

Standards matter

Also, do not believe the prevalent assertion that good writing is something that's virtually impossible to define because—as the notion goes—what's "good" is ultimately a subjective call. Absurd! Clarity, conciseness, cogency, and word flow are instantly recognizable and clearly definable. Don't let any such fashionable academic skepticism (or like-minded excuses for failure, on the part of students or educators) impede your plans for succeeding in college.

Do take care of grammar and punctuation first

As for grammar, I urge you to purchase the most recent editions of John C. Hodges, *et al.*, *Harbrace College Handbook* or H. Ramsey Fowler, *The Little, Brown Handbook*, or a similarly detailed guide to mechanics and style. Don't wait until you enroll in freshman English to undertake a thorough review of grammar and punctuation with one or more of these books. If possible, do so *on your own* before arriving for your freshman year of study. If you are fortunate, your freshman English class will cover grammar and punctuation. If not, you'll still be ready to improve your writing skills on your own.

The history behind my approach to editing

The editing approach that I recommend here has its origin in an intensive expository writing seminar that I administered for several years at the University of Texas at Austin. The students who enrolled in this program were high-school seniors who had been accepted for fall admission into Plan II, a highly esteemed university-wide honors program. They lived on campus for a six-week summer session *preceding* their fall enrollment as freshmen. My goal was to elevate their writing skills to junior- and even senior-level competency before they returned in September to begin their freshman year of study.

The course was a grand success. These high-school seniors, with much hard work, improved dramatically within six weeks—to the point where their prose was sometimes mistaken for that of graduate students.

The fifty-four editorial categories

The course described above was structured around the mastery of fifty-four editorial categories pertaining to *organization, argument, style,* and *form.* These editorial categories were the ones with which I had observed students having the most trouble over the previous ten years of my experience as a teacher of writing.

Mastering "the chart"

After seeing students make the same mistakes over and over in their writing, I came up with an idea of tracking their errors, as well as their progress, on a chart. You can see the chart at the back of this section (you'll likely become very familiar with it as you learn the art of self-editing). This chart enabled students to spot mistakes they made repeatedly, and also provided a visual representation of their progress in the course generally.

Tracking progress

When the students made mistakes in their writing, I filled in the appropriate block on the chart and had the students revise. Because I charted their mistakes, praised their progress, and finally demonstrated how to revise if they were slow to grasp the concept, they ultimately learned the art of editing.

After six weeks, most of these students had internalized the categories and no longer needed the chart. The fifty-four categories became integrated into their permanent editing habits and allowed many of these students to earn extremely high GPAs throughout their college careers (one became a Rhodes Scholar). Moreover, as years pass, I sometimes receive letters and e-mails from students who have by now become highly successful in various professions. They attribute part of their success to the editorial prowess they acquired through a dedicated effort at mastering "the chart."

You, too, can become your own editor

Here's a quick preview of how to use this editing chart:

1. Write the rough draft of your essay.

2. Print a hard copy of your essay, double-spaced. (At first, don't try to do your editing on the computer. Reading your essay on the computer screen will not reveal all the errors.)

3. Look at the chart and pick a category. Study what that category means (see the examples below).

4. Read through your essay, looking for changes to make for just that ONE category.

5. Circle items that need revision; then hand-write the corrections on the hard copy of the essay.

6. Mark the block on the chart to record your error in that particular category.

7. Rewrite your essay to make the corrections that fall into that category and then print another hard copy.

8. Follow steps 3 through 7 for each of the categories. Keep on rewriting with particular categories in mind until you've gone through the chart.

9. Follow this process with ten to twelve essays and you'll start seeing dramatic improvement in your editing (and, therefore, writing) skills.

Start slowly

At first, stick with a single category in order to feel more comfortable with the editing process. If, for example, you're rereading your essay just for "wordiness," then that's all you have to concentrate on *that time around*. You'll be surprised how effectively you'll edit for that one category when you aren't compelled to do everything else at one sitting.

Over time, you'll discover that you have internalized these editing categories. After a while, you'll be able to edit for more than a few categories at a time and eventually you won't any longer need to refer to the chart.

Does that mean you'll have to edit your completed draft fifty-four additional times? Yes—at least at first. But so what? Years of teaching have convinced me that this procedure takes the fear out of the editing process. As time passes and as you absorb the editorial categories, you will eventually edit your papers for every category—and all at the same time. Just take things slowly at the outset.

By becoming your own editor, you will experience a new sense of intellectual empowerment that paves the way for success in multiple enterprises entailing written communication.

Examples for each editorial category

Below you'll find examples for each of the editorial categories. Professors may tell you that they expect you to edit your papers thoroughly, but they usually don't have the time to offer detailed instruction about how do so. Here, therefore, are the categories that will help you master the entire editorial process:

Organization

1. Generate a good opening paragraph

An opening paragraph should get the reader interested in the topic and then advance a thesis. The thesis should imply, "Friend, here's what you stand to learn from this essay that otherwise would have escaped your notice and left you with a less sophisticated grasp of this topic." In other words, your thesis should imply that the average educated reader is likely to encounter something new and exciting about the topic—even if he is already generally familiar with it.

2. Write a strong concluding paragraph

A strong concluding paragraph reiterates the point of your essay, brings forth a saved piece of key data around which you structure concluding remarks, and suggests that your argument and conclusions have implications and ramifications for others who might plan to explore your topic.

3. Advance a progressively unfolding thesis

The index-card approach (discussed above) will guarantee your ability to meet this requirement. If you have a blueprint of index cards dictating the logical flow of your overall argument, each new paragraph will more likely form a new stage in a progressively unfolding argument.

If, on the other hand, you haven't used an organized approach to gathering research data or generating ideas, but have instead relied upon spontaneous inspiration the night before your essay is due, buckle up for a bumpy ride to nowhere.

4. Have your paragraphs be "the right size"

In college, you'll double-space nearly all of your paragraphs. Although it's impossible to say precisely how long any given paragraph ought to be, most will average one-third to three-quarters of a typewritten page. Occasionally a paragraph may be longer or shorter. If your paragraphs tend to be lengthier on a regular basis, you should learn to edit down to the main point. Readers like to pause over a concise block of information and take a moment to ponder it. Proper paragraph length allows them to do that. If your paragraph is too long, break it into two paragraphs or be more selective about the information provided.

5. Have emphatic three-fold transitions at the beginning of new paragraphs

As illustrated above, three-fold transitions are vital at the beginning of all paragraphs other than the opening and concluding paragraphs. A three-fold transition (1) ever so quickly refers back to what you've just said, (2) reiterates, in new language, the overall thesis of your essay, and (3) points forward to the next stage of your argument, suggesting, in tone, that you've arrived at a new and exciting stage of your argument. (If you haven't already read it, see the prior chapter, "The Basics of the College-Level Essay," to learn more about the three-fold transition.)

You may find that you sometimes should forego a formal three-fold transition, simply because the elaborative point of that paragraph does not call for one. But use three-fold transitions as often as possible. They consistently orient readers, leaving them comfortable about where they've been, where they're going, and what you're arguing.

6. Begin new ideas with new paragraphs

This category should pose no problem for students who faithfully use an index-card approach to researching, structuring, and composing essays. Failure to do that often leads students to "wing" an essay, repeating the same idea and failing to move into new stages of a progressively unfolding argument.

7. Avoid sentences that detract from the flow of your thought

When you're proofreading, constantly ask yourself whether you have inserted sentences that are "off-task." Such sentences break the flow of argument, diminish the reader's ability to follow your ideas, and end up compromising the cogency of your essay. It's painful to delete what we feel is a brilliant observation, but do so if a sentence has no direct bearing on your argument.

Argument

8. Faulty logic in an argument

Most faulty logic results less from illogical thinking than from faulty phrasing or faulty grammar that renders a thought absurd. Take, for instance, this classic dangling participle:

> Walking around the corner, the Empire State Building appeared.

Because buildings don't walk, the sentence is illogical. The author obviously means to say, "Walking around the corner, I saw the Empire State Building." When you proofread your papers, constantly ask yourself whether the modifiers (i.e., describers) in each and every sentence would sound logical to someone else. Also, check closely for erroneous references (item 44 below) and faulty parallelism (item 48 below), since those likewise result in inherently illogical observations.

9. Avoid direct address in formal prose

A direct address refers to "we" or "you." Thus, a student might write, "If we were to avoid using drugs, our society would be better off," or "If you stop shoplifting, then the price of food in supermarkets would go down." The average reader, however, is neither using drugs nor shoplifting. Thus, direct address would become something of an insult to the gentle reader. Say, instead, "Our society would be better without drug abuse," or "Less shoplifting would help lower prices in grocery stores." The heart of the matter is the fact that most essays in college feature semiformal prose— that is, writing directed toward people whom the essayist does not know personally. Thus the address of these readers as "you" seems more than a little presumptuous.

10. Paraphrase at least some quotations

More often than not, we can summarize quotations through paraphrase. Quote only the author's words that are so vital as to serve as unique proof or data to advance your thesis. Otherwise summarize a quotation in your own words. Do so, if possible, with fewer words than appear in the original quotation, and be sure to cite the source of your paraphrase. Thus, if you're about to quote James Duban's opinion that

> "Melville's cosmos was charged with incessant battles between the powers of good and evil, of polar struggles that typify the unending balance of positive and negative cosmic forces"

you might instead paraphrase as follows:

> Duban argues that Melville's works posit the opposition between good and evil forces, both terrestrial and cosmic.

You make the same point, seem more in control of the material, and allow the reader to move on with *your* writing. Simply footnote the source of the paraphrase the same way you would cite a direct quotation.

One of the problems pertaining to the overuse of quotations (especially those that extend two or more lines) is a subconscious response of readers to your prose. Too many quotations lead readers to think that you're becoming incapable of speaking in your own authoritative voice, even as you gather quotations to illustrate your knowledge and authority. Paraphrasing also eliminates a distracting diversity of writing styles in *your* essay, especially when the quoted writing style is less concise than yours. Be faithful to your source, but use as few words as possible from the original quotation.

11. Avoid asking rhetorical questions

Because writers should advance an argument rather than beg the reader's clarification, *questions* compromise your authority. Thus, rather than ask,

> Can anybody deny the contribution made by Jonas Salk's discovery of the polio vaccine for twentieth-century immunology?

simply say, with added authority,

Jonas Salk's discovery of the polio vaccine was among the most significant advances in twentieth-century immunology.

Every now and then, of course, a quick, sharp rhetorical question might heighten your authority, especially if you're challenging a prevailing view ("Are we supposed to take such a perspective seriously?"). But use such questions perhaps only once in your essay—in a context when the question is so "clever" as to bolster rather than to compromise your scholarly tone.

12. Avoid summary-like tone; sound argumentative (i.e., persuasive) instead

Remember, the key to persuasive writing resides in your having a cogent argument supported by impressive data. Still, even when many students have met these criteria, they too often fail to put an argumentative "spin" on their prose, assuming, instead, that readers will somehow intuit the logical point of their essay.

Frequently, though, what sounds "persuasive" to the writer comes across as merely observational to the reader. In fact, the writer's utterance strikes readers as simply summarizing what they would have deduced from the evidence on their own, without the benefit of the essay at hand.

This is the most pervasive problem with argumentative writing on college campuses today. It is also the most difficult for teachers to explain, and for which to offer remedial suggestions. When proofreading, therefore, you have to ask yourself, with a fresh glance at every sentence, whether your argument *sounds* more like summary than like an argument. If it does, then fix the problem.

Here is an example of the process of editing that resolves the dilemma. Elsewhere in this book, I referred to my son's essay about Hawthorne's sketch concerning young Benjamin Franklin. The youthful Ben, you'll recall, stood to learn that a wrong doesn't translate into a right simply because a person commits that wrong in the name of the public good. One part of my son's original essay read as follows:

Ben was summoned before his father. After being asked why he would take property not belonging to him, Ben explained how he did it only for the public benefit. His father made haste in correcting him and in explaining that the end does not justify the means, since evil can breed only evil.

My son here failed to use rhetoric (that is, words achieving a certain effect) suggesting that the ethical insight and explanation are *his*, and that he's *arguing* this point. He erroneously assumed that everyone will simply understand that and generously credit his insight. But in most instances readers actually won't!

Here's the revision, which sounds authoritative and persuasive:

> Although Ben seeks to convince his father of the propriety of the theft—with a lame reference to public benefit—his father ends up offering far more than what initially appeared as a mild reprimand. Implicit in the elder Franklin's insistence that the end does not justify the means is vital ethical instruction that has immense pertinence, beyond Ben, for the moral education of Hawthorne's readers. Indeed, the reader unwittingly stands admonished with Ben before his father by the end of Hawthorne's sketch.

Notice how the second, expanded utterance, foregrounds the argumentative bent of the writer. You'll notice the use of such judgmental words as "lame," "far more," "vital," and "indeed."

The new paragraph also advances a *claim* that the incident turns out to have equal relevance, beyond Ben, for the ethics of the reader. The difference in the two passages is the difference between summarization (which the writer simply trusts will be persuasive) and truly persuasive prose that leaves the reader feeling grateful for new insight about the primary data.

13. Restrict the use of phrases like "I feel" and "I think"

We readers already know that you "feel" or "think" or "believe" such and such, because you are stating it. (Otherwise you would be a hypocrite.) So, rather than say, "I feel that Melville explores the more somber aspects of human nature," straightforwardly assert that "Melville explores the more somber aspects of human nature."

Occasionally, however, "I feel," "I think," and "I want to suggest" can serve a useful function, especially when you've summarized the scholarship of others but wish to advance an innovative reading. You might write, for instance, "At issue, I think," or "At issue, I feel," or "At issue, I want to suggest," implicitly acknowledging that some very intelligent people (whose studies you have cited in a footnote) may well disagree with you, but that you're willing to venture *your* innovative reading. Still, employ "I feel" or "I think" sparingly—at the most once per essay, and usually in the context of a polite challenge to existing scholarship or popular opinion.

By extension, I urge you to avoid inserting yourself autobiographically into an academic essay. In some circles, professors value a paragraph (or far more) about your own life, but such writing usually strikes the instructor as highly impertinent and self-indulgent.

14. Failure to conclude a paragraph argumentatively

When readers arrive at the end of a paragraph, they appreciate an emphatic reiteration of the point of the paragraph. Thus, if we return to item 12, above, the concluding sentence for that paragraph could be:

> This dimension of Hawthorne's sketch offers a memorable lesson for anybody aspiring to be a moral leader.

Too many students end their paragraphs blandly, providing little connection to the main thought of the paragraph. That shortcoming compromises their tone of authority and air of contribution. (The problem often emerges when, in a paragraph's last sentence, students seek to anticipate the subject of their next paragraph rather than drive home the point of their current paragraph. Remember, it's preferable to save transitional devices for the first sentence of new paragraphs.)

15. Avoid flowery rhetoric and sweeping generalizations

Rather than writing, "Throughout all of recorded history, scholars have sought every conceivable avenue to make stunning new contributions to their particular fields of study," simply write, "Scholars have traditionally sought to make new contributions to their fields of study." Passionate or grand assertions can't take the place of documented evidence and succinct observation.

16. Lapse of scholarly tone

You might be surprised at the degree to which "street talk" has crept into college-level essays. "Yeah, right!" or other exclamations that might prove popular in hallway discussion have no place in academic essays. If you want to express praise for or doubt about something someone has written or said, don't say, "Way cool!" or "Yeah, right!"; suggest, instead, that this person's position is "on the mark," "misguided" or "questionable." The same advice applies for any idiom that might compromise the reader's faith in your scholarly objectivity or intellectual maturity.

17. Failure to use secondary scholarship effectively

The main reason for citing, quoting, or paraphrasing secondary scholarship (books, articles, or published reviews about your topic) is to demonstrate that you're familiar with what's "out there," and that you have something fresh to add to the dialogue. If you read a collection of secondary articles and, even with proper citation, merely reiterate the substance of those articles, you're not adequately using secondary scholarship as a point of departure to advance your own idea.

To use secondary scholarship correctly, cite existing studies that tend to corroborate your somewhat differing approach, or suggest that your research calls into question the finding of others, whom you may choose either to quote or paraphrase (with proper citation). In any event, never convey the impression that you're simply showing off what you've read about your topic. Make us feel that there's an innovative *purpose* that you're making of secondary scholarship.

18. Don't quote out of context

Students sometimes place an unwarrantable "spin" on an author's words. Thus, when proofreading, recheck primary and secondary quotations to make sure that you're quoting them fairly—that is to say, in a way that accurately reflects the significance that those words possessed in the first instance.

19. Don't hop back and forth between ideas

Students most often do this in the traditional "compare and contrast essay." If you are comparing two separate texts, advance your thesis about the relation between the two, but then treat each text separately (with only casual reference to the other) before intermixing quotations and ideas from both texts in the same paragraph(s) of your essay. Readers then will feel well grounded in the two emphases of your essay rather than having the sense that, because you keep hopping back and forth, they are learning nothing coherent about either.

20. Failure to intermix sufficient quotation

Readers expect paragraphs to have at least two or three *quite brief* quotations amidst your paraphrases and interpretive sentences. By quoting pertinent words or phrases from your primary research, you convey the impression that your thesis is grounded in verifiable data and that you're not simply riding a hobby horse of your own making. I can usually tell when students are "out in left field": they fail to intermix brief quotations from primary research. Instead, they tell us more about their own preoccupations than about the subject matter of the essay.

By primary research, I mean those data about which you are writing. In a literature class, your primary research and data could be a poem, novel, or the an author's diary; in a government class, primary research involves published documents; in a history class, primary research would examine the personal letters of a figure, or facts about his life revealed in period newspapers or pubic records; in psychology, primary research might center around experiments and statistical analysis. Stated otherwise, primary research forms the core of your essay, whereas secondary research reviews and comments on what others have said about your topic.

21. Failure to use a thesis-oriented title

The title of an essay should hint at your main thesis. Suppose, for instance, that this is your theme:

> Beyond the obvious hypocrisy of Dimmesdale, a more subtle public hypocrisy is recurrent in Hawthorne's *The Scarlet Letter*.

Then the title of your thesis might read:

Shared Hypocrisy:

Public and Private Behavior in Hawthorne's
The Scarlet Letter

Do not, as some students do, simply title your paper *The Scarlet Letter* (look, Hawthorne already wrote that!) or "Paper One." Professors get a sense of your professionalism and authority from the titles of your essays. Set a knowledgeable tone.

And don't overdo the artistry of your title page. There's no reason to have the title of your essay be larger or more stylized than words in the body of the essay. Cool it with the computer graphics. When professors submit articles for publication, they seldom change their own font when typing the titles of essays. Such graphics come across as juvenile. (Only a publisher will stylize the titles in either the published journal or book.)

Style

22. Avoid wordiness
Reread every sentence to see if you can rid your essay of words that serve no purpose, but only clutter the sentence.

Thus, you might rephrase the sentence above as follows: "Avoid wordiness." Shorter sentences lend themselves to items 23, 25, 27, and 31. Shorter sentences also facilitate the sort of sentence combination that allows you to alternate your sentence structure.

23. Failure to cut down and combine sentences
Once you eradicate wordiness, you're in a better position to combine sentences. Take the following example:

> Vietnam and Watergate will undoubtedly haunt us for many years. But those incidents were not entirely worthless. We learn some lessons from everything.

Just cut away some of the verbiage and combine:

> Although Vietnam and Watergate have haunted Americans for many years, those events were not without their lessons.

The point here is that sentence combination, as well as alternating sentence structure, depends, in large measure, upon sentence condensation.

24. Avoid repetition of key words in close proximity
Professional writers avoid repetition of key words. Stated otherwise, once we hear the word "repetition," for example, we don't want to see it again for another eight to ten pages. Otherwise the reader reaches conclusions about the writer's laziness in not seeking synonyms.

25. Duplication of thoughts, or redundancy
You'd be surprised how many students will make an assertion and then repeat the same point, in slightly different words, within the next sentence or two. *Build* upon your point; do not simply *repeat* it.

26. Avoid stop-and-go sentence structure (choppiness)
Readers appreciate a smooth read. A flowing prose style enhances your scholarly tone and professional "voice." Thus, avoid choppy prose:

Example 1
Therefore, these options, of and by themselves, offer little assistance to the majority of deaf people in bridging the communication gap, as noted above, between the deaf and the hearing worlds.

Revision 1
These options themselves do little to bridge the communication gap between persons who can and those who cannot hear.

Example 2
The dreary weather, mainly rain, which never seemed to stop, and my problems with my parents (very serious problems) upset me, especially on weekends.

Revision 2
I often felt upset because of the unending rain and serious problems with my parents.

Note how the revisions have absolutely no stop-and-go qualities. That smoothness, in turn, will permit the writer more easily to subordinate one of these sentences to another that may follow, allowing for an enhanced sentence combination.

27. Avoid repetitious sentence structure

Repetitious sentence structure usually takes a subject-verb form. Although repetitious sentence structure is not in itself grammatically incorrect, it lessens the writer's authority by sounding tedious.

Many students erroneously assume that the "cure" for repetitious structure resides in simple alternation of sentence structure, leaving the same number of sentences in place. I, however, urge students to eradicate repetitious sentence structure by condensing two sentences into one or by subordinating one to another.

Two examples
Man is a complex mixture of instincts, drives, and emotions. The ability to control these things is what sets him above other species in nature's scheme.

Eliminate subject-verb repetition by condensing
Man's ability to monitor his instincts, drives, and emotions sets him above nature's other species.

Eliminate subject-verb repetition by subordinating
More intellectually versatile than other of nature's species, man can monitor his instincts, drives, and emotions.

As suggested in numbers 22 and 25, above, your ability to undertake several revisions on the chart hinges on your ability to delete wordiness and choppiness. Those skills, in turn, enhance your capacity to alternate your sentence structure.

28: Avoid triteness, colloquialism, and jargon
Stated otherwise, avoid street talk, sports lingo, or buzzwords in semiformal writing. Write for posterity, not for the hour. "Dissing," "props," "lifestyle," "interface with," and "rad" have no place in an academic essay until they become widely accepted terms. Likewise, profanity cheapens a paper and undermines its tone.

29. Inappropriate passive voice
The passive voice of verbs often leaves readers with a vague sense of who or what is engaged in the action of a sentence. The active voice of a verb is usually more effective. Why write, "Help was needed by the soldier" when you can say, "The soldier needed help"? Still, there's a time and a place for the passive voice. Use it to emphasize how something was passively acted upon. If, for example, you are a journalist and wish to emphasize the plight of bank tellers who "were robbed," that's just fine. You thereby compose your sentence from the point of view of the victim, allowing readers more vividly to experience that perspective.

Passive-voice construction is especially harmful in sections of scholarship application forms where students seek to demonstrate what they have done either in the community or in the laboratory. When they write, "Up to twenty hours a week were spent assisting at a nursing home," or "the specimen was warmed to a temperature of 70 degrees," they implicitly distance themselves from their own accomplishments and initiatives. In fact, the passive voice may wrongly suggest that *somebody else* did the work. Although many scientific journals habitually use the passive voice to emphasize the experiment rather than the personality of the scientist, the passive voice is quite disappointing when you are attempting to demonstrate your own initiative in a particular endeavor.

159

30. Failure to blend your prose with that of the quotation

When you offer a quotation in the midst of your own sentence, make sure that the quotation blends into the syntax and flow of your prose. Thus, the inexperienced essayist might write,

> Business executives give good reasons for "sound ethics is good business."

The problem is that the sentence literally says, there are "good reasons for sound ethics." While that is true, it is not the point that the writer is trying to make.

The following revision more smoothly and logically integrates the quotation into the syntax of the writer's sentence:

> Business executives aptly argue that "sound ethics is good business."

31. Delete self-evident rhetoric

This problem is akin to wordiness, but it has a special twist: the writer fails to realize that the reader easily "gets" the point without the added explanation.

> *Example*
> We should revise our current tax forms, especially those that contain the multitudinous loopholes which accountants and lawyers so frequently seem to utilize.

> *Revision*
> Tax forms should contain fewer loopholes.

32. Failure to use intra-paragraph transitions

Just as three-fold transitions guide us from one paragraph to another, so intra-paragraph transitions guide us gracefully from one sentence to another *within the same paragraph*. While such words as "Nonetheless," "Still," "But," "Moreover," and "Consequently" are useful in this regard, intra-paragraph transitions ought to do more. Indeed, in getting us from one sentence to another, the intra-paragraph transition should also enhance the argumentative dimension of our writing.

Thus, in the preceding sentence, the intra-paragraph transition which does just that is: "Indeed, in getting us from one sentence to another, the intra-paragraph transition should...."

Optimally, then, intra-paragraph transitions should enhance the persuasive tenor of your prose while clarifying the relationship between two consecutive sentences.

(*Note*: In the preceding sentence, "Optimally, then, ..." is the intra-paragraph transition that simultaneously conveys a tone of authority and persuasiveness.)

Be especially attentive to the need for intra-paragraph transitions after you've offered a quotation. Quoting then-President Ronald Reagan, one of my students continued as follows:

> President Reagan said, "In the nuclear era, the major powers bear a special responsibility to ease these sources of conflict and to refrain from aggression. And that's why we're so deeply concerned by Soviet conduct." Ronald Reagan has been called the "Great Communicator."

I pointed out that the sentence following the quotation did not explicitly refer back to the quotation, and the student revised the second sentence as follows:

> Close analysis of this statement helps to explain why Reagan has been called "The Great Communicator."

Note how the new intra-paragraph transition enhances the student's scholarly tone by suggesting that she is clarifying something that otherwise is evasive. Thus, the intra-paragraph transition clarifies the relationship between two consecutive sentences (even when one of those is a quotation) while bolstering the scholarly credentials of the writer.

33. Tagged-on rhetoric at the end of a sentence

This problem often occurs when students don't take time to figure out where every fact in a sentence ought to fall; instead, they simply "tag on" information at the end of the sentence, usually by using a comma, followed by the conjunction "and."

Example
To make moral decisions, an individual should take into account personal conscience and social codes of behavior, and then there are factors relating to mitigating circumstances.

That added-on statement gives the impression of laziness. The writer did not take time to revise these several statements into one smooth sentence.

Revision
Moral decisions will encompass personal conscience, mitigating circumstances, and social codes of behavior.

34. Avoid run-on sentence structures

This flaw occurs when writers fail to punctuate their sentences properly, running one sentence into another without appropriate punctuation. If a period doesn't appeal to you after writing a subject and a predicate, consider employing a semicolon and a conjunctive adverb; do not, however, simply run two complete sentences together. Sometimes this error is called a fused sentence:

> Every person who can read a book owes a debt to a teacher hardly ever does anyone return to thank anyone for this miraculous favor.

35. Avoid run-on concepts, due to lack of commas

Run-on concepts often occur in the absence of a vital comma. Although we often drop the comma after a short prepositional phrase (Behind the door was the missing shoe.), we should not do so when the absence of a comma creates an illogical utterance, such as:

> Behind the door pinned to the wall, was a calendar.

Because the door is not pinned to the wall, we need another comma after the word "door." Similarly, the title of this entry, "Avoid run-on concepts, due to lack of commas" would be difficult to read without a comma after "concepts." Readers might initially read, "Avoid run-on concepts due" and have to backtrack to figure out that they must insert a comma after "concepts" in order to create the necessary brief mental pause that lets them make sense of the utterance.

36. Avoid comma splices

A comma splice occurs if you separate complete sentences with commas rather than with periods or semicolons: "Thomas Jefferson was a wealthy planter and U.S. president, he led a war against the Barbary pirates beginning in 1801." As noted elsewhere, you may connect complete sentences with commas only when the sentences are extremely short, well balanced, and part of a series: "Study hard, be good, and phone home once in a while."

37. Avoid inappropriate semicolons

Semicolons have two main functions. They either separate independent clauses that are intimately related, or they separate elements in a series containing internal commas. Here's one example:

> Separate complete statements with a semicolon when they are closely related; indeed, why stop with a period when a semicolon contributes to the "flow" of your prose?

Note how an inherent relation exists between the two sentences that makes the second sentence an extension or elaboration upon the first. Hence, you use a semicolon (half of a colon) rather than a full colon (reserved for major emphasis).

There is another construction that calls for semicolons:

> At the store, I purchased coffee, which had just been ground; vegetables, which were very fresh; and a pastry, which, despite its numerous calories, proved magnetic.

Note how the internal commas make it impossible for us to read this series unless we separate the main elements of the series with explanatory semicolons rather than with commas.

38. Avoid non-functional commas

Commas allow readers to pause for a moment, principally to avoid the effect of a run-on construction, which is precisely the case with the commas in this sentence. Beyond their use with appositives, and keeping straight the names of cities from states, commas also help us separate elements of a series. Still, students periodically pepper their essays with commas for no apparent reason. *Don't.* When proofreading your essays, ask yourself whether you can justify each and every comma. (The trend these days is to insert fewer commas than was the case through most of the twentieth century.)

39. Failure to use colons for elaboration

Use colons to introduce elaborative lists or explanatory utterances, even when those do not take the form of a list.

Example 1 (when listing)
I went to the store and bought five kinds of fruit: grapes, apples, lemons, pineapple, and oranges.

Example 2 (when emphasis is desirable)
Before you write an essay, remember the most important rule of college-level composition: since nothing can come from nothing, structure your writing with the help of index-card data.

In Example 2 notice how I've used a full colon rather than a semi-colon because the phrasing of the first sentence led us to expect major elaboration.

40. Avoid awkward or rushed phrasing

Granted, students don't mean to write in an awkward or rushed way, but they often do. Although a particular sentence or phrase may make perfect sense to *them*, they don't realize that it perplexes the rest of us. The more a writer can predict the reader's confusion over first-draft phrasing, the better the process of editing will be. When proofreading your work, constantly ask yourself whether you would be able to understand everything you've written if you were not the author. Whenever the answer is "no," simply revise for clarity and conciseness.

I've found two methods that especially help students recognize awkward or rushed phrasing. First, lay your essay aside for a few days before returning to it with a fresh eye. Second—and for purposes of proofreading—print your essay, double-spaced, in a font that you seldom use. This allows you to encounter your work as if it were somebody else's prose, distancing you from the proprietary pride you might otherwise take in each and every word, phrase, and sentence.

41. Avoid too many polysyllabic words in long sentences

I here join the great British essayist George Orwell in believing it wise to cut down, when possible, on polysyllabic words (such as "po-ly-syl-lab-ic"). Thus, rather than say that we wish to *corroborate* somebody's findings, we might suggest that we wish to *confirm* their findings. Or rather than say that something is *especially* or *extraordinarily* useful, why not say that it's *quite* useful?

Words with fewer syllables help you combine sentences and improve their flow.

42. Get incidentals up front in your sentence

You don't want to end your sentence with words that qualify its main point. Rather, you should introduce qualifying points as early as possible in the sentence. For instance, this sentence has a qualifying point at the very end of the sentence:

> The military will launch new space satellites only once per year because those are so expensive.

The sentence would read better with this structure:

> So expensive are space-satellite launches that the military will launch those only once a year.

The main point of the sentence is that the launches occur just once a year. The expense of the launch helps to explain *why*. Thus, edit your prose to get "incidentals" toward the front or middle of your sentence.

43. When possible, avoid "it is," "there is," and "there are"

These formulations are wordy. Rather than say, "It is probable that he will arrive at noon," say, "He will likely arrive at noon." And rather than write, "There is no reason for him to leave," simply say, "He has no reason to leave." Similarly, "There are no reasons that justify her actions" becomes "No reasons can justify her actions."

44. Avoid indefinite or erroneous references

These most often occur in pronoun references: "The scientists examined the monkeys, reminding *them* of similarities to human beings." Since the scientists did not remind the *monkeys* of anything, "them" is an erroneous reference. The sentence ought to read, "The monkeys reminded the scientists of human beings."

The pronoun "it" often introduces erroneous reference: "Before noon arrives, it will be difficult to complete the task." Because of the erroneous reference, the sentence literally says that *noon* will have difficulty completing the task. Revise to avoid indefinite pronoun reference: "They will likely not complete the task by noon."

Erroneous references therefore result in faulty logic (see item 8).

45. Inappropriate use of parenthetical remarks

Reserve parentheses for information that you're offering as a casual remark (a humorous aside would be one such example). Too often, though, students place vital information within parentheses. Vital information does not belong there—just "asides." (Oh, if students could only understand these rules intuitively!).

Placing *vital* data or remarks in parentheses usually reflects a writer's reluctance to figure out how best to work that point of information into the logical flow of a paragraph.

46. Avoid errors in diction

Stated otherwise, avoid using the wrong word. Students sometimes have difficulty distinguishing "then" from "than," "its" from "it's," "your" from "you're," or "lead" from "led," "inequity" from "iniquity." Because errors in diction don't show up in "spell check," have an old-fashioned dictionary at your elbow when proofreading.

47. Avoid errors in subject-verb agreement

Very few students commit blatant errors in agreement. I don't, for instance, see students say "each number are even." In college-level writing, most problems in agreement emerge from a subject separated by intervening plural words from its predicate: "*Each* of the pairs of numbers in the complex series is (not "*are*") even."

48. Faulty parallelism or lack of balance

Faulty parallelism results in illogical utterances. If, for instance, you want to say that John was both an excellent poet and a baseball player, you would not want to write (as many students do), "He is as fine a poet as a baseball player." That implies that John is as fine a poet as the average baseball player is. The problem resides in a lack of parallel structure. To convey your proper meaning, the sentence should read, "John is as fine a poet *as he is* an accomplished baseball player." When correcting for parallelism, you may wish to avoid the repetition of the verb "is" by revising differently: "John is both a fine poet and an excellent baseball player."

Lack of parallelism results in faulty logic (see Category 8, above).

I usually group "faulty parallelism" with "lack of balance," since each reflects the writer's failure to align one segment of a sentence with another. Lack of balance often occurs when a writer fails to achieve consistency among elements in a series.

Example
The professor entered the classroom, opened the book, lectured an hour, *and he was conveying vital information.*

Since the elements of a series ought to be balanced, revise as follows:

> The professor entered the room, opened the book, and lectured informatively for an hour.

There's nothing wrong with having more words in some elements of a series than in others, as long as the grammatical forms of the series are parallel and well balanced. You can help assure balance in a series by arranging the words and syllables from the fewest number to the greatest. I did just that in category 39, above: "grapes, apples, lemons, pineapple, and oranges." You are usually able to arrange a series this way—unless your doing so violates logical sequencing. For instance, if you were writing instructions for maintaining and using a fire extinguisher, you wouldn't want to place "point at the fire" before "make sure that the extinguisher is fully charged before using."

49. Avoid the generic "he" when possible

In general, avoid using the generic "he" when speaking about men and women. The awkward way of revising is to say, "he or she," or, worse yet, "he/she." Evade the entire problem by creating a plural. Rather than say "If a student works hard, he will succeed," simply say, "If students work hard, *they* will succeed."

But be careful. Many students are now accidentally mixing singular and plural rhetoric when seeking to avoid sexist rhetoric, as follows: "If *a student* works hard, *they* will succeed." Because you must maintain consistency when using singular *or* plural nouns and pronouns, avoid this sort of illogical mix. Finally, judge your audience in cases where plural phrasing is not quite to the point of your meaning, and where "he or she" sounds cumbersome. An occasional generic "he" sounds better than interrupting the reader's thought process with a forced and intrusive "he or she" or a "he/she." If your professor disagrees, then write "he or she" for him/her. (In this book, you will find several instances of the generic "he" or "she" because "he or she" struck me as awkward, or because constructing a plural "they" was inappropriate.)

Form

50. Use proper footnote or endnote form

Footnotes vs. endnotes. Footnotes fall at the bottom (i.e., foot) of a page; endnotes appear on a separate page at the end of the essay. If you create a separate page for notes, simply label that page "Notes." Although your computers have the capacity to generate footnotes, I'd suggest that you use endnotes. They are easier to manage, for one thing. When professors submit articles for publication, their manuscripts contain endnotes. When the article appears in print, the publisher may or may not choose to convert those into footnotes. Since that process is more expensive and raises problems with typesetting, fewer and fewer journals and books any longer feature footnotes. In your college manuscripts, use endnotes, unless your instructor requests otherwise.

All standard grammar and style handbooks have chapters on proper footnote form for books, articles, newspapers, or the Internet. Simply consult those chapters for numerous examples of how to cite your sources properly. (The sciences and social sciences have their own citation forms.)

Manuals of style: In formal essays, you'll most often choose between the *Chicago Manual of Style* citation method and the Modern Language Association of America (MLA) form. The Chicago style stipulates that you create an endnote, with complete source information, directly after you initially paraphrase or quote; the MLA style directs you to assemble a complete bibliography of all primary and secondary texts, and then simply offer parenthetical citation as you go. Having worked with both formats, I have come to find the MLA style preferable.

Parenthetical citation: When using MLA citation style, you need only open parentheses and enter the name of the author and the page number of the work.

As an example, your bibliography lists the following work:

> Duban, James. *The Nature of True Virtue: Theology, Psychology, and Politics in the Writings of Henry James Sr., Henry James Jr., and William James.* Madison, N.J., and London, England: Fairleigh Dickinson University Press and Associated University Presses, 2001.

If, for example, you wish to cite my opinion that the elder Henry James engaged in "quasi-revolutionary posturing" (Duban, 135), you need only do so like this, working the quotation and parenthetical page reference directly into your text.

Most writers now drop the "p" before the page number (or the pp. before a page span: pp. 12-15). In years gone by, the rule was to include the "p"(s) for all page numbers from books, as well as for all parenthetical and footnote/endnote reference to journal entries. The only exception would be the initial citation, in which a volume number appears—for example, James Duban, "From Bethlehem to Tahiti: Transcultural 'Hope' in Melville's *Clarel*," *Philological Quarterly*, 70 (1991): 475-83. Over the years, most publishers have simply dispensed with the "p"(s) altogether.

When citing parenthetically, you usually mention just the author's last name, and then cite the page number. If, however, your bibliography contains more than one entry by that author, you must also cite a brief version of the title. Were, for instance, your bibliography to feature more than one of my studies, the parenthetical citation above would change to the following: "quasi-revolutionary posturing" (Duban, *Nature*, 135).

Parenthetical citation assists readers by allowing them to encounter a paraphrase or quotation without seeing a cumbersome superscript number that directs them to the endnote page, where they discover a page reference. Part of the object of good editing is to achieve a pattern of rhythm and flow in your prose. If somebody continually has to turn to the end of your essay merely to encounter page references for quotations, that interruption seriously impairs the flow of your rhetoric. Thus, get in the habit of using parenthetical citation.

If you choose to use the Chicago style of notation, you may also modify it to include parenthetical citation. For example, after citing Duban's reference to "quasi-revolutionary posturing"[1]—including the superscript endnote number—you'd simply have the following citation:

1. James Duban, *The Nature of True Virtue: Theology, Psychology, and Politics in the Writings of Henry James, Sr., Henry James, Jr., and William James* (Madison, N.J., and London, England: Fairleigh Dickinson University Press and Associated University Presses, 2001), p. 135; cited henceforth parenthetically in the body of the essay.

That last utterance, "cited henceforth parenthetically in the body of the essay" is vital. It liberates you from any longer having to compose separate endnotes to account for quotations or paraphrases from this one text. Rather, if you later quote from page 201, you need only insert (Duban, 201) after the quotation—right in the text of the essay.

When transforming the Chicago style into one formal endnote followed by parenthetical citation within the body of the essay, do so mainly for *primary sources* that you cite six or more times. You'd cite secondary scholarship parenthetically with the Chicago form mainly for book reviews, since the book under review becomes your primary source, as it were. Otherwise, we readers really don't want to be bothered by recurrent parenthetical citation to a single secondary source; your doing so suggests a failure to speak in your own voice.

Thus, even when using MLA citation, try to cite existing studies quickly and early, not returning to them unless a subsequent segment of your own essay is indebted to the words or concepts of those studies. Remember, your job is to offer something new, not to keep reiterating what's already out there.

51. Failure to space properly after punctuation

Typewriter spacing: Before computer-generated word processing, there were typewriters. Typing on a typewriter had slightly different spacing-after-punctuation rules. If you're typing on a typewriter (yes, people still do this occasionally), add two spaces after a period, question mark, exclamation point, and a colon. Add one space after a comma and semicolon. Don't add any space before or after a dash.

Desktop publishing: Word processing software today, however, knows how to space after each of these punctuation marks. You need only space once and the word processing program will adjust the spacing so it looks good to the eye.

No justified spacing: But to have the computer at least approximate the conventional spacing, *do not justify your right-hand margin.* Justified right-hand margins achieve evenness by distorting conventional spacing between words and after punctuation. Thus, to the eye trained in typing, your "justified" typing looks out of control, relative to rules of spacing. You don't want professors, aged 40 or older, asking themselves why this student doesn't know how to space after a period; you want us concentrating on the integrity of your ideas. Justify your argument, not your right-hand margin and paragraphs.

Dashes: Form a dash with two consecutive hyphens. Your word-processing program will probably turn the double hyphen into a dash for you. (Computer operating systems also allow you to access less well known characters, such as the "em dash," the longer dash used in publishing. Microsoft Windows, for instance, provides the Character Map in the System Tools folder.) Do *not* space before or after the two hyphens. Many students erroneously form a dash with only one hyphen. When doing so, however, they create ludicrously hyphenated words—really! In the preceding sentence, a non-extant word, "words-really" would have occurred had I used only one hyphen when forming the dash.

52. Use ellipses properly when deleting words in a quotation

In quoting, use ellipses to signal your deletion of words either within a sentence or between sentences. When deleting a word from a quotation, be sure to use precisely three periods, with appropriate spacing of those periods: James Duban said, "In quoting, use ellipses to signal your deletion of words … between sentences."

When quoting two or more sentences within the same paragraph, and when deleting intervening sentences, use four (evenly spaced) periods, as above, but have the first period fall directly after the last letter of the word preceding the ellipses. (The first such period actually denotes the omitted period in the deleted sentence.)

53. Punctuate in correct proximity to quotation marks

When you are not using parenthetical citation, here is the correct placement of punctuation, relative to quotation marks (see the table below).

Quotation marks and punctuation		
Punctuation name	**Character**	**Example**
Period	."	John said, "Have a good day."
Comma	,"	When John said, "Have a good day," I responded, "You, as well."
Question mark (quoting a question)	?"	Carol asked, "Who's coming?"
Question mark (when a sentence is a question)	"?	Can you believe that John said, "Have a good day"?
Exclamation point	!"	The student exclaimed, "I'm thrilled!"
Dash	"—	The first sailor to spot the shoreline yelled, "land-ho!"—just what you would expect.
Semicolon	" ";	John said, "Goodbye"; then he waved farewell.

Illustration 19.1

171

When you're offering quotations and using parenthetical page citation, though, the rules change. Punctuate as follows, always leaving a space between the quotation mark and the parenthesis (see table below).

Quotation marks, parenthetical citation, and punctuation	
Punctuation name	**Example**
Period	John said, "Have a good day" (p. 58).
Comma	When John proved "inadequate" (p. 5), the manager sent in a new pitcher.
Question within declarative sentence	When she asked, "Who's coming?" (p. 85), she learned that her worst enemy would be at the party.
Question when your quotation is exclamatory	Can you believe that he shouted "Fire!" (p. 54) in a crowded theatre?
Semicolon	John said, "Have a great day" (p. 4); he then waved farewell to his friends.
Exclamation point	Quite early in the narrative, the student exclaims, "I'm determined to learn the rules!" (p. 66).
Dash	The first sailor to spot the shoreline yelled, "land ho!" (p. 88)—the very response one would have expected.

Illustration 19.2

54. Avoid back-to-back quotations

Always insert some of your own words between quotations; never directly follow one quotation with another:

Example

He was very appreciative, saying, "Thank you," "that's very kind of you."

Revision

To express his appreciation, he said, "Thank you," then added, "That's very kind of you."

Beyond the chart

The task of becoming your own editor is *yours*; you must revise countless times before submitting your essays. But you must know what to look for. The following editing chart and the preceding explanations will help considerably. But take even more initiative by seeking out professors who are willing to offer extensive notations and editorial suggestions. Tell your professors that you would value their severest criticism of your writing because you really want to improve.

Note: You can download a free single-page version of the editing chart from my website, www.college-achiever.com.

Conclusion

In my experience, practice alone does not make perfect when it comes to mastering the art of writing top-notch, persuasive, scholarly essays. You need intensive feedback, criticism, and encouragement to become an accomplished writer.

The 54-Category Editing Chart						
Organization						
1	Poorly structured opening paragraph					
2	Weak concluding paragraph					
3	Failure to advance a progressively unfolding thesis					
4	Paragraphs are either too long or too short					
5	Weak thesis-oriented transitions between paragraphs					
6	Failure to begin new ideas with new paragraphs					
7	Sentences that detract from flow of thought					
Argument						
8	Faulty logic					
9	Avoid direct address					
10	Quoting obvious points (paraphrase instead)					
11	Avoid asking questions of your readers					
12	Avoid summarization; sound argumentative instead					
13	Restrict use of "I think" and "I feel"					
14	Failure to conclude a paragraph argumentatively					
15	Avoid flowery rhetroic and sweeping generalizations					
16	Lapse of scholarly tone					
17	Failure to use secondary criticism effectively					
18	Quoting out of context					
19	Hopping back and forth between ideas					
20	Failure to intermix sufficient quotation					
21	Failure to use a thesis-oriented title					
Style						
22	Wordiness					
23	Failure to cut down and combine sentences					
24	Repetition of words in close proximity					
25	Repetition of thoughts or redundancy					
26	Stop-and-go sentence structure (choppy)					

Illustration 19.2

The 54-Category Editing Chart					
Style, cont.					
27	Repetitious sentence structure				
28	Avoid triteness, colloquialisms, and jargon				
29	Inappropriate passive voice				
30	Failure to blend your prose with your quotation				
31	Failure to delete self-evident rhetoric				
32	Failure to use intra-paragraph transitions				
33	Tagged-on rhetoric at the end of a sentence				
34	Run-on sentence structure				
35	Run-on concepts (due to lack of commas)				
36	Comma splice				
37	Inapppropriate semicolon				
38	Non-functional commas				
39	Failure to use colons for elaboration				
40	Awkward or rushed phrasing				
41	Avoid too many polysyllabic words in a long sentence				
42	Generally, get "incidentals" up front in your sentence				
43	Generally, avoid "it is," "there is," and "there are"				
44	Indefinite or erroneous reference				
45	Inappropriate use of parenthetical remarks				
46	Error in diction				
47	Error in agreement				
48	Faulty parallelism or lack of balance				
49	Avoid the generic "he" when possible				
Form					
50	Improper footnote form				
51	Failure to space properly after punctuation				
52	Failure to use ellipses properly				
53	Failure to punctuate in correct proximity to quotation marks				
54	Avoid back-to-back quotations				

　　　Illustration 19.2

Section 5 ::
Being a College Star

Chapter Twenty

Taking Your Ideal College Education Beyond the Classroom

These days, the ideal college education involves a broad range of achievement—both in and outside the classroom. By the time you graduate, you'll want your record to reflect your well-roundness, passionate commitment to a field of study, and likelihood for distinction in graduate school, professional school, or your chosen vocation. We thus far focused on success in the classroom and on developing professional relationships with your professors. Now it's time to talk about success beyond the classroom.

Beyond the classroom

You should seek out opportunities to distinguish yourself within the university environment. On-campus opportunities include:

- Participating in a university Honors Program
- Joining a professor's research team
- Working on an independent research project
- Writing for campus publications and competing for academic prizes

Such campus activities testify to your initiative and self-reliance.

Beyond the campus

You'll also want to branch out and explore the world; in other words, think "outside the campus." Plan to study abroad; network with other students and future colleagues in professional organizations; and try to get published (either as author or co-author) in your field's academic journals. Also seek internships or part-time employment within your field of study to demonstrate your professional acumen and capacity for growth.

Within the campus

While it's in your best interest to create professional links and relationships off campus—whether through internships or part-time employment—you should still enjoy (literally) *the time of your life* during your undergraduate years. By that, I do not mean excessive partying; rather, I'm referring to social interaction with fellow students that can and should be part of the ideal college experience. Make new friends; frequent campus coffee houses; go to plays, concerts, lectures, symphonies, and poetry readings; and by all means cheer on your campus athletic teams.

Also, don't miss those "heavy" student discussions that sometimes extend into odd hours of the night. Years later—in your first corporate job (or however you start your career)—you're unlikely to find Camus, Dante, Nietzsche, or Sophocles the chat of the snack room. Learn from the many diverse points of view and experiences your fellow undergraduates bring to campus. College, after all, should be a place where you discuss and define humanity's core values and principles while determining the life worth living that is best for you.

I think back fondly on many such hours during my undergraduate experience at the University of Massachusetts Amherst and wouldn't trade them for the world. Remember, though, that you *will* graduate—and sooner than you think. It's in your best interest to build bridges to the "real world" at the same time you immerse yourself in campus life.

Conclusion

The ideal college education entails much more than success in *required* courses. College is a multi-faceted experience that involves social engagement, intellectual curiosity, and major commitment beyond the classroom.

Chapter Twenty-one

Plan to Study Abroad

Students should, if possible, study abroad for a summer, a semester, or a full year. Doing so is part of the ideal college experience. Travel abroad expands one's perspective, aids in foreign-language acquisition, and demonstrates maturity and self-reliance. Students who study abroad become cosmopolitan, are comfortable in new situations, and are better able to engage in meaningful dialogue.

Personal growth

Having navigated the challenges of studying abroad, such students are often able to handle most anything else that comes their way. The unknown is less frightening and more of a challenge. They also establish an international network of friends and—perhaps most importantly—memories that are usually impossible to duplicate once that first mortgage, child, or full-time job comes along. There's always retirement, but do you really want to wait that long to travel?

Studying abroad helps you to stand out in the competitive global market

Studying abroad also makes a student more competitive in the global economy. Employers are impressed by the maturity of students who have studied in a foreign country, while fluency in foreign languages lends itself to the expansion of world markets. Also, imagine how impressive it will be to have a glowing letter of recommendation from one or more professors at universities in other countries. That's truly "external validation" of merit.

Studying abroad increases your chances with scholarship foundations

National scholarship foundations (Rhodes, Marshall, Truman, Rotary, and Udall) are likewise impressed by students who have traveled and studied abroad. Study-abroad experiences are especially useful in the "personal essay" segment of national scholarship applications. Students who have studied abroad are at an advantage in being able to recount interesting episodes in a foreign country and what they learned about the differences and similarities spanning various cultures. That figures in the deliberations of employers and national scholarship foundations: they are making an investment in students and often count on the best returns from somebody who, by virtue of international travel, possesses significantly enhanced maturity and intellectual development.

Ditto for graduate schools

Moreover, the same assumptions often hold true for law schools and medical schools looking for "well-rounded persons." There is no better evidence of that than when students demonstrate that they have broadened their horizons internationally.

The finances

What at first glance may seem financially prohibitive is often manageable. Many universities have study-abroad offices that arrange worldwide exchange programs. Exchange programs can also feature arrangements involving "locked" tuition scales. Thus, relative to tuition, students end up paying no more than they would for the same number of semester-credit hours at their home university.

Discount, too, the saved cost of maintaining your automobile and its insurance for a year (there's your round-trip airfare!). Finally, many universities offer study-abroad scholarships to help defray the expense of studying abroad, while one national scholarship (the Annette Kade Scholarship) specifically assists students on study-abroad programs in France or Germany.

Your graduation schedule

You might be wondering if you will significantly delay the date of graduation by studying abroad. Maybe yes, maybe no. In the event that you do, regard the excursion as an invaluable part of your education. If you take five years to graduate, the experience of having been abroad is worth it. At the same time, however, some study-abroad programs have long-standing arrangements with foreign universities that allow a transfer of credit hours to your home institution. Stated otherwise, you should seek to take courses that your home institution will "count" towards your degree. Thus, even if you're gone for a year, you can—if you plan ahead—arrange to graduate on schedule.

Be aware that many study-abroad programs last either a summer session or for a single semester rather than for a full year. In many cases, this assists in the logistics of studying abroad at a reasonable expense.

Moreover, if you're still in the process of acquiring foreign-language proficiency, you can begin your study-abroad experiences in an English-speaking country.

I write from personal experience. As an undergraduate, I went on a study-abroad summer program to Oxford University and studied literary criticism under a well-known British "don" (their expression for professor). That was one of the most thrilling, inspiring, and intellectually challenging experiences of my life. It was there that I resolved to become a professor of English.

Consider who your professors are when you study abroad

Relative to letters of recommendation garnered from study-abroad programs, I strongly urge you to consider programs that actually place you in the classroom of a professor who is a full-time faculty member of the university where you'll be studying. Quite often, professors from American universities lead study-abroad summer excursions and teach the classes themselves. They are usually excellent teachers and go out of their way to make your experience marvelously educational and enjoyable. The only drawback is in the geographical distribution of letters of recommendation that you will ultimately have. This is an issue that only you can resolve after appropriate deliberation about the spectrum of study-abroad opportunities available through either your university or other universities. Universities customarily seek students from around the country to help them enroll the maximum number of students for their study-abroad programs.

The Rotary Ambassadorial Scholarship

You may also qualify to travel abroad, prior to your senior year of study, on a $26,000 Rotary Ambassadorial Scholarship. The Ambassadorial Scholarship funds a year of study in most countries where you would have language proficiency (including English-speaking countries—England, Ireland, Scotland, and Canada, for instance).

Rotary International urges you to visit major cultural centers not only in your host country but also in nearby or distant countries ($26,000 can go a long way). And while taking courses or conducting research in your major field of study, you are also encouraged to interact with the local population and local Rotary clubs. Stated otherwise, the scholarship not only places you in a position to study abroad; it actually helps you structure a year of meeting hundreds of people in that country. Since there's a year's delay between the time you win the scholarship and the time you travel abroad, you have a year to prepare for the adventure of a lifetime. See the chapter "Nationally Competitive Scholarships" for more details about Ambassadorial Scholarships (as well as related national scholarships) that subsidize a year or more of study abroad.

The Fulbright Grant

The Fulbright Grant, in one of its several forms, is designed for seniors who are about to graduate, or for graduate students. It offers a year of cultural enrichment entailing an intensive course of research at a foreign university. Students who have traveled abroad *before* their senior year are at an advantage—with respect to cosmopolitanism and "contacts"—when they apply for the Fulbright and other international scholarships, such as the Rhodes, Marshall, or Mitchell Scholarships.

You can also study for a semester at other universities in the U.S.

Finally, if you cannot travel abroad, look into university-sponsored National Student Exchange programs that allow students at one U.S. university to study for a semester at another U.S. university. Such programs often let you to pay the same tuition at the host university as you would pay at your own university. So the goal here, if you are studying at a state university, is to spend a semester at a prestigious private university, or a well-known state university in another state. I know one student who enrolled in two programs of this sort; she broadened her horizons and was able to obtain wonderful letters of recommendation from several famous scholars.

Where to get assistance for studying abroad

Several campus offices may sponsor study-abroad programs. Check with your Dean of Students Office, with the International Programs Office, or with the director of your university honors program. Even academic departments may offer study-abroad programs, such as an English department that sponsors a "Study-Shakespeare-in-England" type of course.

It's possible to learn about summer-abroad opportunities by viewing websites or by word-of-mouth. I would, though, strongly urge you to consult with the professionals on your own campus when you decide to study abroad: people who have coordinated a study-abroad center know how reliable the various programs are and can attest to the happiness or discomfort experienced by previous students. Most importantly, they will know whether the courses you might take abroad would count on your U.S. transcript as certified, transferable credit hours (toward either your major or your electives).

Conclusion

Study abroad to enhance your personal growth, international awareness, foreign-language skills, national scholarship prospects, attractiveness to graduate schools, and competitiveness in the global economy. Pick a study-abroad program that stands to offer the best courses, setting, and prospects for letters of recommendation.

The Benefits of Studying Abroad

Jared Crebs (right), a student from the University of North Texas, won a $25,000 Rotary Ambassadorial Scholarship to study flamenco guitar in Spain, at La Escuala de Música Creativa. Jared is here pictured in Plaza Mayor with his flamenco teacher, Carlos Del Rio. At UNT, Jared majored in Jazz Studies and minored in Music Theory and Spanish. Jared's year of study in Spain fueled his entrepreneurial spirit. Following his return to the U.S., he wrote and published his first ebook, *The Beginner's Guide to Unlocking the Guitar—Learn How to Easily Play the Guitar in Just One Weekend* (www.unlocktheguitar.com).

Chapter Twenty-two

Why You Should Enroll in Honors Programs

There may very well be more than one honors program on your campus. Some honors programs are sponsored by specific academic departments, such as English Honors or Biology Honors. Other, frankly more prestigious, honors programs are university-wide and not housed in any particular department. Your campus may possibly have more than one of these university-wide programs, or even an honors college.

You should make it a point to apply for admission to all such programs. Participation in honors programs significantly enhances the quality of your education and will provide you with a built-in support group of students having similar interests and high educational goals.

The department-level honors program

Let's focus on some of the advantages of being in a departmental honors program. First, honors classes are usually smaller and are more likely to be taught by the department's most effective professors. The smaller class size is a "carrot" that attracts the best and brightest faculty members to teach in the program. The smaller class size also provides you with more individual attention in exchange for your educational investment. If, for example, you're at a state university that averages thirty or more students in a conventional class, and if the departmental honors program tops off at fifteen to twenty students per class, then you get the benefits of a small college for far less tuition.

Course requirements to complete a major

If you're concerned that taking honors classes may delay your graduation, don't be. The honors classes in the program usually correspond to the courses you'll need to complete your major degree plan. Thus, if an English department requires that you take a course in nineteenth-century American literature to fulfill part of the English "major," the departmental honors program might feature a course in "Hawthorne, Melville, and the Transcendentalists." This honors class would have an interesting angle, offer in-depth reading in a particular area of literature, be taught by a professor who has published on this topic, enroll outstanding students, and often meet one of your graduation requirements.

Before enrolling in an honors class, though, check with the honors program director to see which honors classes correspond to your major's graduation requirements. Nonetheless, do not resist enrolling in an honors program simply because one or more of its courses do not "count" towards graduation. Simply take those courses on an "elective" basis.

More interaction with top-notch professors

Departmental honors classes are often taught by professors known for their scholarship in that specific area; so you may well come to know a well-published professor in an area of interest to you. Moreover, if you need to write a senior honors thesis to graduate with departmental "honors," then one of your honors professors may sign on as your mentor. Professors are extremely busy and sometimes reluctant to supervise honors theses of students about whom they know very little. They are far more willing to direct a thesis when you propose to elaborate upon a dimension of a course you took with them. In short, continuity appeals to student and professor alike.

The senior honors thesis

Let's elaborate upon the senior honors thesis. If you are to graduate with "Special Honors," many honors programs expect you to write an in-depth paper in your senior year. That project is generally called a senior honors thesis. They range in length from 40 to 120 pages and reflect a year or more of research. A "scholarly" thesis seeks to present an innovative perspective about an issue or concern in the student's field of study and can later serve as the foundation for a master's thesis or even—if the student sustains interest in the concept—a Ph.D. dissertation. In fact, I know one student whose senior honors thesis underwent that metamorphosis and ended up, twelve years later, as a major book in her field of study.

Then there are "creative" theses—collections of art works, musical compositions, poems, short stories, or even a student's first attempt at a novel. Senior honors theses can exist both within a departmental honors program *and* a university-wide honors program. When I directed the English Honors Program at the University of Texas at Austin, I often granted permission for students to coordinate one thesis to satisfy the requirements of both programs. If you end up participating in two honors programs that sponsor honors theses, I'd urge you to seek permission to develop *one* thesis that counts for *both* programs. The research and writing otherwise can be too formidable for a student to tackle two such projects at the same time.

University-wide honors programs

Now let's look at the university-wide honors programs (or honors colleges within universities). Those require you to take a certain number of courses within their program and, if you wish to graduate with university-wide honors, to write a senior honors thesis or to complete a "capstone" seminar. The courses offered in the university-wide honors program (or college) will generally fulfill many of the "core" classes required for graduation.

I cannot overstate the importance of being associated—beyond departmental honors programs—with university-wide honors programs. To attract the best students, the honors director or honors dean usually seeks out the most exciting professors on campus to teach honors courses. In honors classes, moreover, two (or even three) of the brightest professors on campus (and from *different* departments) may sometimes team-teach a course. And bear in mind that those professors often compete to teach within the program and therefore are at the top of their game when teaching. Honors classes are traditionally small enough to encourage discussion.

Thus, if you're in both departmental and university honors programs, you can meet many of your core and major requirements in intimate settings and graduate with additional distinction.

Learning often entails more than rote memorization; honors classes usually provide sophisticated adult-level discussions among students and cultivate more creative and profound thinking and writing.

Additional offerings from honors programs

University-wide honors programs feature guest speakers, conferences that orient you to the world of research, public-events discussion sections, community-outreach projects, or study-abroad opportunities. Honors directors typically have generous budgets that allow them to obtain extra benefits for their students.

Affiliation with either a departmental or university-wide honors program provides a home-away-from-home and the very best peer group. In honors programs, students rise to the level of their peers and become involved in programs and projects they might not otherwise have contemplated.

More opportunities to shine

Many honors programs also feature "honors magazines," various project committees, and yearly academic prizes. Thus, being in an honors program often represents a good chance to get published, to take leadership initiatives, and to be able to boast academic "prize" distinction on your vita or résumé.

Bigger feathers in your graduation cap

Moreover, since honors students are usually held to a higher academic standard, you enhance your odds of being able to impress graduate programs, national scholarship foundations, professional schools, and employers with your undergraduate record of achievement. This is so because the most ambitious honors programs are now promoting research opportunities that encourage advanced knowledge and insight, all the while leaving students more qualified to compete successfully in national scholarship competitions.

Whereas professors outside of honors programs are sometimes over-committed to the point of being unable to supervise additional undergraduate research projects, the case is often otherwise in honors programs that encourage professors to become involved in those research projects. Thus, in honors programs you are more likely to find more paths to research than you might otherwise locate on campus. Again, that research will have an immense impact upon your prospects for post-graduate employment, national scholarship competition, and admission to graduate school or professional school.

What I mean when I say "research"

Research has varied meanings across academic disciplines. Yes, when research occurs in a science laboratory we think of test tubes, computers, microscopes, or experimental projects relating to the great unknown. But college-level research is cross-disciplinary. In literature, for instance, you might research the relation between a given novel or poem and the political climate in which the author wrote those works. In sociology, research might entail inquiries into population or immigration trends. In anthropology, one might explore how religion influences politics or consumer-based advertising. Your honors professors will be able to explain what "research" means in their fields of study and will be able to guide you towards a meaningful project.

There's something impressive about students who are able to claim that they were in an honors program and graduated "with honors" because of a major research project or honors thesis.

Additional institutional support

Finally, your enrollment in an honors course will place in you close contact with the honors program director, usually a professor of distinction who is greatly concerned with your academic and personal well being. Beyond the director, honors programs usually feature internal "advisors," highly trained professionals accustomed to navigating course requirements, semester loads, and the intricacies of scheduling for an optimal sequence of courses. Elsewhere on campus you will seldom find such an array of persons whose mission is to help you organize the optimal college experience.

Ronald E. McNair Post-Baccalaureate Achievement Programs

Across the country, the Department of Education funds the existence of a good number of Ronald E. McNair Post-Baccalaureate Achievement Programs. Named for the deceased *Challenger* astronaut Ronald E. McNair, these programs seek out promising "first-generation" college students whose family incomes allow them to meet the criteria for admission to the McNair Programs. Students are recruited in their sophomore year of study and immediately paired with a research mentor.

The goal is to have all McNair students earn the credentials that will allow them to enter graduate school and earn a Ph.D. At the undergraduate level, funding often exists for students to undertake research projects during the summer and to continue that momentum year round. McNair students travel to student-oriented national conferences to "present" their research, and McNair research mentors often take their students to national-level professional conferences, where McNair students and mentors sometimes co-author presentations and mingle with the "Who's Who" in that field of study.

McNair students and their mentors frequently co-author publications. Moreover, McNair programs consistently feature guest-speakers who lecture about everything from national scholarship competitions to preparing for the Graduate Record Examination. (The GRE is a standardized examination required for entrance into many graduate programs.) In various ways, therefore, McNair Programs can be compared to honors programs and are well worth your consideration if you meet the criteria for admission.

Conclusion: Honors programs are a win-win situation

There's really no question about it: if your university has honors programs—either departmental or cross-disciplinary—apply for admission to all for which you qualify. If you gain admission, take whatever extra courses are necessary to be a member in full standing. You won't regret this decision.

Chapter Twenty-three

Working Outside the Classroom: Independent Research, Research-Team Participation, Internships, and Employment

Bridging the gap between learning and doing

Much of your ideal college education will occur beyond the classroom in quasi-work environments. You'll still be learning, but you'll also start to practice your craft and branch out into your likely profession. These quasi-work environments fall into roughly four main categories:

1. Conducting independent, on-campus research.

2. Being a member of a professor's research team.

3. Participating in an internship.

4. Getting part-time or summer employment relating to your field of study.

Unlike these experiences, conventional classes encourage you to master a body of knowledge for which you are accountable on examinations. But there's a huge leap between studying anthropology, let's say, and being an anthropologist; between studying mathematics and working in a place where you use mathematics to get a job done; and between studying chemistry and devising new products to detoxify soil or water. In many ways, it's the difference between theory and practice, knowledge and application, or youth and adulthood—between, then, unemployment and a job.

Off-campus: Internships vs part-time employment

Whether in the quasi-"working" environment of an internship or in another "hands on" arrangement, there should be somebody willing to have a mentoring attitude towards you. Try to get training from someone who wants to see you rise in the profession and who is willing to offer guidance to get you off to a solid start. In an internship, you will likely labor for free—in exchange for that mentorship and good will.

But don't assume that mentoring will inevitably be part of the deal in an *off-campus* or *for-pay* job. That's why I would favor internships over outright employment, if possible: the mentoring aspect of your free-labor commitment is accepted up front by everyone.

Shortening the training time for future employers

Business people time and again confirm that you never really learn your subject matter until you're on-site and actually participating. Since that period of training is expensive for companies hiring college seniors, students who have work experience "outside the classroom" are at an advantage. They've demonstrated that they can take initiative and be responsible to others. They have practical experience and are therefore all the more attractive to employers and to graduate-admissions officers.

Sometimes your major may *require* you to perform an internship (such as a student-teaching job for an education major). But nearly all college students—whether or not they have financial need—should make some effort to get practical experience. However, give the commitment enough forethought and planning so as not to over-schedule yourself. Don't forget that you'll likely be engaged in outside-the-classroom-work while still being enrolled in twelve or more hours of college credit per semester.

Let's talk about each of the quasi-work categories individually.

1. Independent research

Independent research within your field of study often occurs in a specialized project under the general supervision of a professor for one or more semesters. You usually write an extensive paper that discusses something new and makes a contribution to the field.

More often than not, you will earn course credit for independent research. Most departments have a special section titled "Independent Study," or some course that allows professors to take on students in a formal capacity and set those students loose to conduct research and periodically report in for feedback. This sort of research, along with that type of professorial relationship, can lay the groundwork—even in your undergraduate years—for a later master's thesis.

Another situation that would fit into this category is the multi-page thesis (often called the senior's honors thesis) required by an honors program.

Examples of independent research

In the humanities, for instance, a student might visit his university's Rare Book Room and see what manuscripts or collections are housed there. It's always interesting to compare the manuscript of a poem or novel to the published version(s) to see what revisions the author undertook and what conclusions about the creative process can be drawn from that research.

In the social sciences, independent research might entail the study of census data and population trends, or interviews with various members of different ethnic or age populations to assess educational and vocational goals and achievement. In the physical sciences, on the other hand, a professor might recommend any number of projects—ranging from marine biology, to neuroscience, to chemical analysis—that would provide students with a semester or more of valuable, independent research. Your professors will be able to direct you initially, though the outcome should demonstrate that you've learned how to direct *yourself*.

With whom should you do independent research?

Generally, only professors who have come to know you quite well will want to supervise your external research project. Thus, it's probably best to approach professors with whom you've already taken a course or two. You should have a particular subject you want to investigate, usually one that has arisen from the class you had with the professor. You'll want to work with the professor to determine how you might make a contribution to the existing body of scholarship.

Also, in addition to locating professors who have confidence in your research abilities, be sure to be a competent writer by the time you seek to undertake independent research. Professors are understandably reluctant to take on a student whose writing is so shaky as to require incessant criticism and revision from the professor.

When to start your independent research

You would likely want to be able to talk about your external research accomplishments by your senior year (when you're applying for graduate-school admissions or national scholarships). In that case, you will want to be able to start this project as soon as is reasonably feasible before your senior year, with the aim of impressing a professor or two with your potential to become *somebody* in their discipline of study.

When possible, try to begin the research for your senior honors thesis in the second semester of your junior year, or over the summer leading into your senior year. That allows professors who write recommendations to account for the research you've been conducting for several months leading up to the letter of recommendation. In some cases you'll already have results to show for your research; in others, the ongoing research will serve as an impressive foundation for the professor to speculate about the likelihood of your being able to handle the business of the profession.

2. Research-Team participation

Similarly, seek to gain admission, if appropriate, to a professor's research team. Research teams generally exist in the physical and social sciences. (You're far less likely to encounter research teams in the humanities, where faculty members traditionally work individually on books and articles.)

Becoming part of a research team carries immense benefits. Aside from "doing" the business of the profession on a research team, you're demonstrating that you know how to work well with other people. I have, for instance, seen letters of recommendation in which scientists praise the student's knowledge, initiative, and ability to be a team player. When you later interview for corporate jobs, prospective employers will always wonder how you're going to "fit in"—that is, whether you'll be a team player or, less attractively, a Lone Ranger disinclined to work productively with the group.

Thus, by working on a research team, you're fortifying—beyond your claim to practical experience—the social dimension of your future letters of recommendation. To the extent, moreover, that you emerge as a student leader on a research team, you enhance your "leadership" credentials. Both employers and national scholarship foundations are always interested in leadership potential.

How to get on a professor's research team

Below are various tips I've gathered from my math and science students who successfully participated on research teams.

- **Study with the professor**
  As suggested above, the first rule of thumb is to approach a professor with whom you've studied. There's nothing wrong with

finding out who has research teams and then studying with that professor in order to position yourself to make a later request to be on his or her team. When you enroll in that professor's class, make sure to go to office hours regularly (but not overwhelmingly), prepared to discuss concepts in greater detail than classroom discussion might have permitted. That initiative will allow professors get to know you and to appreciate your initiative, which they may value for their lab.

- **Knock on doors**

  The other way is simply to knock on doors and make your interest known when you're aware that a given research team exists under the domain of that professor. If you've got lots of accomplishment, bring a vita sheet or a résumé. If you don't as yet have an impressive list of achievements, just bring yourself and your enthusiasm. The same goes for guided research in the humanities. If a professor is an expert on Shakespeare, and if you've taken a Shakespeare course and now wish to conduct more advanced research, knock on doors—preferably that of the professor with whom you've studied.

- **Research the professor's research online**

  In the sciences, it is often possible to examine a professor's research online, since many science departments make a point of publicizing their faculty's research on the Internet. They post such information as a way, in part, of attracting companies or foundations that may wish to fund various research endeavors. Some professors even host their own web pages, elaborating there upon the research and the personnel in their labs.

  Once you find an attractive area of research, and after you've closely surveyed the website, send an e-mail to the professor and express your interest in pursuing whatever is happening in his or her lab. Seek an appointment to visit the professor during an office hour.

  When you meet with the research director, make it clear that you wish to commit yourself to that research experience for two or more years, and mean what you say. That will help justify the professor's and the teaching assistant's investment of time in training you to participate meaningfully in that lab. In the sciences, research professors are often resentful when somebody works for them for a brief time (let's say, just one semester) and then, upon leaving, asks for a letter of recommendation. They feel "used."

If you are particularly advanced in your knowledge of the research endeavor, you might express your wish eventually to work on your own project within that lab, though you should make it quite clear that you are willing to start out in whatever position will help you get your foot in the door.

- **Keep your options open**

  You should also make appointments with several professors and—if you are fortunate enough to attract two or more invitations—not necessarily take the first position that becomes available. Learn if that professor has a reputation for working well with undergraduates, and if he or she really enjoys doing so. Ask around to see if the professor is willing to assign personal responsibility to lab assistants, or whether those students remain mere lab jockeys for two or more years. (Graduate students are often ruthlessly frank when asked questions like this.) Also assess whether you feel in a position to rise to the expectations of the research professor, given your other responsibilities.

What to do once you're on the team

Once you get on that research team, go "all out"; never be lazy, and never let your director down. When possible, try to identify a part of the project to which you might make a special contribution. That might entail your taking on responsibility that others either don't want or don't have time for. The important thing is your eagerness to assume responsibility in whatever way the professor finds useful. Realize that working in a lab is a two-fold commitment: half involves your mastery of specific tasks; the other half entails cooperation and compatibility with the other members of the lab, whether they are undergraduates, graduate students, postdocs, or professors.

To the extent that your other responsibilities permit, demonstrate complete immersion and devotion to your research experience. I once received an e-mail from a student who was working in one of my colleague's biology labs. The student said something like, "Sorry if this e-mail is incoherent; I think it's 3:00 a.m." When I discussed that e-mail with his supervisor, we both agreed that the sentence, "I think it's 3:00 a.m." summed up the dedication of this student's research attitude. It wasn't so much that he had stayed up until 3:00 a.m. to work on the research;

rather, it was the fact that he had lost track of time; all that mattered was the research.

Make your opinions and observations known to the team, so as not to become a mere lab jockey; have your lab partners regard you as an essential team member. Students who excel in laboratory environments affirm that enthusiastic commitment *and* a winning personality are vital to a successful laboratory experience and to the professional advancement that may result from that. Indeed, I have heard scientists affirm that social skills are often vital for success in a multi-person laboratory setting. Your accomplishments as both a researcher and as a valued member of the research team will figure in letters of recommendation from research mentors. Those letters will be among the most vital parts of your dossier when you apply to graduate school, professional school, or for a job.

3. Internships

Just as you should aim to join a research team, so you should seek either year-long or summer-length internships in your academic discipline. Some fields of study require such internships: for example, elementary, middle-school, and high-school teachers must first be student teachers. Similarly, nurses are required to have worked in hospital settings. That makes perfect sense. Why not, then, apply the logic to other fields of study?

Experience, not pay, is the key issue. Supervisors of internships often write stellar letters of recommendation on professional letterhead. Students in internships get to know—really know—how their field operates *in practice*. As somebody who constantly reads letters of recommendations, I am impressed when I see both an internship supervisor (off campus) and an on-campus professor praising a student with similar enthusiasm. They each back up the other and add reassuring credibility to the praise.

If you plan a career in industry, or if you aspire one day to have your own start-up company, seek out an internship in a large corporation to learn how a well-run company operates. I've had students report that, in the sciences, for instance, they learned far more than cutting-edge technology when interning for a major corporation. They discovered how to deliver complex designs, on a tight schedule, when hundreds of workers are involved. They also acquired risk-management skills that would serve them well in the future.

There are a number of books dedicated to finding internships among numerous fields of study. For instance, check out *The Internship Bible*.

Work that "counts" as research experience

Quite often real-life work experience can "stand in for" an internship when the work experience is highly related to a student's future career or discipline.

Sometimes you might find work experience on campus. For instance, every school newspaper has a student editor, and I can well imagine that any student in journalism would obtain experience resembling research from being an editor for one or more semesters. I can also imagine how a political science major would shine in that position, conducting research and writing daily editorials about key social and political issues. In a related vein, universities often have radio stations that employ students who aspire to be television anchors, news commentators, or disc jockeys.

Similarly, a student interested in becoming an elementary-school teacher might do well to work in a child-care facility for a year or more. Nothing like being out in the trenches! The point—whether in a formal research assignment, in an internship, or in a work-related job—is to get genuine experience that illustrates your fitness for advancement within your field of study or in the profession that awaits you after you earn your bachelor's degree.

4. Part-time employment

Part-time, paid experience in one's field of study can also serve as an invaluable credential. For instance, a business major would improve his or her credentials (and better understand business concepts) by having worked in a bank, mortgage company, or investment firm. Again, you're not only bridging the gap between theory and practice; you're advertising to future employers that you won't be as expensive to train. That's especially the case if you end up working full-time at the same company. I have one acquaintance who, as an engineering student, worked part-time with the Lockheed Martin Corporation. He is now president of one division of that company.

Other quasi-work experiences

There are other outside-the-classroom activities that would work, too, but you should focus on keeping the activity related to your field of study. Just think to yourself: "What can I do, outside the classroom, that demonstrates my commitment to my field of study and that would later be helpful in producing a "personal statement?"

Artists can arrange art showings on campus or in a local gallery; English majors can try to get poems published in a student journal; radio/

television/film majors can write movie reviews for the campus or local newspapers.

Also volunteer your time and "major" skills to charitable organizations. Many a charitable organization could use the short-term services of graphic designers, web developers, accountants, writers, counselors, psychologists, nutritionists, librarians, etc. However, don't let the time you invest in a volunteer job undermine your ability to do well in your college classes. Your grades are too important. Also, be careful not to get in over your head by trying prematurely to deliver professional-level services. Note, too, that there are some unscrupulous businesses out there that solicit the services of students for free labor and have no interest in fostering a mentoring relationship; do be wary of such situations, since it's unlikely you would get a letter of recommendation that will help you in the future.

Conclusion

At every possible turn, think of demonstrating that you are so committed to your field of study that—whether for pay or not—you look for opportunities to engage in the practice of your future profession or field of graduate study. Again, the point is to regard classroom interaction as the *starting point*, not the end point, of an ideal college education. Internships, research experiences, and pertinent part-time employment will greatly contribute to that educational experience, making you more desirable to employers and graduate-school admissions officers.

Working outside the classroom

Photo by Irene Wong

Walter Gribben, a senior at the University of South Alabama in Mobile, is majoring in history and minoring in chemistry within that university's pre-med program. In addition to maintaining a very impressive academic record that earned him a four-year Whiddon Honors Scholarship covering most expenses, Walter has consistently extended his education far beyond the college classroom. Active in student clubs and president of the campus chapter of Mortar Board, Walter participates in community service projects. During the summer of his freshman year Walter began volunteering in a local hospital. He got to know most of the medical profession-als and established a reputation of reliability. But Walter also knew he wanted more "real-world" medical experience. The next summer he completed the American Red Cross Nursing Assistant Program (a four-week, full-time course) so that he could be hired as a Patient Care Technician (PCT) in the hospital's emergency department. Walter has since spent many hours assisting doctors, nurses, and other medical personnel with the usual emergency-room gamut of illnesses and injuries. Now promoted to PCT II, Walter has developed the kind of "hands-on" experience that best complements a stellar academic résumé. He plans to start medical school next year.

Chapter Twenty-four

Taking the Initiative: Winning Awards, Getting Published, and Networking

When it's time to *leave* college, you'll want to impress prospective employers, Human Resource Departments (which used to be called Personnel Departments), future clients, graduate school admissions committees, or national scholarship award committees. (And don't forget about future in-laws if you're planning on getting married soon.)

In any case, you'll want to stand out from the crowd and have several "gold stars" on your résumé. Many other undergraduates will earn good or great grades; and a number of those students will also have the work or research experience that shows commitment to their fields of study. So how will *you* distinguish yourself from *that* crowd?

You'll do so by showing initiative, taking a chance, putting forward your best effort. Here are a few of the tried-and-true ways to round out the college experience with distinction: win awards, get published, network. Along the way, you'll get extra practice and learn to enjoy the element of risk, feeling less and less apprehensive of failure or rejection.

On-campus awards

Consult your university's catalogue; then visit department advisors and the Dean of Students Office to learn about various awards for outstanding freshmen, sophomores, juniors, and seniors. There are also other scholarships within academic departments. Those awards may not be well publicized, so you'll need to do some poking around.

Once you learn about prizes on your own campus, determine who the supervisors and coordinators are; discuss with them the customary academic profile of winners. After that, take steps to earn the credentials that will allow you to compete successfully. For instance, a "Best Essay" or "Outstanding Student" award in your major department amounts to an immensely impressive credential, as do other scholarships dedicated to academic excellence and artistic accomplishment.

Here's a personal example. I was able, in my sophomore, junior, and senior years of study, to win the "best essay by a male undergraduate award" in the English department. Though each award brought me only $25.00 (for which I was quite grateful!), the distinction of those awards had lifelong positive implications. The most immediate of those was admission to graduate school with a very generous fellowship provision worth the equivalent of $120,000 today.

Publication

If possible, get published, in some manner, either as a co-author or as solo author. Publication can be in the form of poetry for undergraduate journals; newspaper editorials, guest columns, movie reviews; or academic publication for scholarly journals. It's worthwhile to list a category titled "Publications" on your résumé. This indicates that somebody besides your mother has genuine interest in what you have to say.

In the case of scholarly essays, publication indicates a genuine contribution to the field of study. When undergraduates publish in scholarly journals, they often do so by being named co-authors in a professor's research project.

By extension, therefore, take the initiative to get onto somebody's research team in the sciences and work your way up to meriting co-authorship. Short of that, have poster presentations where you exhibit your work—and preferably in competitive, award-winning environments. Prizes thus earned suggest that you are a person of diligence and accomplishment. Poster and essay presentations lend themselves nicely to a "Presentations" category on a résumé or vita.

Networking

Take the initiative, as well, to network within your field of study by joining whatever honor society exists for undergraduates in your major, and by attending, if possible, either regional or national conferences frequented by professors in your discipline of study. Those conferences may feature an "undergraduate panel discussion" or an opportunity for undergraduate paper presentations. You could thereby earn the credential of having presented an essay or having participated in a panel discussion. In the process of doing that, you would meet the faculty leaders in your discipline, several of whom might hear you speak and perhaps remember you when, down the road, you apply to their graduate programs.

Professional organizations often have membership discounts for students. Join any local groups and attend meetings as often as your schedule allows. If the professional group has a website, visit it regularly. You can learn a great deal about your future career by following the topics in e-mail listservs or discussion groups. That networking circle will become invaluable and is these days easily accessed and maintained through e-mail correspondence.

Entering off-campus contests in your major field of study

The point of entering contests is not always to win first prize, but to get *any* prize that can enhance your résumé and introduce you to a company or college graduate program where you may end up working or studying. Even a couple of Honorable Mentions can go a long way.

Conclusion

Countless other opportunities for "initiative" will present themselves—service roles, leadership positions, student-newspaper assignments, etc. The point is to leave your television at home, get off your chair, and make things happen. Opportunities recognized and seized lead to further opportunities; one achievement leads to other invitations. Campus leaders are not born; they create themselves through early and sustained initiative.

Section 6 :: Reaping the Benefits of the Ideal College Education

Chapter Twenty-five

Keeping Your Focus on the Finish Line: Achieving the Ideal College Education

To achieve an ideal college education, as I have defined it in this book, you must *plan* for it. Of course, the "ideal" college education will have different meanings for different people, so you'll ultimately have to decide which meaning works for you. My suggestion—based on over twenty-five years of teaching and advising college students—is that you should use one or more national scholarship applications as a marker for charting your ideal education. When, as a college freshman, you look at the various questions in those applications, you'll get a sense of what "ideal" signifies within national-level competitions.

Where to start ... where to start ...

At the end of this chapter you'll find URL addresses to access scholarship applications for Rhodes, Marshall, Truman, Goldwater, Udall, Rotary, National Science Foundation, and Jack Kent Cooke scholarships, among others. Read these applications and others that suit your interests (see the Resources section at the end of this book). Beyond taking account of the advice in this book, make a list of goals that you wish to accomplish before you get to your senior year of college; have several of those goals correspond to the expectations governing the scholarships that you've targeted. Start thinking *now* about how you can accomplish those goals.

The really big prize is an ideal college education

The point is not whether you will necessarily win one of these scholarships. While I hope that you do, those opportunities are highly limited. More important is whether, by the middle of your junior year in college, you have charted and attained the sort of college career that—while proving intellectually stimulating and rewarding—also leaves you with viable *options* for your future, including the prospect of applying for national scholarships and graduate-school fellowships. You will then have structured a highly impressive college education that—beyond being intrinsically valuable—will appeal to prospective employers and graduate-school admissions officers.

The guidelines in this book will position you, in particular, to apply for national scholarships, since this model of an ideal college education corresponds to the expectations outlined in those scholarship application forms. By following the guidelines in this book, you will (by the time you graduate) prove to yourself and others that you:

- Engage in critical thinking and meet high expectations in course work

- Possess a passionate competency in a particular field of study

- Can make new contributions to your field of study

- Have a capacity for innovation, exploration, and creativity

- Take responsibility for your own self-learning

- Have real-world experience in your chosen profession

- Know how to network among professional colleagues

- Are seriously targeting specific career goals

- Show compassion for your fellow human beings through community service

- Exhibit leadership skills among your peers

- Communicate well in a variety of circumstances

- Manage your time well

- Enjoy the competitive spirit

- Are a well-rounded citizen of the nation and the world

You will, in other words, be leagues beyond students who have sought merely to make As and Bs in their courses.

Other benefits of applying for a prestigious scholarship

Let's assume that you do end up applying for at least one prestigious scholarship. Even if you don't win the scholarship, you'll still be left with multiple benefits. For one, you will have undertaken an important project and seen it through to its conclusion. You'll have learned more about yourself and your plans from the application process, and you'll have communicated with professors and advisors who agreed to write comprehensive letters of recommendation.

Another tangible benefit of applying for prestigious scholarships resides in the essays that you will write. You'll generate concise statements about your intellectual passion for a field of study, and you'll be able to recycle those essays for other applications—whether for scholarships, graduate/professional school admissions, or cover letters that accompany your employment résumés.

Graduate school fellowships: The other potential prize

Don't forget that graduate-school programs can offer financial assistance to help you earn your advanced degrees. A four-year graduate school fellowship covering a master's degree and Ph.D. can be worth as much as $150,000–$175,000. If you earn one of those fellowships, then all of the months of preparation for a national scholarship would be amply rewarded, even if you don't win the national scholarship. I know a student who applied for the British Marshall Scholarship but did not receive it. She then took a day to revise her essays into a graduate-school application due the same week. She ended up winning a five-year fellowship that allowed her to earn her Ph.D. at a major graduate program.

And the job market

Similarly—for those entering the job market—an excellent education, accompanied by superb communication skills, will allow you to be innovative, advance in your profession, and never have to fear that your company-wide memo will compromise your reputation.

When to start ... when to start ...

Yes, I'd finally suggest that you must vigorously prepare for those national scholarship competitions as early as your freshman year. But first you must mentally prepare by recognizing that those scholarships reward only ideal educations. That's what you're getting ready to undertake; a national scholarship competition simply recognizes which students have done the very best job of creating optimal college educations. Thus, do everything you can to craft an ideal education rather than naively suppose that there's an automatic checklist guaranteeing you a national scholarship.

In the end, it's up to you

It's up to you to achieve your ideal college education, so enter programs designed to help you get there. Get involved, for instance, in honors programs, since university honors directors constantly seek to cultivate ideal educations. If you're at a community college or a large state university, plan ahead and structure your education so that you can rise to the achievements anticipated by various questions and categories on national scholarship applications. Any university—Ivy League or otherwise—will at best merely make available the building blocks of your education; *you* yourself must structure those blocks optimally. An ideal education—beyond acquainting you with the best that has been thought and said—leaves you intellectually empowered in communication skills, social engagement, academic mastery, leadership initiatives, and world travel—each opening successive doors of opportunity.

Major national scholarships and their URL addresses

Now's the time to read through these applications and decide for yourself how you plan to achieve your ideal college education. The following list is not meant to be comprehensive, but is rather a sampling of links to application forms to download and examine yourself. Look for common themes and expectations. Think about how you would like to be able to respond to the various inquiries in these applications four or five years from now. In particular, I recommend that you review the application forms for the following scholarships (several of which I describe in later chapters):

- **Rhodes Scholarships**
  www.rhodesscholar.org
- **Marshall Scholarships**
  www.marshallscholarship.org
- **Truman Scholarships**
  www.truman.gov
- **Rotary Ambassadorial Scholarships**
  www.rotary.org/foundation/educational/amb_scho/rotarian/award/type.html
- **Barry M. Goldwater Scholarships**
  www.act.org/goldwater/
- **Ford Foundation Predoctoral Fellowships for Minorities**
  www.fordfound.org
- **Morris K. Udall Scholarships**
  www.udall.gov

- **National Science Foundation Research Fellowships**
  www.nsf.gov

- **James Madison Fellowships**
  www.jamesmadison.com

- **Paul & Daisy Soros Fellowships for New Americans**
  www.pdsoros.org

- **Fulbright Scholar Grants**
  www.iie.org/templatefulbright.cfm?section=Fulbright1

- **Andrew W. Mellon Fellowships in Humanistic Studies**
  www.woodrow.org/mellon/competition_2005.html

- **Jack Kent Cooke Foundation Graduate Fellowships**
  www.jackkentcookefoundation.org

- **Gates Cambridge Scholars**
  http://trust.gatesscholar.org/

- **Jacob K. Javits Fellowships**
  www.ed.gov/programs/jacobjavits/index.html

Note: Web addresses are notorious for changing unexpectedly. If you go to any of the above URLs and don't find the web page you're looking for, use an Internet search engine to find the scholarship sponsor's website and then locate the application form by using the website's navigation system.

Conclusion

Plan your ideal college education early to maximize your post-graduate options. While planning that ideal education, seriously consider the common expectations of various national scholarship competitions.

Chapter Twenty-six

Taking a Closer Look at Actual Scholarship Applications: Common Themes

At the very beginning of this book we talked about the fifteen specific goals for experiencing the ideal college education. If you accomplish all of the goals in that list, you'll not only have a superior education and many opportunities for personal advancement, but you'll be in a fantastic position to do any of the following:

- Apply for scholarships to travel abroad or continue with your postgraduate education.

- Apply to prestigious graduate or professional schools, with the hope of receiving financial assistance.

- Seek a job in your chosen profession.

- Do your own thing, such as start a business or otherwise carve out a place for yourself in the world.

And how do I know this? Because I've read many, many scholarship and graduate-school applications, and I've come to realize they are all looking for the same thing—that special student who has achieved the ideal college education.

You don't have to take my word for it, of course. Let's look at the common themes and expectations in the applications for some of the more well-known scholarships, such as the Rhodes, Marshall, Truman, Fulbright, Rotary, George J. Mitchell, Barry M. Goldwater, Jack Kent Cooke, Morris K. Udall, Andrew W. Mellon, and National Science Foundation scholarships/fellowships. We'll be learning more about these specific scholarships in the next section, if you're curious about them (and you should be!).

As for the applications' common themes—notice how they are in line with the essentially practical approach to the ideal college education articulated throughout this book. We'll be looking at:

- Employment related to college major
- Specific career goals
- Research/Internships/Field experience
- Community service
- Leadership
- Well-roundedness
- Letters of recommendation
- Communication skills
- Academic excellence
- Awards and prizes

Employment related to college major

Several national scholarship competitions (for example, the Udall, Rotary, Truman, and Jack Kent Cooke scholarships) asks for employment information. I once heard a national scholarship judge remark that he read the job listings expressly to see whether students were interested enough in their major fields of study to have sought out work in those areas.

Specific career goals

The Barry M. Goldwater Scholarship and the Morris K. Udall Scholarship ask applicants to explain their professional aspirations. Similarly, the Goldwater Foundation asks students to write about their professional aspirations and specify how their current plan of study will prepare them for that vocational goal: "Indicate in which area(s) of mathematics, science, or engineering you are considering making your career and specify how your current academic program and your overall educational plans will assist you in achieving this goal."

Some scholarships expect you to look even farther down the road. A recent copy of the Jack Kent Cooke Scholarship application asked applicants to envision themselves as a successful person ten years from now. "Why are you successful? How did you get there?" The Marshall Scholarship application, in turn, requests a paragraph about "future career aims," while the Truman Scholarship application asks students, "What do you hope to do and what position do you hope to have upon completing your . . . studies?" For related reasons, the Truman application asks students to list three significant courses they've taken to prepare for a future career.

Clearly, national scholarship foundations regard career placement as a legitimate and optimal outcome of an ideal college education, and they expect students to be thinking in those terms. I once heard a high official of the Truman Foundation remark that they were not looking for diamonds in the rough, but for polished diamonds. The pursuit of a career has everything to do with that polish. Stated otherwise, scholarship foundations don't want to take a risk; they seek sure bets.

Research/Internships/Field experience

Many of the national scholarship foundations expect students to have conducted research or to have engaged in internships related to their future fields of study. The Goldwater application asks applicants to account for research activities and then to compose a two-page essay pertaining to a research project and its relevance. The National Science Foundation Pre-Dissertation Fellowship application requires that applicants write about their previous research and their proposed plan of research. The Udall Scholarship asks applicants to describe an activity that has helped them clarify or strengthen their commitment to the environment, implying that hands-on commitment, beyond the classroom, is a *must*.

To compete, moreover, for a Fulbright Scholarship, graduating seniors must compose a detailed plan of research to justify a scholarship that will allow them to study abroad for a year of cultural and academic enhancement. In line with these expectations, the Marshall Scholarship application asks students to demonstrate "practical experience." Even in the humanities, students who apply for Andrew W. Mellon Fellowships, Rhodes Scholarships, and Marshall Scholarships are at a clear competitive edge when they can furnish paragraphs devoted to research and practical experience in essays qualifying as "personal statements."

Community service

Examples of public service seem to be in demand because they are intrinsically worthwhile and because they alert national scholarship foundations to something vital about an applicant's character. The Truman Scholarship questionnaire asks applicants to recount their most satisfying public-service activity. The Rhodes Scholarship application expects students to have "an interest in one's fellow being." That interest usually manifests itself through public-service commitment. The same criterion emerges in the Jack Kent Cooke application, which asks applicants to chronicle their "participation in unpaid internships, volunteer service activities, and other school, civic, professional, or community activities."

Public service is also an assumed dimension of any Rotary Scholarship application, since the phrase "service above self" is at the core of Rotarian values. Similarly, the Udall Scholarship application requires applicants to "describe … any public service and community activities associated with your interests in the environment, Native American health care, or tribal public policy in which you regularly participate." The phrase "regularly participate" is vital: short-term public service, for purposes of résumé padding, won't cut it. Prolonged engagement with public service (especially in leadership roles) suggests something valuable about a student's heart and mind.

Leadership

The Truman Scholarship application asks undergraduates for a paragraph-long example of their leadership, while the Marshall Scholarship application solicits information about the applicant's "leadership roles." The Mitchell Scholarship application says that applicants will be expected to show "a record of leadership." On the Jack Kent Cooke application, leadership is implicit in the request that students "describe a recent experience in which you made a difference. Explain what was accomplished." And all of the above are compatible with the stipulation, from the Rhodes Trust, that applicants have "moral force of character and instincts to lead." Leadership, it would appear, is here regarded as another outcome of the ideal college experience.

Well-roundedness (including travel abroad)

This is the category that balances the vocational emphases. The Marshall Scholarship application demands that students provide "personal interests and non-academic activities," also asking applicants to list languages, other than English, in which they have proficiency. In a related vein, Jack Kent Cooke Scholarship applications have, in the past, asked students to describe a work of art that they find interesting. For related reasons, the Mitchell scholarship application speaks about "participation in extracurricular activities," while even the Goldwater Scholarship application (oriented towards science) asks students to list school activities "such as clubs, publications, debating, dramatics, music, art, and student government." The point here is that vocationalism ought to be balanced with well-roundedness.

Letters of recommendation

All national scholarship agencies require letters of recommendation—anywhere from two to eight. Each of these competitions therefore expects that students will have impressed their faculty enough to receive several comprehensive letters of endorsement. Those letters need to reflect upon, and even expand upon, the student's academic excellence. Letters of recommendation should show a professor's *personal knowledge* of the student and indicate professorial interaction with the student beyond the classroom. In many cases, letters of recommendation are just as important as high grades—sometimes even more so—in helping students achieve their long-term goals.

Communication skills

All national scholarship foundations expect students to have excellent communication skills. If students have a track record of publication—whether in the student newspaper, in university honors journals/magazines, or in scholarly journals—that's an excellent index of proficiency in the area of written communication. Moreover, the application essays that students compose indicate whether they have learned to express themselves clearly and forcefully. The Truman Foundation underscored the importance of writing at one of its conferences for scholarship advisors by distributing materials to help students put together their applications; among those handouts was a copy of Strunk and White's famous book, *Elements of Style.*

As for verbal skill, I have heard more than one foundation representative (along with several judges of these competitions) emphasize the importance of succinct, coherent, informed, and friendly conversation. And why not? Think, for example, of the $26,000 Rotary Ambassadorial Scholarship. Anybody who wins one of those has the responsibility of giving talks at a large number of Rotary clubs about themselves, their studies, their year abroad, and how all of that relates to the values of Rotary. How can Rotarians do anything *but* respect excellent communication skills? Having been involved in national scholarship coaching for nearly two decades, I am convinced, moreover, that most students either win or lose a scholarship in the first half minute of an interview. The rest of the interview merely corroborates the judges' first impressions, one way or another. The point is this: paper credentials are just the beginning in scholarship competitions requiring an interview. Communication skills reflect a vital dimension of an outstanding college career and are therefore essential to winning national scholarship competitions.

Academic excellence

In most scholarship competitions, academic excellence is a given. The students whom I have personally coached for Rhodes, Marshall, Truman, Udall, Goldwater, Andrew W. Mellon, and National Science Foundation scholarships/fellowships have typically earned grade point averages ranging from 3.8–4.0. Moreover, most of them have been associated with one or more honors programs. I can, in fact, recall a conversation I had with one foundation scholarship judge in a shuttle-bus going from the advisors' conference back to the airport. I distinctly remember his saying that he expected really outstanding students to have been enrolled in their university's honors program. I can understand why. Students who have "honors" credentials naturally stand out and are perceived to have had the ideal college experience.

Awards and prizes

Just about all of the national scholarship application forms ask students to list awards, prizes, or like distinctions. The more awards, the better. The bottom line is that past accomplishment has always been, and will always be, a key measure of future success. Awards affirm that this graduate is intellectually gifted and willing to enter the arena of competition. Employers welcome that evidence and take it as a prophecy of future success.

So you can see that accomplishing the undergraduate goals we've talked about is intrinsically worthwhile and will pay off big-time when it's time to sit down and start filling out applications and résumés. In fact, if you achieve the ideal college education, your problem will be to stay within the word limits stipulated by the applications (a nice problem to have!).

Conclusion

Chart an undergraduate education consistent with the demands of national scholarship applications: career goals, research/internships/field experience, community service, leadership, well-roundedness, great letters of recommendation, awards and prizes.

Let's move on, then, to examine these scholarships in closer detail.

Chapter Twenty-seven

Nationally Competitive Scholarships

As suggested earlier, the ideal undergraduate education leaves you poised to compete for merit-based national scholarships: some can fund your junior and senior years of study; others will fund postgraduate study.

A sampling of undergraduate scholarships

Knowing a little bit about what's out there will help you understand and anticipate common expectations among the better-known undergraduate-level scholarships described below. There are, however, many others. For help with finding and applying for scholarships of interest to you, see the resources section at the end of this book.

Barry M. Goldwater Scholarship

The Goldwater Foundation seeks to identify this country's most promising undergraduates in the areas of math and science. This scholarship pays college students $7,500 to complete their junior year of study, and then another $7,500 in their senior year. If you have maintained an extremely high GPA in your freshman and sophomore years, and if you have managed by the end of your sophomore or junior years to complete a research project in math or science, you should compete for a campus nomination for the Goldwater Scholarship. After graduating with the B.S., Goldwater Scholars often receive large fellowships from graduate programs in the sciences. Thus, winning a Goldwater Scholarship can ultimately lead to postgraduate funding in excess of $150,000.

Morris K. Udall Scholarship

These scholarships fund juniors and seniors at $5000 per year to pursue courses of study that stress environmentalism and environmental public policy. The Udall scholarships go to outstanding students in any number of fields, ranging from journalism and political science to philosophy, biology, or to nearly any discipline having a link to environmental concerns, or to Native-American tribal healthcare. Like the Goldwater Scholarship, the Udall is very prestigious, brings a lifetime of recognition, and can open still other scholarship/fellowship doors. Students who are named Goldwater and Udall Scholars in either their sophomore or junior years of study often compete for Rhodes and Marshall Scholarships (the next chapter of this book discusses those in greater detail) in their senior year of college.

Jack Kent Cooke Scholarship

The Jack Kent Cooke Scholarship targets two audiences—transfer students who will complete their college educations at a four-year university, and college seniors who plan to enroll in graduate school. The second category funds graduate-level study, up to $50,000 per year for as many as six years. Beyond excellent grades, the Cooke Scholarship demands that students compose highly creative essays, be able to demonstrate an appreciation for the arts, and discuss some significant life challenge that they successfully met. In many ways, the Cooke scholarship seeks to reward the truly well-rounded and creative student. The Cooke Foundation does take financial need into account.

Rotary Ambassadorial Scholarship

This scholarship allows college juniors and seniors (as well as graduate students) to travel abroad for a year of cultural enrichment. It pays $26,000 per year. You may compete for the Rotary Scholarship as early as your freshman year of study because, after you win, there is a twelve-to-fifteen-month delay before you go abroad. Thus, if you win this scholarship in your freshman year, you will stay at your university during your sophomore year and then travel abroad in what would have been your junior year. For the same reason, college sophomores who win this award travel abroad in their senior year of study, while college juniors can earn a splendid graduation present for themselves.

Inasmuch as Rotary International values "service above self" and outstanding communication skills, students who excel in those areas, while maintaining impressive grade point averages, have the best chance of winning. Along with the Harry S. Truman Scholarship, the Rotary Ambassadorial Scholarship has an implicit emphasis on volunteer work and public service. Businessmen and businesswomen, along with other professional members of the Rotary organization (physicians, dentists, attorneys, clergy, and politicians) conduct these interviews. While they are certainly receptive to applicants who want to pursue master's degrees or Ph.D.s, they also encourage applications from students who plan to enter a specific vocation. Rotarians would value a proposal that explains why a year of study abroad would enhance your professional abilities while permitting you to spread good will.

Harry S. Truman Scholarship

This scholarship grants college juniors $3000 to complete a senior year of study. Following graduation, they then receive another $27,000 to apply towards the graduate program of their choice. Students may also apply for the Truman Scholarship when they are seniors—but only if they've completed all their undergraduate courses so promptly as to graduate after only three years of study.

The Truman Scholarship rewards exemplary students who plan careers in public service and who have already demonstrated—through both internships and course work—that they aspire to become "change agents" in the area of U.S. domestic or international public policy. Thus, the Truman Foundation expects applicants to go beyond volunteer work and eventually influence local or national policy that affects the lives of thousands or hundreds of thousands of people. Truman Scholars are also expected to be well-read, to write well, and to be effective public speakers. Thus, like other national scholarships, the Truman Scholarship rewards students who have had an ideal undergraduate education.

What is more, because most Truman Scholars receive the award in their junior year of study, they usually gain admission to the graduate programs of their choice—often with immense fellowship support (to which they then add their remaining $27,000). And better yet—the Truman Foundation encourages its scholars to compete for Rhodes, Marshall, and Mitchell Scholarships (Truman Scholars simply defer the Truman Scholarship until they have finished their stints abroad as Rhodes, Marshall, and Mitchell Scholars). Finally, the Truman Foundation, perhaps more than any other national scholarship organization (with the exception of Rotary) makes you part of a "family" and works diligently to open up further doors for your development and success.

The William E. Simon Fellowship for Noble Purpose

Named after former Secretary of the Treasury, William E. Simon, the Simon Fellowship for Noble Purpose encourages undergraduates to pursue educations that will contribute to a lifetime of service above self for the benefit of mankind. The website for the fellowship emphasizes that successful applications will display qualities of passion, dedication, self-direction, and originality "in pursuit of a goal that will strengthen civil society." In its first year of existence, the sponsors (Interscholastic Studies Institute) offered one $40,000 and two $5000 scholarships—along with several honorable mentions. Students who are great candidates for either Rhodes, Truman, or Rotary should also compete for the Simon Fellowship.

Chapter Twenty-eight

Graduate-Level Scholarships and Fellowships

These days there is little difference between a graduate-level *scholarship* and a *fellowship*. Technically speaking, a fellowship implies that you've joined an esteemed group and are now a member (or "fellow") of that group. But recipients of fellowships are still receiving a financial award, the equivalent of a scholarship. "Fellowship" sounds fancier, though group identity and interaction only occasionally justify the name.

Although these awards fund graduate study, most applicants begin to fill out application forms in the spring of their junior year and apply in the fall of their senior year of study. If successful, the student then earns funds to sponsor one or more years of postgraduate study. First-year graduate students may often apply for a number of graduate-level scholarships and fellowships. After that first year of graduate school, however, students often must wait until they are writing their doctoral dissertations to find other external funding opportunities.

The following are some of the better known graduate-level scholarships. For a list of additional nationally competitive scholarships (including descriptions), visit the National Association of Fellowships Advisors (NAFA) website at: www.nafadvisors.org/scholarships.htm.

A brief note on valuation

Some scholarships have a particular monetary value publicized in advance. Others fund a certain number of years of study and sometimes require the completion of a degree. For instance, the Rhodes Scholarship covers all educational expenses, a living stipend, travel expenses to and from Oxford, and study-related travel for a two-year period. Such funding is in line with similar provisions for other scholarships (several of which are listed below). The monetary "value" of such scholarships will vary according to the educational cost of attending graduate programs at different universities and the length of a time the scholarship spans. That said, a rough estimate of these scholarships would be between $25,000 and $35,000 per year.

The Rhodes Scholarship

This scholarship allows eligible college seniors and graduates to earn their next degree, usually over a two-year period, at Oxford University. Most Rhodes Scholars now earn a "taught" master's degree at Oxford; some scholars there locate assistance to stay on for the Ph.D. In either case, the experience of being a Rhodes Scholar is its own prestigious reward.

During their second year at Oxford, the master's candidates often apply to the graduate or professional program of their choice back in the United States. They are frequently assured of admission—often with immense scholarship or fellowship support. Without question, the Rhodes Scholarship caps an ideal education, part of which may include the way the students have already demonstrated their capacity to organize a major community outreach project or program. Earlier in this book, I quoted from a memorandum that I send to prospective recommenders of Rhodes Scholars. The key phrase, "breadth and scope of knowledge," best captures the relation between an ideal college education and this fantastic opportunity.

The Marshall Scholarship

Founded by an Act of Parliament in 1953, the Foreign & Commonwealth Office of the British government finances this scholarship. It commemorates the ideals of the U.S. Marshall Plan. This scholarship resembles the Rhodes, save for the fact that the Marshall Scholarship allows students to study at *any* university in the United Kingdom (whereas the Rhodes Scholarship sends students exclusively to Oxford University). Many students who vie for the Rhodes end up applying for the Marshall as well. Like the Rhodes Scholarship, the Marshall likewise comes with a lifetime of distinction that transcends fiscal benefits.

The George W. Mitchell Scholarship

Sponsored by the U.S.-Ireland Alliance, this scholarship takes students to any one of nine Irish universities for a year of postgraduate cultural enrichment and enrollment in a degree or certificate program. You would usually compete for the Mitchell Scholarship during your senior year of study.

The Gates Cambridge Scholarship

Funded by the Bill and Melinda Gates Foundation, the Gates Cambridge Scholarship allows students to earn their next academic degree at England's Cambridge University. The scholarship funds students for several years of postgraduate study. If students apply for this scholarship during their senior year of study, they must have a highly specific research interest, the materials or resources for which reside exclusively at Cambridge University. Regardless of your field of study, you would have had to achieve unusual research distinction as an undergraduate and then be able to argue convincingly that the resources for your advancement to the master's and Ph.D. levels of study exist exclusively at Cambridge University. In that sense, the Gates Cambridge Scholarship is less about "finding oneself" abroad than it is about being at Cambridge University to "read" in a highly specific area while making use of specific research facilities (whether in the humanities or the sciences) and engaging in conversations with some of the world's leading figures in your field of study. Thus, you must first be accepted into a course of postgraduate study at Cambridge University before you are allowed to apply for a Gates Cambridge Scholarship.

The Fulbright Grant (U.S. Student Program)

Sponsored by the Department of State, Fulbright Grants (of which there are different varieties, including Pre-Doctoral Fellowships) emphasize cultural enrichment and a highly specific research program best suited to the host country and university. It is not uncommon, therefore, for students who apply for Rhodes and Marshall scholarships to apply simultaneously for a Fulbright Scholarship. The Fulbright does differ, however, in its demand that students be able to articulate *in great detail* a program of research they would undertake during the year abroad.

National Science Foundation Pre-Doctoral Fellowships

These fellowships fund graduating seniors and first-year-graduate students up to $110,000 (plus tuition and fee wavers for these years) to pursue their master's and Ph.D. degrees in the sciences. The NSF has a broad definition of the "sciences." Those include, among others, the physical sciences, computer science, mathematics, the social sciences, and political science. I have worked with students who have won NSF awards in such diverse fields as chemistry and archeology. They had been deeply immersed in research projects as undergraduates. That gave them something "real" to write about in the various "research" essays that make up part of the NSF application. Many universities are so delighted to enroll students with an NSF subsidy that they will arrange for supplementary fellowships or teaching assistantships to make up the difference in outstanding tuition, fees, or living expenses over a four-to-five year period.

Andrew W. Mellon Fellowships in Humanistic Studies

These fellowships encourage a new generation of students in the humanities to become college teachers and researchers. The fellowship pays nearly all expenses associated with the first year of a combined master's and Ph.D. program in such fields as history, English, art history, and comparative literature. The fellowship pays tuition, fees, and a one-year stipend of $17,500. But there's more: most major graduate schools are eager enough to have a Mellon Fellow enter their program that they arrange for a series of internal fellowships and teaching assistantships to help subsidize the student's remaining years of study for the Ph.D. degree.

Note: In an August 2005 memo, the Andrew W. Mellon Foundation announced a one-year suspension of competition for the one-year Fellowship in Humanistic Studies (effective in the 2005-2006 academic year, for fellowships that would have helped to fund the 2006-2007 academic year). The Mellon Foundation, in partnership with the Woodrow Wilson National Fellowship Foundation, is reassessing the rationale for one-year fellowships in the context of multi-year funding "packages" offered by many graduate programs in the humanities. A review is underway to reconfigure the best way of supporting graduate students and young scholars in the humanities. Stay tuned and check the Mellon website for updates in policy (www.mellon.org/programs/highered/research/research.htm).

Keep updated

Be sure to check the websites of these scholarships for more detailed information. But also know that sometimes specific aspects of a scholarship or fellowship program can change. Even if you have familiarized yourself with a scholarship of interest, you should still periodically check for updates in submission policy, application requirements, deadlines, and benefits. (This advice, by the way, applies to any undergraduate or graduate scholarships mentioned or described in this book.)

Chapter Twenty-nine

Entering Your Professional Life

Rather than move on to some sort of graduate study, many of you may seek employment directly after graduating. The ideal college education, as defined in this book, will leave you positioned not only for finding a job but also to do well once you're there.

Let's review some of the goals I've encouraged you to accomplish while you're in college, and see how those will enable you to prosper in the "real world."

High grades

Your pursuit of excellence as an undergraduate often figures in your later business and professional success. If you have worked diligently to earn high grades in college, employers will likely assume that you will work energetically "on the job." If you have shown a passionate interest in your major field of study, you'll likely show a passionate interest in your job. So while high grades may not bridge the gap between theoretical and practical knowledge, they do suggest how hard you're willing to work.

Communication skills

The ideal education will prepare you to master tasks and to communicate effectively with your colleagues and clients. You will not have to fear writing a memo or sending an e-mail to several, scores, or hundreds of people. The voice of authority you develop in your college essays will resonate throughout your correspondence. Moreover, the power of dialogue that you master through classroom participation and study groups will help define you as an effective public speaker in your profession.

I have conversed with a good number of executives in various fields of employment. Setting aside actual subject matter of their professions (which they usually feel requires on-site experience), they all lament the deterioration of communication skills among recent college graduates. Employers will be especially impressed by your history of publication and speaking engagements.

Branching out intellectually; learning to take responsibility for your own education

Employers will likely assume that if you made contributions to your field of study during your undergraduate years, you will make similar contributions in your new job. Evidence of undergraduate innovation, exploration, and creativity will be viewed as indicators of vocational success in related areas, or even in new pursuits demanding intellectual curiosity and a disciplined approach to learning.

Indeed, an undergraduate track record of taking responsibility for self-learning will indicate your readiness to keep up with cutting-edge thinking in your new profession and to adjust to changing circumstances, technology, and approaches to your profession.

Experience in the field

For related reasons, your experience "in the field"—whether in paid jobs or volunteer internships—will indicate that you understand the difference between theory and practice, and that you won't take as long or be as expensive to "train."

Initiative and networking

Your professional-associations credentials will likewise be attractive to prospective employers. Students who are members of professional organizations, and who have a track record of "networking" at conferences or meetings, will likely be compatible workers and represent an employer well in public.

Campus involvement and community service

The same goes for students who establish track records of campus involvement and community service. When you consider that many of a community's most successful business men and women are Rotarians, and when you recall that "service above self" is a motto of Rotary, you begin to understand the degree to which prospective employers might value a community-oriented individual.

Leadership skills

Much the same can be said of students who have taken documented leadership initiatives. Having "made things happen" while at college illustrates to prospective employers that you have the capacity to take initiative, inspire others, and see things through. Your various college projects also suggest that you have superb communication and time-management skills.

The pertinence of national scholarship essays for employment prospects

When, as an undergraduate, you apply for national scholarships, you generate comprehensive essays that are easily adaptable to the kind of cover letters you submit as part of your job search. The essays that you previously wrote and refined will illustrate your commitment to a specific endeavor and convey your passionate interest in that area of study (later, in many cases, that area of employment). The essays will also speak to the breadth of your learning and to your involvement in community service. And just as importantly—if you've applied for national scholarships—your professors will already have written comprehensive letters of endorsement that they can alter appropriately to help you gain employment.

In brief, all of your college initiatives and accomplishments speak worlds about your ability to set goals and to meet them. After all, you graduate at a "commencement" ceremony. In other words, as you leave college, you are ending one part of your life and beginning another. The ideal college experience will have provided you with the breadth of knowledge to be a well-rounded person. Yet you will also have a sufficiently comprehensive grasp of a specific branch of knowledge to commence either graduate school or your new vocation with fervor and accomplishment.

The professional schools

Note, also, that the ideal college education sets you up just fine for making applications to law or medical schools, which also require letters of recommendation. When you've gone the extra mile in college, professors notice; so do honors-program directors and internship supervisors. They will usually write praiseworthy letters that attest to your excellent character, intellect, attention to detail, as well as to the likelihood that you will one day make significant contributions to your field of study or chosen profession.

Your college résumé

Following through on your ideal college education will leave your résumé chock-full of accomplishments that will catch the eye of prospective employers. When there are far more job applicants than there are positions, who will be more impressive—someone who has simply met the requirements to graduate or somebody who has taken the extra steps in the various ways recommended above?

What still comes to my mind is a conversation, some thirty years ago, with the chairman of an academic department at Cornell University. He was talking about how he and his colleagues would hire one or two candidates in a highly crowded job market. He said that he always went to yearly academic conventions with his mind already made up about whom he planned to hire. He made this decision simply on the basis of the stellar records of achievement represented in résumés. Assuming that nothing turned out to be "wrong" with the candidate in person, he or she would be hired on the basis of past accomplishments; *those*, he insisted, were usually the most reliable indices of future success. My personal observation over the years leads me to second his sentiment and to maintain, therefore, that your willingness to undertake an ideal college experience can have a dramatic impact on your vocational options.

Don't downplay, then, the importance of the résumé over other aspects of obtaining employment, such as how well you perform in a job interview. Still, you won't get an interview unless someone is first impressed by your résumé. What follows is a résumé of a student who, in my opinion, had an ideal college education at the University of North Texas. She became a Harry S. Truman Scholar and later worked as a Rural Development Specialist Desk Officer in the National Partnership Office, Washington, D.C. She then won a full scholarship to attend Texas Tech Law School.

Conclusion

A résumé illustrates how the ideal college experience occurs both within and beyond the classroom. An ideal college education translates into a spectacular résumé.

Résumé

Sharon Young, LMSW [pseudonym]
5802 North Branch Blvd
Dallas, TX 76384

Education

University of Texas at Arlington
Master of Science in Social Work
Focus: Administration/Community Practice
Diploma, May 2000
GPA 3.9

University of North Texas, Denton, Texas
Bachelor of Social Work
Minor: Business Administration
Diploma, December 1998
GPA: 4.0 Class Rank: 1 of 1,277

Professional experience

National Partnership Office (NPO), Washington, DC, administration office for the National Rural Development Partnership (NRDP)—The NRDP enables rural institutions to work together more effectively by bringing together partners from local, state, tribal, and the federal government and the for-profit and non-profit private sectors. The NPO is housed in the U.S. Department of Agriculture, which provided most funds for the NRDP Rural Development Specialist Desk Officer—June 2001 to June 2002. Duties, responsibilities, and accomplishments:

- Provided technical assistance and guidance to 20 of the 40 State Development councils' (SRDC) Executive Directors and Council members, and helped design and implement a new compliance system to assure that SRDCs are meeting their cooperative agreement requirements.

- Reviewed and processed over 64 cooperative agreements, work plans, and budgets for SRDCs, and participated in the Office of Community Development's Empowerment Zone application review.

- Calculated what 40 SRDCs received per federal obligation, prepared documents for the National Finance Center, approved SRDC payment requests, and created NRDP FY01 budget reports.

Harry S. Truman Scholarship Fellow—June 2000 to June 2001. Duties, responsibilities, and accomplishments:

- Served as Executive Assistant and Secretary to the NRDP Executive Board, served as Strategy Manager to the National Knowledge Network Team, maintained a variety of databases for the NPO, and managed subscriptions to and maintenance of seven NRDP listservs.

- Coordinated orientation sessions for new SRCD Executive Directors, NRDP new members, and new Truman Fellows.

- Edited the NRDP 10th Anniversary Historical Book, the weekly reports for USDA Secretary, the Texas SRDC Resource Team Annual Report, and the NRDP USDA Transition Book.

- Performed same budget and accounting responsibilities as listed above.

Licensed Master of Social Work (LMSW). Authorized and licensed in Texas as a LMSW by the Texas State Board of Social Work Examiners, May 2000. Previously authorized and licensed in Texas as a licensed Social Worker (LSW), October 1999.

Lockheed Martin Corporation. Graduate Social Work Intern (LSW)—August 1999 to May 2000. Assisted the Administrator of the Employees' Con-Trib Club, a 501(c) (3) non-profit, Fort Worth, TX. Duties, responsibilities, and accomplishments:

- Reviewed grant-seeking proposals from non-profit agencies, investigated these agencies, wrote reports on the agencies for the Board of Directors' consideration, and assisted in allocating funds to the agencies.

- Interviewed employees seeking financial assistance, made weekly presentations to the Emergency Aid Committee as the consumers' advocate, and maintained the Emergency Aid database.

- Helped organize the 2000 U.S. Savings Bond Drive, the Employee Community Volunteer Projects, and the Con-Trib Club Campaign.

Judith Granger Birmingham Center for Child Welfare, Graduate Research Assistant—July 1999 to May 2000. Researched child welfare issues and helped create the certification exam for the Texas Child Welfare Academy, Arlington, TX

Texas Department of Protective and Regulatory Services, Children Protective Services Specialist Investigator—February 1999 to June 1999. Investigated cases of child neglect and abuse in Unit 96: Hurst, TX

Texas Department of Protective and Regulatory Services, Children Protective Services Social Work Intern—July 1998 to December 1998. Assisted investigations, organized the Foster Families' Christmas Party: Denton, TX

Families United Program, Social Work Intern Team Leader—June 1998 to September 1998. Researched the effects of divorce on children, conducted social histories, and supervised parent visitations: Dallas County, TX

State Representative Lon Burnam's District Office, Social Work Researcher—April 1998 to August 1998. Compiled a demographic report about the well-being of District 90's children: Ft. Worth, TX

Denton Regional Medical Center, Social Work Intern—January 1998 to May 1998. Assisted a LMSW with caseload. Worked with consumers of all ages, ethnic groups, religions, and social classes: Denton, TX

Community Involvement

National Rural Development Council, Member—June 2000 to Present: Washington, DC

Women in Rural America Task Force, Member—June 2000 to Present: Washington, DC

Welfare to Work Task Force, Member—June 2000 to Present: Washington, DC

Higher Achievement Program, Mentor and Tutor—October 2000 to May 2001: Washington, DC

Arlington, Texas Community Fair 2000, Organizer, Culture Diversity Team Leader—January 2000 to April 2000

Women's Health Clinic Volunteer—October 1997 to April 1998: Denton, TX

Voter Registration Volunteer—October 1997 to April 1998: Denton, TX

Metroplex Hospital's Social Service Department Volunteer—May 1997 To August 1997: Killeen, TX

Texas Special Olympics for Area 11 Equestrian Competitions—April 1997: Justin, TX

Riding Unlimited, Therapeutic Horsemanship Program, Volunteer—February 1997 to May 1997: Justin, TX

Awards

National

- Harry S. Truman Scholar 1999
- Phi Kappa Phi Award of Excellence 1999
- George Mitchell Scholarship Finalist 1999

Campus

- University of North Texas School of Social Work Alumni of the Year Award 2002
- University of Texas, Arlington, Peter Gaupp Scholarship for Administration MSSW Students 2000
- Fannie Belle Gaupp Outstanding University of North Texas Student in Social Work Award 1999
- President's Scholarship for University of North Texas 1996 to 1998
- French Studies Scholarship 1996

Affiliations

Phi Kappa Phi Honor Society—January 1999 to Present
Alpha Chi National Honor Scholarship Society—April 1998 to Present
National Association of Social Workers—May 1997 to Present
Phi Eta Sigma National Honor Society—April 1997 to Present
Alpha Lambda Delta Honor Society—April 1997 to Present
Golden Key National Honor Society—April 1997 to Present
Student Association's Freshman Interns, President—Sep 1996 to May 1997

Special skills

- Program Evaluation, Community Assessment, Policy Analysis Experience
- Grant Proposal Writing and Fundraising Experience
- Direct Practice Social Work (communication and facilitation skills, dealing with interpersonal relationships)

Section 7 :: The Scholarship Application Process

Chapter Thirty

How to Find Scholarships

We've talked extensively about structuring your ideal college education around the goals and credentials associated with one or more national, merit-based scholarships. Let's assume that you'll follow the guidelines in this book and, by the beginning of your senior year of college, be qualified to apply for a scholarship, graduate-school fellowship, or professional-school grant. Or, perhaps you've found, earlier than that, that you're ready to apply for undergraduate-level national scholarships. This section will help you get started with the scholarship application process and offer tips for writing personal essays and preparing for the interview process.

Starting the search

Of course, first you have to identify which scholarships are of interest to you and whether the prerequisites for those are compatible with your own accomplishments. I would recommend that you keep a notebook to store information about different scholarships; since there are so many scholarships (and they each have specific details, descriptions, sources, amounts, deadlines, requirements, etc.), keeping track of your scholarship research can quickly become overwhelming if you are not well organized.

Here are some ideas to get you started in locating scholarships you'd like to focus on:

- **Campus scholarships**
  First and foremost, explore all of the on-campus scholarships, financial-aid opportunities, and academic awards, grants, or prizes that are available through the university you plan to attend. (Note: From now on, I'll generally refer to any award having some sort of monetary or publicity value as a scholarship.) Your best chance of winning a scholarship is usually through these on-campus possibilities. These scholarships can

range from financial-need awards for incoming freshmen, to merit-based scholarships for students with outstanding talent, to "best sophomore in Chemistry" or "best student in English."

To locate campus-based scholarships, first visit the Financial Aid Office. Then try the Dean of Students' Office to learn about campus-wide or university-related scholarship competitions. Search out department-level scholarships by consulting the chairman of the scholarship committee within your academic department.

- **Community scholarships**
  Keep your eyes open for local community scholarships (by "local" I mean your and your parents' home town). You may come across newspaper write-ups concerning winners of local scholarships, or you may find that certain banks, credit unions, businesses, or religious federations sponsor scholarships (checking websites and making direct phone calls can help here). Even if the scholarships are small and not particularly high-profile, apply for them. After you've gone through the application process several times, you won't be intimidated when it's time to apply for larger, more prestigious scholarships.

  Smaller scholarships also become great credentials to help you earn larger scholarships. Any scholarship suggests that some organization or group was willing to invest in you because they had faith in your past achievements and future potential. Smaller scholarships therefore serve as credentials to help you earn larger awards. Scholarship committees like to fund students whom they consider "sure bets." Your being considered a "sure bet" by one committee greatly increases the odds that another committee will see you the same way.

- **External scholarships**
  Be attentive, as well, to the thousands of external scholarships. The "Resources" chapter at the end of this book includes many websites, books, and other publications you can consult to find scholarships that are of interest to you and in line with your qualifications.

Searching on the Internet

Let me mention here a few Internet search opportunities that I regularly recommend to my students.

- **Cornell University Graduate School Fellowship Database**

  To my mind, the best "major scholarship" search engine is the Cornell University Graduate School Fellowships Database (www.cuinfo.cornell.edu/Student/GRFN). You can search there for hundreds of mostly senior-level and graduate-level scholarships. You may do so by field of study (simply type your major into the "search" box) or through broader categories (such as "social science," "biological sciences"). You may also search for scholarships for women, for minorities, or for students who wish to study abroad. The search engine will immediately generate a list of pertinent scholarships and allow you to click on each name for further information, including a description of the scholarship, the amount of the award, eligibility rules, and where to obtain application forms. The great thing about the Fellowship Database is that, even if you find a scholarship that's available only to graduate students, you at least learn that those funds are out there, and you can apply at some more appropriate time down the road.

- **Minority or specialty scholarships**

  A splendid resource exists in The United Negro College Fund website search engine (www.uncf.org/scholarships/index.asp). Minority students enter specific information about themselves and then receive a list of likely scholarships.

  Also, visit the web pages of Reference Service Press (www.rspfunding.com/prod_bookscol1.html) for a stunning collection of scholarship directories (both print and electronic). Your library may own several of these publications, probably housed in the reference section. Or, you may be able to access a Reference Service Press eBook through netLibrary, an eBook subscription service for libraries.

- **Other search engines**

  For a far more comprehensive web search, containing many lesser-known scholarships, log onto www.fastweb.com or www.brokescholar.com. These sites will put you in touch with over 650,000 scholarships. It's not as easy as it sounds, but at least you know that you're in touch with highly comprehensive scholarship search engines.

Keep a sharp lookout

Hang in there with the search—even if nothing of interest pops up in a search engine or appears on a bulletin board in a Financial Aid office. You're more likely to notice a pertinent scholarship if you're constantly on the lookout; the earlier you start the better.

But note that some scholarship-locating companies are under investigation, and people should be very skeptical about paying for this kind of information.

Conclusion

- Research all campus-based scholarships and awards.

- Be aware of prestigious national scholarships.

- Consult search engines for thousands of other scholarship possibilities.

Chapter Thirty-one

Locating Advisors to Help You in the Application Process

You should find a guide to help you through the scholarship application process. There are often people on campus whose job it is to offer assistance; some of those persons may even be prepared to shepherd you through the intricacies of specific scholarship applications.

Identify campus advisors for scholarships

First scout out who your advisor (or advisors) might be. There may be several people on campus who can offer guidance, or you might be able to find someone who specializes in scholarship advice. You should identify your potential advisors as soon as possible and make an appointment to introduce yourself, even if you're not sure for which scholarships you'll ultimately apply. A good advisor can help you identify suitable scholarships.

Centralized offices for national scholarships

Many campuses now have centralized offices for national scholarships. Those offices have such titles as:

- The Office for Nationally Competitive Scholarships
- The Office of Postgraduate Fellowships
- The Office for Prestigious or National Scholarships and Fellowships

The director of this office—if such an office exists on your campus—is your "best bet" advisor. To learn if your campus has this kind of office, contact the university's Dean of Students' office. Also consult the website of the National Association of Fellowships Advisors (www.nafadvisors.

org/scholarships.htm) to see if your campus is represented in that organization, and to obtain additional information about nationally competitive scholarships.

Finding a faculty representative for specific scholarships

The following national scholarships have "faculty representatives" on most larger campuses: Rhodes, Marshall, Truman, Fulbright, Madison, Udall, Mitchell, Mellon, Goldwater, and Jack Kent Cooke. The faculty representative is the registered faculty person to whom the different scholarship foundations relay vital information, including application forms, deadlines, and special instructions. The faculty representative also organizes nominating committees for that scholarship (if such a committee is necessary) and arranges interviews for applicants. He or she recruits year-round for students who have a chance of winning any of these scholarships.

If a centralized office for national scholarships exists on your campus, the director of that office may be the faculty representative for most of the more prestigious scholarships (but not necessarily all of them).

If you don't have a centralized office for national-level scholarships, and if you can't locate a specific faculty representative on your campus, use the scholarship's website to see if it names your university's faculty representative. To find the scholarship's website, try entering the name of the scholarship foundation in an Internet search engine (such as www.google.com) and look for the scholarship in the search results. Once you connect to the scholarship's website, you'll usually find a list of faculty representatives, including one for your campus.

Again, touch base with that faculty representative as soon as possible—even three years in advance of the time you'll apply for a national scholarship. You want to know from the outset exactly what you have to do to gain a nomination on your campus. Don't wait until your junior or senior year to inquire.

What if your campus doesn't have a faculty representative or an official national scholarship advisor?

Approach the Dean of Students' office with comprehensive website information about the scholarship. Ask the Dean of Students to appoint a faculty member to serve as a campus representative so that you and others may apply for the scholarship, assuming that scholarship mandates an official university nomination.

Note that some applications require university nomination and endorsement. Indeed, several national scholarship foundations (Rhodes, Marshall, Mitchell, Goldwater, Udall, Jack Kent Cooke) prohibit you from applying directly to the foundation. Rather, you must first submit your application to a campus nominating committee and earn the nomination of those faculty members. They, in turn, either submit your completed application to the scholarship foundation or authorize *you* to do so. Moreover, a number of scholarships—Rhodes, Marshall, and Truman, for example—also ask the nominating committee to compose an "institutional endorsement" to accompany your application packet. The endorsement is often a letter of recommendation drafted by the nominating committee and sometimes signed or cosigned by the President of your institution. The institutional endorsement takes account of your letters of recommendation, your transcripts, the information gathered in interviews with you, and any special circumstances regarding your academic career or personal situation. This institutional endorsement is the "big picture" recommendation. Most foundation-based judges read this endorsement *first*—to place in perspective the many details of your application, personality, academic accomplishments, and civic engagement.

For applications requiring institutional endorsement, you should begin to compose your essays up to ten months before those are due. Why? Because you need to perfect your essays for a nominating committee that may have an internal submission deadline several months ahead of the time when they need to nominate you. That early application deadline gives the committee adequate time to read through numerous applications, to interview and nominate likely winners, to make suggestions for further revision of your essays, and to draft a comprehensive endorsement sponsored either by the university nominating committee, the university President, or both.

Other possible on-campus advisors

If your campus doesn't have a centralized office to assist students with scholarship applications (especially external scholarships), you should still be able to seek guidance from other campus personnel to prepare for competitions. Especially critical are your essays, which must be clear, concise, and grammatically correct. Students are frequently too closely involved to see the shortcomings in their own essays. Nor do students usually understand the sort of essay that "works." Do not try to apply without some guidance.

Directors of honors programs

One potential resource for national scholarship competition is an honors-program director. On a number of campuses they oversee national scholarship competitions and possess a vested interest in having their honors students apply and, when possible, win. Honors directors typically write the very best letters of recommendation because they are well versed in the "culture" of these competitions.

Professors who have sponsored past winners

Seek out professors who have sponsored past winners. These faculty members take great pride in the success stories of their students and are always on the outlook for new candidates.

Professors in your field of study

When your application deals with a specific field of study, you should ask a professor in that field to read your essays and comment upon the logic of your responses. After the professor in your field does so, approach an English professor and ask that person to comment on the style, tone, and structure of your essays. Do not reverse the order here. It makes no sense for an English professor to offer stylistic feedback when a specialist in your field may tell you that the basic formulation is faulty.

Past winners of scholarships

See if you can locate past winners of scholarships on your campus. They have the "inside track" and can offer good advice.

Don't forget the thank-you note

Whether you win or lose in a scholarship competition, always write a pleasant thank-you note to the faculty or staff members who offered feedback throughout the application process. Aside from appreciating that courtesy, those persons will likely include your heartfelt letters in their annual faculty-review packets, demonstrating the commitment of time they invest in students like you. (Remember, too, that you might need their help again for later scholarship competitions or job interviews.)

Conclusion

- Identify campus advisors for scholarships.
- If no one on your campus has that specific responsibility, consult the Dean of Students' office, Honors Directors, or individual faculty members.
- Don't be a Lone Ranger when preparing for national scholarship competitions. Seek guidance.
- Arrange for feedback on your application essays well in advance of deadlines.

Chapter Thirty-two

Breaking Up the Application Process into Eight Steps

Applying for a large or prestigious scholarship can be a daunting process; like all big projects, however, it gets done one step at a time. At all stages, be prepared, have a plan, and seek guidance. Here's a brief overview of eight essential steps in the scholarship application procedure:

Step 1: Get a copy of the application form—*now*.

Step 2: Read the application and make a to-do list.

Step 3: Start a notebook to record your ideas and to hold all related materials.

Step 4: Make contact with a faculty member or campus advisor.

Step 5: Complete the application form.

Step 6: Obtain or make arrangements for additional items that accompany the application.

Step 7: Assemble and deliver the application packet.

Step 8: Prepare for the interview process (if one is required).

The process isn't so difficult when broken into eight steps; so let's look at each step in detail.

Step 1: Get a copy of the application form—now

After you choose a national scholarship for which you want to apply—even if you intend to apply two or three years down the road—get a copy of the application form *now*. You are usually able to do that online by visiting the website of the scholarship foundation; or you can send an e-mail to the scholarship foundation to request an application form.

Step 2: Read the application and make a to-do list

Don't worry about practicing on an outdated application form until a new one becomes available. The idea is to study it and anticipate what you will need to say and do by the time you apply for the scholarship on a "current" form. You may find that the application requires essays about issues that you have not yet addressed in your studies or extra-curricular concerns. Or you may be surprised to find that the scholarship application asks for information about your community involvement or well-roundedness. No time like two years before the application deadline to learn this—and then *to do something* about any gaps of knowledge or experience.

Step 3: Start a notebook to record your ideas and to hold materials

Whether you're filling out an application—for real or for practice—start a notebook in which you create a checklist of things you must do, and by when you should complete those tasks. Continually add material and ideas for rounding out that application. For instance, keep track of the contact information for anyone you hope will write a letter of recommendation (and stay in touch with that person through occasional office visits). In this notebook, keep all materials that might be helpful to you—such as exams, essays, and publications. Also include an updated list of your achievements that might be of interest to recommenders or scholarship nominating committees.

Keep separate notebooks for each application process. Also remember to make backup copies of essays for future applications (and other purposes).

Step 4: Make contact with a faculty member or campus advisor

Bring your notebook and all relevant materials to your campus director of national scholarships (or to the faculty member charged with oversight of that particular scholarship, or to whomever else you've chosen as your official guide). Ask, "Am I on the right track?" The two of you should work out a specific game plan as to what ought to happen and *when*. I once had a college sophomore visit my office and declare that she planned to become a Rhodes Scholar. "I just need to know what to do over the next two years," she said. We charted a game plan; she followed her plan; she became a Rhodes Scholar. Another student told me that she would definitely win a Truman Scholarship if she set her mind to doing so and if she knew what to do, step-by-step. She became a Truman Scholar. Each student stuck to a rigorous game plan and schedule.

Also, ask the faculty representative for permission to view as many past winning applications as may be on file. You'll get to observe the form, style, and tone of a winning application. For that reason, the Truman Scholarship Foundation publishes successful applications to serve as models; other scholarship foundations, alas, do not. In those cases, two resources can provide immediate access to model application essays: Joe Schall's *Writing Personal Statements and Scholarship Application Essays: A Student Handbook* (Eden Prairie, MN: Outernet Publishing, 2006) and the new website "Live to Learn: An Online Resource by Students for Students" (www.livetolearn.com).

Step 5: Complete the application form

At such time as you're filling out the application form for actual submission, make sure to get constant feedback about your ideas and writing from the national scholarship advisor, or from the faculty representative for that particular scholarship. In cases where your application will have to be endorsed by a campus nominating committee, the faculty representative will be able to anticipate his/her colleagues' possible objections to your writing style and emphases. If you maintain regular contact with the faculty representative for a particular scholarship, you will end up submitting an application that has a better chance of gaining university endorsement.

Writing the various essays

Nearly every scholarship application calls for multiple essays—some very short; others ranging from one-to-three pages, single-spaced. Tackle those essays one at a time; don't ever try to complete the application all at once.

In cases where the application form instructs you to compose a separate personal essay (of 1000 words, for example), generate that essay on your computer and then print a copy having the title "Personal Statement—Your First and Last Name." You can then show copies of this personal statement to your faculty scholarship advisor to receive suggestions. Double-space the essay when circulating it for feedback.

Word limits mean ... word limits

Never exceed the specified word limit, and never resort to shrinking down your font to squeeze in more words. Scholarship judges know that you're evading the instructions by doing either. They give you a specified word limit because they feel you ought to be able to respond to the question within that amount of space. If you can't, then you're virtually disqualifying yourself. All the more reason to start your writing months before the submission deadline. Part of the main challenge of completing a scholarship application form is to edit down your life's story into a thousand or fewer words. This is no small assignment. Start early—very early.

Be honest

When filling out an application, you should be completely honest. Do not exaggerate and do not misrepresent any award or achievement. Any sort of scam can come to haunt you during an interview and damage both your reputation and that of your university. Keep in mind the fact that most interview questions originate from claims you've made in your personal statement.

Round out information

Make sure to round out information that others may not be in a position to understand. If, for example, you won a named award (let's call it the John Doe Award) for "best essay in English," don't simply list "The John Doe Award"; rather, list "The John Doe Award, 2004 (for the best essay in English)." Most scholarship judges have absolutely no idea about why various students have received particular "named" awards. Clarify those achievements.

How important is neatness?

Rule No. 1: Neatness is a must.
Rule No. 2: See Rule No. 1.

Also, absolutely none of these:

- Grammatical errors
- Spelling errors
- Scratched-out items
- Answers left blank

- Obvious failures to follow directions (such as ignoring prompts)
- Answers extending out into the margins of the application form
- Using a damaged or stained application form

Any one of these failures will probably discredit your application. Most scholarship competitions have vastly more applicants than scholarships. That causes judges to look eagerly for reasons to eliminate contestants. Don't make that job easy for them through silly or careless errors.

Areas of space in the application form

Application forms contain two types of space for you to enter information. First, you usually encounter short-answer spaces that have lines on which you type standard information (name, address, and so on). The other kind of space is more open (ranging in height from two inches to a full page) and dedicated to either short or long essays.

To type is better than to print

Most scholarship applications ask that you print or type your answers. You want to type, rather than hand-print, onto designated lines because the application will look far more professional that way. People reveal a great deal about themselves in their printing—or so we think. You do not want judges coming to prejudicial assessments of you because of your printing, whether it is upright or slanted. Typing looks neutral.

Therefore always type when filling in "lined" questions (that is, on specified lines printed on the application form). By "type," I mean use an actual typewriter, not a computer and printer combination. Locate an erasing typewriter (ask around campus for an IBM Selectric typewriter—I keep several in my office just for this purpose) and learn how to use that kind of typewriter for typing on narrow lines.

Essay blocks

When responding to essay questions, first type your essay onto a computer (using Microsoft® Word, Corel™ WordPerfect®, etc.) and then use a printer to have the essay fall exactly where it's supposed to on the application form. You'll need to make multiple photocopies of the relevant application page in anticipation of having to print the essay many times. As you print the essay, keep adjusting the margins and placement of the essay on the computer so that your paragraphs eventually fall exactly where they must when you run the application page through the printer. Don't be surprised if it takes five to ten tries before you succeed.

Be sure that your essay is able to fit into designated spaces on the application form. If the essay is too long, edit down. Only after it fits onto the actual application form should you print out a further copy of that essay in double-spaced format—and on standard white paper—to present to your scholarship mentor for stylistic feedback. It makes little sense for a faculty member to offer comments if your essay will not fit into the allotted space on the application form. (You would end up having to delete prose that the faculty member has edited for clarity.) This advice holds true even if you are completing an online scholarship application. Cutting and pasting text you have generated in another software program directly into the essay sections of online applications is easier than trying to type your essays into the form itself.

How to make sure your essay "fits"

As just described, compose your essays on the computer and adjust the margins so they line up with the margins on the application page. Print up each essay and then see if it will fit into the space allocated for it on the application page. To test whether it fits just right, press a printed copy against the segment of the application form that has the blank space. Hold both the form and the white paper against a light to see if the essay fits. If it doesn't (especially if it is too long), just revise your essay "down" until it matches.

Avoid, if possible, having the essay crowd either the upper or lower lines in the block. Generally fill up at least ¾ of all blocks, and then center the essay (to camouflage any leftover space).

Avoid shrinking the font to make an answer "fit." I have heard national scholarship judges say that they grow resentful of students who do this. It makes for a tough "read" and strikes the judges as slightly dishonest. Most scholarship applications specify the minimal font size. In cases where they don't, simply use a font that is comfortable to read, normally twelve point pica. Don't make readers squint.

The ping-pong feedback process with your advisor

Now you will start the process of getting feedback from your advisor, who will look over your essays and let you know if you are making sense, or if you need to remedy stylistic flaws or gaps in your essays. The length and intensity of this process will vary from advisor to advisor. You'll likely have to revise a good number of times (I've seen even excellent writers revise a thousand-word essay ten or more times).

This ping-pong process of feedback and revision can be a very long game. You should therefore begin to compose your major and minor essays months in advance of scholarship deadlines. Several of the students whom I've coached have spent up to six or more months preparing their applications. You cannot afford to have any flaws in your essays—in style, tone, or content—so you should anticipate devoting considerable time to your essays.

Some words of advice

Try to stay focused on one essay at a time when getting feedback from your advisor. I have found that students are usually eager to perfect a single paragraph, but that they feel overwhelmed by a dozen pages of criticism aimed at different parts of the scholarship application. Similarly, the professor feels more at ease in this process if he or she is playing "ping-pong," as it were, with one essay at a time.

While you are always at liberty to ignore the advice of a professor (after all, it is and remains *your* application), you should be mature enough to understand the nature of the professor's criticism and to compose a revision that eliminates the need for that criticism.

You will become a much better writer in the process of completing a major scholarship application. In fact, one of the key benefits of applying for national scholarships is the way students are finally forced to be responsible for each and every word they write, not to mention the enhanced tone, organization, and punctuation they must master. The process of completing a national scholarship application resembles that which you'd undergo in a well-taught class devoted to advanced expository writing.

Once an essay has the "thumbs up" from your advisor, don't mess with it—no matter what the temptation. Students who do so inevitably introduce new typos or grammatical errors. Most of the typos that I've seen on applications have resulted from "late insertions"—and after the student assured me that the application was "perfect."

Printing the final drafts onto the application page

After you've finished revising (to your and your mentor's satisfaction) you will have to use trial and error to print your essay or essays onto the actual application pages. Place your original application in a safe place—where it won't be susceptible to a coffee-ring stains or mustard smears (I've seen both!). Until you're ready to laser-print right onto the original application, use photocopies of each page to see if your essays fall directly into the assigned blocks after you run trial copies of the application pages through the various screens of your computer program containing the answers to different pages. (This is where multiple copies of the original application form prove handy. If you need to print only one essay to a page of the application form, keep positioning your essay on your computer screen so that, when it prints onto the application page, the essay falls exactly where it must. If you need to get more than one essay on the page, place those essays onto one page of the computer screen and keep adjusting their position until they fall exactly where they're supposed to when you run a copy of the application page through your printer.

Printing onto the actual application

Before you print on the official copy of the application, make sure that the correct side is facing either up or down in your printer. (If you're printing onto pages that you can easily download from a website, then you don't have to worry about this sort of mistake.)

Computerized templates

Some scholarships now have computerized templates that allow you to type directly onto the lines, and then to print out the completed application. The problem with using some computerized templates is that you may not be able to "save" your work. Thus, if you later notice a typo, you may have to retype the entire page.

You will one day be able to generate all essays on computer templates that allow you "save as you go." Until that time, use the preceding methods. Doing so will allow you to avoid introducing typos once your scholarship coach has given your essay the "thumbs up." You never want to have to retype something that's already accurate (you *will* inevitably add typos).

Submitting applications online

Certain scholarship foundations (including Mitchell, Fulbright, Truman, Marshall, and NSF) require that the application be entered into templates and then submitted online. Several programs demand, as well, that letters of recommendation and institutional endorsements be submitted online. In such cases, perfect your application as you would normally do, but allow at least three days to complete the online submission process. Also, rather than giving your recommenders two weeks' notice, provide them with at least two-and-a-half weeks' notice. This will allow both you and them to deal with any "uploading" complications (there have been countless cases of those) without missing your deadlines. Some scholarship foundations actually turn off their computers at midnight of the stipulated submission date. If you have last-minute technical problems, you're wiped out.

The longer essays

Many applications require longer essays—for example the "personal statement" and a description of your creative or research project. You may usually print these essays onto a large space on one or more pages of the application, or you may sometimes just print the essays on white paper that you include in the application packet. (Or, as suggested above, you may be able to copy and paste the text of longer essays created in text-editing programs directly into sections of the online application.)

The personal statement

Nearly every scholarship application requires a personal statement. Assuming that your grades and letters of recommendation are up to snuff, the personal statement sometimes makes or breaks an application. The personal statement is vital because, all things considered, nearly all applicants for scholarships have fine grades and highly supportive letters of recommendation. Scholarship agencies accordingly place immense importance on the personal statements, believing them to reflect the essential quality of the applicant. Stated otherwise, the personal statement allows them to see what makes you tick and if you really are "the right stuff."

Writing the personal statement is not as easy as it sounds

Lots of things make us tick, but what is the scholarship foundation "looking for"? Many students virtually disqualify themselves by writing about matters that end up having little importance for scholarship judges. Personal essays can also sound so egotistical as to disqualify a candidate right off the bat. Writing about ourselves is difficult, and few students do it well the first time around.

The personal statement: Linking who you are to your field of study

So what's the key? I would suggest that, in most scholarship applications requiring a personal statement, you structure observations about yourself that progressively lead up to—and reinforce—the commitment you feel to a certain field of study or degree program. After all, scholarships reward people who look like they will make a difference in their fields of study or chosen professions; so personal statements that reveal "who you are" *relative to a field of study or vocational goal* stand to have the best chance of impressing the judges. Stated otherwise, your personal statement allows

255

judges to *invest* in somebody whose experiences and perceptions—from childhood through adolescence and young adulthood—reflect an extraordinary personality heading towards a distinguished future *in a specified profession or field of study*. (The same applies to non-conventional, older students, who enroll in college after having experienced some other career. Briefly account for your life's story and then concentrate on your new academic endeavor and future plans in your new field of study.)

A few of your favorite things, as those relate to your field of study

Personal statements should thus demonstrate that you live and breathe the subject matter of your discipline—indeed, that you're off in your own universe of discovery and ideas, and that you simply love to talk about past experiences that have led you to your current academic or vocational commitment, as well as about the things in your field of study that you most enjoy contemplating. Have you ever heard the song "My Favorite Things" from *The Sound of Music*? Intellectual and professional interests are the favorite things that most personal statements should contain. In Truman Scholarship circles, one often hears judges speak approvingly about an applicant's "passion." When you discuss the momentum of your life, try to sound reasonably passionate about your intellectual commitment to your area of study. At the same time, include paragraphs that explore some of your other interests—including even sports, and reading, or musical and artistic talent—to show the breadth of your personality.

Include public service, connecting it to your field of study, if possible

Spend at least one paragraph demonstrating ways in which you have valued the notion of service above self. If you don't have this credential, get out there and acquire it. You'll find that public service is its own reward, besides ultimately enhancing your personal statement. If you can have your public service be consistent with your area of study, so much the better (for example, a math major might tutor needy students in math at a nearby middle school).

Don't aim for the scholarship—aim for your field of study

When you write the personal statement, never "play for the scholarship"— that is, don't start to mention the scholarship and why you want it and need it (that is, unless the prompt specifically asks you to mention your financial need). More often than not, national scholarship judges want to be swept off their feet by the prose of somebody whose essay is vibrant, original, and engaging. Rather than write something which suggests that you have a right to the scholarship, based on financial need, cause readers to think, "This person is so interesting, and so likely to make contributions to her field of study, that we can't afford *not* to award a scholarship to such a talented, creative, and devoted person."

Develop dual themes—you and your field of study

Thus, when writing the personal statement, go out on a limb: the limb that you balance on will be the personal experiences that make up the essential you. But always hang on to the limb above you; that limb will be your devoted commitment to your field of study and to a set number of academic/vocational interests. My years of coaching successful scholarship applicants suggest that this is the winning combination of emphases in a personal statement.

The research essay: Describe your research project in terms that anyone can understand

Several national scholarship applications demand, beyond a personal statement, that you describe a research project you've undertaken in college. Whatever your discipline, you must learn to write these descriptions in language that a non-specialist can understand. Even if a scholarship form says to assume that a specialist will be reading your essay, you should aim for a degree of clarity most people can understand, or can at least pretend they understand. Thus, when you find it necessary to offer very advanced and complicated utterances, you might have a follow-up sentence reading, "In other words, ..." The non-specialist will respect the fact that you've gone out of your way to clarify. Nobody likes to feel ignorant; it doesn't enhance your prospects for winning a scholarship by making the judges feel vaguely puzzled or uninformed.

Emphasize your original contribution when writing a research essay

Always try to end the first paragraph of your research essay with an emphatic statement regarding your contribution to the research team, or (if you conducted independent research) with a summary of the main outcome of your research. Why? Because scholarship agencies are making an *investment* in you. These agencies and foundations are therefore most likely to invest in a student who is poised to contribute to an area of study in which he has already shown himself able to undertake a significant research project. That project, in turn, usually goes well beyond the letter grade of A to suggest that the student is now on the threshold of practicing the real work of the discipline or profession.

Show that you're on the cutting edge in research

In an essay devoted to your research project, have the first paragraph allude to some leading studies in your area of interest, and briefly suggest—by way of introducing your unique contribution—how your work goes beyond existing outlooks, or how it stands to change the way we think about a particular issue in your field of study. That will enhance your "investment value." Why else would a scholarship foundation ask you to describe past research unless they want to gauge the likelihood that you will one day take your field of study beyond current states of knowledge?

Learn to use the active voice in your writing (to emphasize your initiative)

When writing descriptions of your research and its outcome, always use the active voice, not the passive voice. By this, I mean that you should say, "I then gathered ten samples of such and such" rather than, "Ten samples of such and such were then gathered." The first example actively demonstrates your initiative, while the passive "Ten samples were gathered" suggests that you didn't have a direct hand in this part of the research. The latter problem is especially pervasive in scientific writing, since many scholarly journals in the sciences favor the passive voice—to draw attention to the research rather than to the scientist conducting the research. Still, in undergraduate (and even graduate-level) research reports, you seriously compromise the reader's sense of your independence, initiative, and resourcefulness by using the passive voice. Save the passive voice for post-doctoral journal articles.

Mention your mentor, but then move on to your own contribution

In your research essays, do, of course, mention your research mentor early on—"I did such and such under the direction of Professor Wonderful, in the spring of 2005"—but try to leave Professor Wonderful increasingly in the background as you go on to stress your personal initiative in his lab or the unique conclusions that *you* drew from the data under consideration. I've seen too many students become mesmerized by affection for their research mentors. Those students feel disrespectful when not citing the influence of those mentors throughout the essay. After mentioning Professor Wonderful early in your response, leave him behind in order to demonstrate that you are your own person, and one whose future is promising enough to merit a scholarship. Professor Wonderful will understand why you leave him behind, for eventually you must do so in real life. Just send an occasional e-mail to say "Hi!" and to see how he's doing.

Save the techno-jargon for the middle paragraphs

If you have to use highly technical descriptions of what you did, save the advanced rhetoric for the middle paragraphs of research essays. As long as most readers have a clear understanding of your project in the opening and concluding paragraphs, they will feel comfortable and informed enough to grant credibility to the project, especially if some of their colleagues on the assessment committee are specialists in that area and can validate the substance of the more highly technical *inner* paragraphs.

Sound excited about your conclusions

Always try to end your research essay by playing up the *significance* of your findings or conclusions. If *you* don't sound enthusiastic about those, then why should the evaluators of your application be excited?

Step 6: Obtain or make arrangements for additional items that accompany the application

Applications for national scholarships almost always require two or three (and sometimes up to eight) *comprehensive letters of recommendation* from professors or other individuals who have worked with you. They also frequently require an "institutional" endorsement (see above).

What is a comprehensive letter of recommendation?

A comprehensive letter of recommendation is one that is longer and covers significant territory about you and your project or studies. It is typically one-and-a-half to two pages in length, single-spaced, with double spacing between the paragraphs. To obtain letters of this sort, approach only professors who know you well enough to be able to fill up all that space with glowing words about your talents and accomplishments.

Short letters are fatal

Even a short letter that says something quite nice is usually the kiss of death. That is so because letters of recommendation are often weighted within a composite score. If your recommender scores "low," so do you. Short letters also convey the impression that you really didn't make all that much of an impression on the author of the letter. Thus when you approach a professor for a letter of recommendation, bring your past essays and exams, and ask, "Do you have time to write a comprehensive letter of endorsement for me? If you don't, I understand." You've got to make it clear that you need a *substantial* letter.

Of course, it's difficult to approach professors with this request—with the exception of those professors for whom you've done research in the past, or for whom you've gone the extra miles in various projects. Yet the payoff for having worked diligently with research mentors resides—beyond what you've learned—in their comprehensive letters of recommendation. Once they compose one for your scholarship application, they'll always have the letter on file for other purposes—graduate school recommendations, for instance. (Make sure you've followed the prior advice on developing mentoring relationships with professors in your field of study.)

Recommendations may also come from off-campus persons (employers, clerics, civic leaders, etc.), but I have typically found their letters to be short and less than compelling—even when they praise the student. I have also observed that some off-campus recommenders will have an employee draft the letter for their signature (Congressmen are notorious for this). Those letters are often weak—despite very large and ornate signatures. In my opinion, you're better off seeking letters from your professors (most of whom write well), with only an occasional "external" letter. You might use an external letter, for instance, in Truman Scholarship competition, where one of your letters must come from somebody who oversaw your "leadership" initiative. The point is this: request external letters only for good reason and make it very clear to the author that you would appreciate a comprehensive letter of endorsement, if they feel they are in a position to compose one.

Since you can't know what a recommender is going to say about you, you might wonder, "How do I know if I can safely approach her for a comprehensive letter of recommendation?" If you must ask that question, then you've just provided the answer: this is *not* the person to ask. If you've put out the extra effort for a professor, and if you've conducted a significant research project under that professor's supervision, then you ought to know in your gut that the professor thinks the world of you and will write a highly supportive and detailed letter about you.

What should the recommender write about?

Many times, the application itself has suggestions about what information the letter of recommendation should contain. (For example, the Goldwater application asks professors to account for your research potential; the Truman application asks recommenders to talk about your leadership, public service, or academic credentials.) Let's call these suggestions "prompts." Politely remind the recommender of any specific prompts on the application form. I have seen both professors and "outside recommenders" write the same sort of "generic" recommendation for everybody, regardless of the prompts available on scholarship cover sheets. Such letters will do you little good. Prompts are there for a reason.

Finally, always give professors at least two weeks notice—and more if you can—when you request a recommendation. Bring the professor all of the papers and exams that you completed in his or her class. Those will provide the professor with further ammunition for a letter of recommendation. Also provide the professor with a one-to-two page summary of your achievements. In cases where the letter of recommendation has a cover sheet containing a specific prompt, the summary of your achievements should address items that legitimately fall within the domain of the prompt. Also, recall (in writing) at least five of the perspectives that you contributed to classroom discussion. In separate paragraphs, detail the nature of the discussion that day and the point that you raised. This will help jog the professor's memory in such manner as to allow him to recollect observations about your capacity to engage in meaningful discussion. Be sure you don't offend the professor by offering these extra aids on an uninvited basis. Simply *ask*, "May I provide a summary list of my achievements, along with my recollections of several incidents of classroom contributions that I remember having made?"

If a scholarship doesn't offer a specific prompt for the recommender to address, then present the recommender with the summary of your achievements, including all the highlights that you'd like to imagine that he would reference in the letter. He may or may not be mindful of any or all of the above; but ask if he'd like to see these materials.

When to approach your recommenders
Approach a professor for a letter of recommendation only *after* you can give that person a completed copy of your scholarship application. The information contained in this form rounds out the picture of the "essential you." The completed application also allows professors to place their letters in the context and values of the particular scholarship.

Step 7: Assemble and deliver the application packet
Most scholarship applications contain a checklist of the materials that you're supposed to submit. Double-check to make sure you've brought together all the items. You'll sometimes be asked to include the professors'

letters of recommendation. In such cases, the instructions will call for the professor to return a sealed recommendation (sometimes with a signature placed over the seal) directly to you, who will enclose those letters in the outgoing packet. Always arrange those outgoing materials in the order in which they appear on the checklist. Some scholarships applications will require that you sign the checklist to certify that you've included every item.

Photocopy rules

If the application calls for two or more copies, be careful to arrange each packet in the same order (in other words, do the collating yourself), and designate the original packet as "original" by using a Post-it® Note). When making photocopies, be sure that each copy looks as dark and clean as the original. (Be sure to ask your recommenders to include the requisite number of copies in their sealed envelopes.) Scholarship foundations that call for extra copies usually have multiple readers. You want each reader to feel as if he or she has an original copy.

Mailing rules

When mailing your packet via overnight mail, make sure to list a street address rather than a P.O. Box, since most overnight delivery services will *not* deliver to a P.O. Box. Always retain a copy of the entire application, save, of course, for letters of recommendation. In cases where the faculty representative has the responsibility of mailing the packet, he or she will likely know how to proceed.

Check and double-check those submission deadlines

Be absolutely sure of submission dates—whether those are your responsibility or that of the faculty representative for a given scholarship. Different scholarships have differing deadlines, and those often change from year to year. Also, be aware that the same scholarship can have various deadlines. For example, when students compete for a Rotary Scholarship, they do so through thousands of Rotary clubs around the country and throughout the world. Each club sets its own submission deadline; moreover, the various clubs within thousands of Rotary districts often have quite varied nomination deadlines. The bottom line is this: it is your responsibility to know all of the deadlines and then (diplomatically) to check up on your recommenders and Foundation representatives on campus to make sure that everybody is on schedule.

Step 8: Prepare for the interview process (if one is required)

A number of scholarship agencies require that you attend one or more interviews. I have included extensive interview advice in the next chapter. If the scholarship you are applying for does require an interview, you don't want to neglect this advice. You'll also need practice (I've yet to meet a college student who already had top-notch interviewing skills prior to practice interviews) and outside help. But more about all that in the next chapter.

Conclusion

You can see after reading these steps how much you need to do when applying for a scholarship (not to mention all the work that allows you to qualify for the scholarship in the first place!). Follow these tips:

- Stay organized, and keep working despite setbacks. All the challenges will turn out to be surmountable.

- Stay focused on each step and see it through to its conclusion; then concentrate on starting and finishing the next step. Eventually you'll reach the final step and complete the application process.

- There's no guarantee that you'll receive the scholarship or prize that you're seeking, but you'll have satisfaction and increased confidence in yourself just by accomplishing—and finishing well—a big project.

Chapter Thirty-three

Advice for Successful Interviewing

In some cases the final step in the application process is "the interview." Several scholarship foundations—including Rhodes, Marshall, Mitchell, Rotary, and Truman—require that finalists travel to district, state, or regional sites for personal interviews. Universities, too, may require interviews for large scholarships. I recently coached a high-school student who was about to interview for a $40,000 freshman scholarship at a major state university; I also coached a young woman who interviewed for a $30,000 scholarship at a small private university. Both students won. Most of the points that I make below about interviews came up in our discussions and practice sessions.

Over the years, I've arranged numerous practice interview sessions for students anticipating (or hoping for) an interview for a nationally competitive scholarship. I've also spoken with many students *after* an interview to find out what went right—and, just as importantly, what went wrong. I've even talked with interviewers about what they look for in a successful candidate. The tips and advice below are a compilation of all these efforts to help students shine in interview sessions.

The basic goal for a successful interview

Most importantly, remember that an optimal interview *becomes an engaging conversation among people with common interests*. In a world where most finalists have the paper credentials to "win," and where practically everybody has great grades and fine essays, the scholarship will go to the person who has the best conversation with the judges. This does not mean that "form" matters more than "substance"; rather, during that day of interviews where *everybody* has great substance, the equally well-qualified candidate with the best *conversational form* will win.

Get outside help if at all possible

Most students do not interview well without assistance from national scholarship advisors, or from faculty who have had experience preparing students for interviews. Almost all students need guidance to learn how to smile more frequently, how to be brief, how to dress appropriately, how to maintain eye contact, how to change a quiz into a discussion, how to handle hostile questions, and how to conclude an interview gracefully. If possible, have your practice-interview coach provide you with video feedback.

Be up on current events

Whereas, in regular conversation, it would often be rude to have politics dominate an initial chat with somebody, scholarship committees often jump immediately into current events, including political issues. Therefore, you should be aware of the leading events and conflicts of the day. In general, you can be "current" by visiting a news website (such as www.cnn.com) twice a day and reviewing the up-to-the minute summaries of the lead stories at home and abroad. Also read a number of newspapers or journals for commentary from both liberal and conservative perspectives. I often recommend *The New York Times*, *The (London) Economist*, *The New Republic*, and *The Wall Street Journal*. In advance of an interview, you should isolate the ten leading issues of the day and have at least five intelligent observations to make about each issue.

What to wear ... what to wear ...

Whether you are a man or a woman, wear a suit to an interview; if you don't own one, and if money is an obstacle, buy one at a resale shop. Women should not wear pant suits but rather skirt suits—preferably dark blue or dark grey, with matching shoes and blouses, along with a modest amount of jewelry. (Be careful about *new* shoes, which may rub a blister and make you physically uncomfortable.) If you wear excessive earrings or rings—or if you otherwise adorn yourself with facial piercing—dump the metal for this occasion.

What to carry ... what to carry ...

Women should avoid walking into an interview with a handbag. Figuring out where to place it is sometimes difficult, and you don't want to end up tripping over a handbag as you leave or, worse yet, forgetting it and having to knock on the door to retrieve it.

Go ahead and chat in the waiting room

If you have to wait in a room with other people who are being interviewed, *do* engage in casual conversation. That will get you in the conversational mode, so that you can simply continue the conversation once you enter the interview. But don't wear out your vocal chords before you get into the interview. Also, don't be fazed by students who refuse to talk in those waiting rooms. Their rudeness is an intimidation technique; don't let it get to you.

Handshake advice

When the chair of the interview committee initially greets you, offer a good smile and a firm, really manly handshake—whether you are a man or a woman. A limp handshake on the part of women may be forgiven by an elderly male interviewer, but the women on the committee won't forgive a weak handshake from a woman. It suggests that you are unaware that women have to play hardball to work their way up in the world. Also, don't shake somebody's fingers. Lock hands (all the way down) and shake firmly.

If members of the committee offer to shake hands, do so with a nice smile and with a brief remark for each committee member ("Hello," "Good to meet you," "A pleasure," "How do you do?" etc.). It's to your advantage to shake hands with everybody when you enter, but never seek do so when you leave (that is, unless the committee initiates those handshakes). Trying to shake hands when you leave gives the impression of currying favor; shaking hands when you enter (if the seating arrangement lends itself to handshakes, and if you can do so naturally) conveys confidence and courtesy.

Adjust your chair

When you sit down, take a moment to adjust your chair—whether you're comfortable or not. Doing so suggests that you're in control of the situation and that you feel confident enough to arrange your chair to your own satisfaction.

Don't worry; be happy

When you're awaiting the first question, don't be distressed by the people who are flipping through your paperwork to remind themselves of the points they've underlined, or who have simply failed to do their homework in advance and who are trying to catch up. Until someone asks you a question, maintain a pleasant smile to suggest that you're already having a good time and that you're going to enjoy this discussion. Most students look very frightened while they're awaiting the first question. That makes them appear young and vulnerable—hardly like a competent peer who merits a scholarship. Look happy instead.

The critical two-second delay before answering a question

Usually wait two full seconds before responding to most questions. That two-second delay shows respect for the questioner and suggests that the question was worth thinking about. If you just jump right into an answer, you're really slighting the questioner and, at some level of consciousness, breeding resentment.

Still another reason to wait two seconds is to give the impression that you didn't expect that question (even if you've rehearsed for it), and that you're really thinking this through spontaneously.

During the two-second delay, try to define in your mind the underlying principle behind the question and your upcoming response. For instance, if you're asked whether a compulsory military draft is in order for all eighteen-year-olds, you might, after two seconds of reflection, say something like, "Well, what appears to be at issue here is whether eighteen-year-olds have an obligation to serve their country at such time as a volunteer draft is no longer working." You could then offer two supporting statements, relative to that underlying principle, and then conclude your response with an emphatic assertion and a pleasant smile. The main point is this: define the *principle*. So many students begin talking without ever defining the point at issue. They usually go full circle from nowhere to nowhere.

Don't look at the ceiling, etc.

When offering a response, never look at the ceiling, the walls, or the floor. Those objects usually offer the most readily available sources of psychological escape, and students think that they appear to be contemplative when looking at one or more of those. Hardly. They instead look scared and stumped. Even if you come up with a good answer, the impression remains that you were at a loss for an answer.

Look at the questioner

When responding, look into the eyes of the questioner. That flatters the questioner and establishes the reality of one-on-one discussion. Consider, too, that the questioner really wants you to offer a masterful response to his question—both to make you feel comfortable and to demonstrate what a skillful questioner *he* is. Thus, if you look in his eyes, he'll likely offer emotional support that draws you out. Ceilings and walls cannot do that; nor can they vote in your favor later that day.

When it's appropriate to "look contemplative"

Perhaps three to four times in an interview, there's a time to look away. That's when you've been asked a question that requires a philosophical or otherwise "deep" answer. So, for three seconds, you enter a contemplative mode, looking just to the left or right of the questioner into your own private space, where you search the innermost depths of your soul and your values for an answer. Then you snap out of that contemplation to return to the eyes of your questioner in order to respond.

Know when to shut up

Try to keep your responses to thirty seconds per question. I once asked the head of a major national scholarship foundation what the main flaw was of most students who interviewed for that scholarship. His response: "They don't know when to shut up."

Bring in personal experience

Try to respond to questions by periodically inserting your own personal experience. Everybody loves anecdotes, and your answer will seem all the more authoritative if you can back it up by showing how a personal experience helped you arrive at your position.

Try to relate questions to your field of study

When possible, connect general questions to your field of study, or to some research project you've undertaken. Why? Many follow-up questions will pertain to something you've just said. By bringing in your field of study, you stand a chance of pitching the next ball directly to yourself and then hitting a home run.

Smile—you're being interviewed

A smile shows self-confidence and suggests that the interviewers are doing a good job. Especially smile when you're about to conclude an answer— unless the question pertains to a somber topic.

Make the questioners feel good about their questions

Make every questioner feel as if he or she has asked the most brilliant question in the world. Never, of course say, exactly, "That's a great question," but respond with a degree of enthusiasm that suggests as much. Remember, interviewers want to look good in front of one another. Younger interviewers especially want to look impressive. They would never admit as much, but they *do*.

Establish soul contact with the interviewers

Establish "soul" contact with several interviewers. Look directly at the questioner for the first eight seconds of a thirty-second response. When you come to a natural pause, simply look at somebody else on the committee and talk to them for a while. Don't just establish "eye contact"; speak heart-to-heart with your interviewers. That's soul contact. You can convey the impression of soul contact with a number of facial gestures and body movements. For example, you can nod your head while making an emphatic point; you can furrow your brow and lean your head slightly to the left; you may occasionally use a hand gesture while bringing your main point into focus; you can change the tempo and emphasis of your voice. All of these gestures suggest your genuine commitment to and conviction about your principles. When you're ready to conclude your response, return to the person who initially asked you the question, smiling as you offer the concluding eight to ten words. Start smiling *before* you get to the end of your response; don't wait until you've finished the whole sentence.

Use the silence

After you make an emphatic point that merits reflection, *pause*. That second of silence suggests that you expect people really to think about what you just said. Most students are afraid to pause in an interview because they fear silence. Use the silence to your advantage when you've just made a solid point. Interviewers will take you more seriously if they have time to think about the value of your remarks. Moreover, by pausing after a good point, you give questioners the ability to generate a follow-up question in that same area of concern. That's to your advantage and enhances the possibility that you can "pitch the next ball to yourself."

And, avoid "and"

Avoid stringing sentences together with "and." Since most students abhor silence, they finish a sentence and move right along to another without pausing or stopping. They simply tag on the word "and" at the end of their sentence and, without pausing, move quickly to another sentence and another thought. Before long, the interviewer can't discern any continuity of ideas. The answer becomes one big scrambled egg.

Use hand gestures sparingly

Every now and then, use hand gestures to punctuate or emphasize a point, but avoid the temptation always to have your hands in motion. People who do that end up spellbinding us with their hands—to the point that we're not really paying full attention to their words and thoughts. Use hand gestures sparingly, so that they have an impact. After making a hand gesture, get your hands back together, clasping one another on a knee. Do not keep folded hands on the table (you'll look like a school kid).

Keep your eyes on the person who is addressing you

When a committee member is asking you a question, never glance away— even for a second—to gauge the response to the question of other committee members. It is highly disrespectful to take your eyes off somebody who is talking to you. Students who do so end up looking as if they're in a poker game, glancing around the table to figure out what everybody "has." The moment you glance away from somebody while he or she is addressing you, you've hurt that person's feelings, though that person will never admit as much to others. Even if someone new walks in the room while an interviewer is talking to you, do not turn away from the questioner to see who's there. If somebody spills coffee, do not look. Just keep your eyes glued to those of the person who is addressing you.

Include the curmudgeons in your eye contact

Avoid the temptation of looking only at committee members who seem to like you. You may already have them on your side; the challenge is to get the doubters on your side. Look at them cheerfully while you're speaking. Switch to another skeptic during the next question. By the end of your interview, have everybody feel that they were part of a real "conversation."

Remember: This is a conversation, not a pop quiz

In that same vein, always try to turn "questions" into discussions rather than into mere "answers." You're not taking a pop quiz; you're having a conversation with adults. Credentials being equal, the person who has the liveliest discussion with an interview panel usually wins the scholarship.

Talk louder than normal (but not too loudly)

When responding to a question, increase your volume to three times that to which you are accustomed. You'll think it sounds too loud, but it doesn't. A louder volume, within reasonable limits, adds authority to your utterance. And besides, it always helps when people can hear what you're saying.

Show that you like to think on your feet (even if you're sitting down)

Remember that, in matters of opinion, there's theoretically no right or wrong answer. Questioners usually want to see how you "think on your feet." Thus, when asked a question, identify the underlying principle that ought to inform your response, and then spend thirty seconds illustrating it. When possible, be upbeat and vivacious. That shows how much you enjoy talking about the subject; it also makes the questioner feel as if he has asked a perfectly brilliant question—one that really drew you out.

Don't take yourself too seriously

I've seen many students who, rather than offering upbeat and pertinent observations, become moody and "philosophical," acting as if the entire world is awaiting the gems of knowledge that may evolve from their contemplative mood. That perpetually serious and meditative mode suggests that you think too much of yourself and your wisdom at the tender age of eighteen or twenty-one.

Smile, even when you're showing you can speak a foreign language

In some interviews, you'll be questioned in a foreign language if you've made claims of proficiency in that language. Only a few committee members will speak that foreign language. Thus, when you respond, speak with a smile. Committee members who don't speak the language will still judge that you appear comfortable and happy speaking the foreign language.

Be ready to talk in depth about anything in your personal statement

Many interview questions arise from the personal statement that you've submitted. So each of your claims becomes "fair game." If, for instance, you've remarked that you enjoy reading Herman Melville, you'd better be ready to respond to questions about his major novels and short stories.

Be prepared to talk about courses you took years before

Recall in advance two things that you studied in each of the courses listed on your transcript. I've heard of students who, when asked about a course they took three years earlier, couldn't, under the pressure of an interview, recall specifics—let alone the name of professors who taught that course.

Two questions you'll almost always get

Always be prepared for two recurring questions:

- "What do you do to relax, when you're not studying?"
- "What have you been reading for fun lately?"

Never say that you don't have time for recreation or that you don't have time for enjoyable reading. Ideally, you're doing both with reasonable frequency, so be prepared with a legitimate response for each of those questions.

When answering those two questions, provide more information than the mere "answer." For example, if you respond that you like to read the poetry of Robert Frost, offer a few observations about several specific poems that you admire. In other words, add information that turns a mere "answer" into an engaging discussion. The same holds for movies. If, for fun, you enjoy attending the cinema, talk about which movie you recently enjoyed *and why*. Somebody on the interviewing panel will have seen the film and will show off by talking about why they either liked it or didn't. Either way is OK—just keep the discussion going.

Recall a point made by a committee member

If possible—and do this only once during the meeting—refer back to what some other committee member said five minutes earlier. That shows that you were really listening, and that you're now using that remark to shed light on another issue. When you do that, you're having a real conversation. But again, do this only once, lest people think that it's simply a device that you're using to curry favor.

How to address the challenging questioner

Never—ever—"get into it" with a questioner. When somebody challenges you, they often want to see whether you can respond courteously and conversationally. They want, in brief, to see how ambassadorial you are. Unless you've said something horribly "wrong"—factually speaking—don't compromise your principles to suit those of the person who is challenging you. Rather, maintain a low smile through the challenge (as if to suggest that this will be fun to talk about) and then say something like, "Well, from the point of view you articulate, I can see how somebody might reasonably hold that perspective." You might even add an observation to show how familiar you are with the possible merits of the position that stands to challenge yours.

Then pause. Continue meditatively and thoughtfully with, "I wonder, though, whether …"—and proceed politely to back up your point without overtly calling into question either the intelligence or integrity of the questioner. Moreover, by saying, "I wonder, however, whether …," you give the questioner the opportunity to respond in a way that may grant part of your point without his seeming to have "caved." Keep smiling through this exchange and speak to several people in the course of those thirty seconds. By doing this you stick to your principles, while showing that you can disagree amiably and conversationally. That makes the questioner feel good about having challenged you. It also makes the questioner look good in front of his colleagues.

Wake 'em up at the end of the day

If you chance to be interviewed at the end of the day—when committee members are weary and ready to go home—you have the challenge of waking them up and demonstrating that you're the best thing they've seen all day. Don't let their weariness pull you into a vortex of despair.

Don't look bored if committee members have a discussion among themselves

Every now and then, two or more committee members will begin to debate a point among themselves. Just smile and watch them go at it. They're showing off for the committee and enjoying the performance. Be thankful that they're "eating up the clock" for you. Smile as they talk; join in if it doesn't seem pushy to do so; but, above all, don't look bored.

Never, ever yawn during an interview

Strange as it may seem, some students think it's OK to yawn during an interview, as long as they "politely" cover their mouth with a hand, or a casually closed fist. *Do not yawn under any circumstance.* If you do, you've just surrendered that scholarship to your opponents.

What you learn when you look at your watch during an interview

Never look at your watch. If you're in the habit of looking at your watch while you talk to people, do not wear a watch during the interview, and avoid wearing one for three weeks leading up to the interview. Looking at a watch when someone is talking to you is an act of consummate rudeness. The only thing you learn when you look at your watch is the exact time that you blew the interview.

Learn how to say "I don't know"

Learn how to say "I don't know" if you really don't know. Don't say, "I'm sorry, but I don't know." Don't offer a dissertation on why you don't know. Just smile and say, "I don't know." The smile shows that your world hasn't fallen apart, and that we're all human. Somebody will jump in with a new question, and everybody will respect your honesty.

Don't be a comedian

If you have an opportunity to make a witty remark, do so once. In a twenty-minute interview don't be witty more than twice. If you can make people laugh once, that's great; if you make them laugh more often, they may feel that you're likeable, but too much of a comedian for an academic scholarship.

The unsettling question: make your answer short

If you're asked an unsettling question, respond in fifteen seconds. By unsettling, I mean a question dealing with a very grisly or ugly topic. Such topics are often newsworthy, and merit serious reflection; still, you don't want that topic and all of the associations surrounding it to become the defining memory of your interview. So keep your response brief and hope that somebody will change the topic. If not, you'll simply have to answer a follow-up question. Do so briefly.

Help create your own questions

Learn to pitch questions to yourself to avoid unexpected questions. Thus, if you're talking about a book you read, you might say that you also like related themes in the works of so-and-so. Somebody may then ask you about so-and-so, and you're good for another thirty seconds.

When you talk about your area of study, look extra cheerful

When talking about your area of study, always do so cheerfully and engagingly. Never look bored or sound matter-of-fact about the area that is supposed to "make you tick."

Avoid "you" when answering questions

Avoid "direct address" when making points. Here's an example. A questioner might ask, "How are we going to stop crime?" Don't answer, "Well, if you kill someone, you should go to jail." Even though you're using "you" in the general sense, the remark still targets the questioner. He or she has neither killed nor will kill anybody. Rather, you might respond, "People who kill others should go to jail or in certain circumstances face the death penalty."

Keep going even if you lose your train of thought

If you slip up and lose your pace or thought pattern, don't look or act frustrated. Just stop for a second, and then keep going. Questioners will respect that. When a figure skater falls on the ice, she does not begin to cry; she heroically gets up and finishes the routine. So should you. Fifteen minutes later, committee members will have forgotten that you messed up.

Have your own questions for the committee

Always come prepared to respond, with the appearance of spontaneity, to the question that often occurs at the end of an interview: "Well, do you have any questions to ask *us*?" Take a smiling two seconds to ponder that question, and then pose a question. Never say "No." By asking an engaging question, you demonstrate that you're an adept conversationalist who wants to know more about the committee members and *their* interests.

Try, if possible, to have your question draw out the interview panelists in a way that will get them talking about themselves and, in essence, elaborating upon the values that they cherish. If, for instance, you are interviewing for an Andrew W. Mellon Fellowship in Humanistic Studies, you might respond, "Hmmm. Well, it would be interesting to know what inspired members of this committee to enter the profession of college teaching. Anyone willing to give me a glimpse?" That's upbeat, it's conversational, and it gets people talking about themselves in a pleasant context. You can sit there and smile as they talk it up.

How to finish up the interview with a flair

When the chair of the committee lets you know that it's time to end the interview, you may feel a pit in your stomach and think, "I didn't have enough time to say everything I needed to say; there's so much more to me than they'll ever understand from the brief twenty minutes I had to explain myself." Stop thinking like that. Rise to the challenge of a smile, thereby indicating that you're quite satisfied with all that has transpired to that point. Then, when it's time for you to get up, do so with a smile. When you're fully standing, look at the committee and say, "Thanks so much; I enjoyed our conversation." As you leave the room, shake the hand of the committee chair if he/she opens the door for you. Look that person in the eyes, and say, "Enjoyed it!"—and say that just loudly enough for the rest of the committee to hear. Stated otherwise, depart the interview with an air of joy; if *you* leave that room with less than the appearance of confidence, why should the judges have confidence in your performance?

Practice, practice, practice

To conclude, both the application form and the interview are the outcome of considerable revision and repeated practice. Still, it makes no sense to practice unless you can recognize the difference between good and poor responses. That's why you should study successful scholarship applications and then locate a scholarship mentor who understands the culture of interviews and who is willing to coach you through a number of practice sessions. Also practice with friends who are willing to ask you questions. When alone, rehearse out loud in front of a mirror. I have my students do that all the time, and they agree that the exercise is very useful.

Conclusion

- Remember that applying for a national scholarship and preparing for an interview is a "no lose" prospect if you consider how much you end up learning about yourself, about public speaking, about advanced expository writing, and about your future prospects in a chosen field or profession.

- Most students who apply for a national scholarship and who undergo practice-interview sessions regard that process as one of the most valuable chapters of their undergraduate or graduate-level education

- The art of the interview is the art of turning a pop quiz into an engaging conversation.

Section 8 ::
College Resources

Chapter Thirty-four
College Resources

College Resources

The list of resources below is a compendium of materials I consider useful to college-bound students. It is not intended to be a comprehensive list of all books, periodicals, and websites relating to college. Please note that the website URL addresses provided below are here for your convenience and enjoyment. Due to the changing nature of the Internet, URL accuracy cannot be guaranteed, even at the time of printing. Commentary about the resources is also provided for your convenience, but no promises are made about any website's accuracy or safety. All Internet users are encouraged to exercise caution and skepticism when visiting any website. To avoid repetition, the "http://" that generally starts a URL has been omitted if the next part of the URL begins with "www".

Main categories

- General information

- College admissions

- Paying for your college education

- The college experience

- Writing and communication skills

- College-level research

- Alternative college learning environments

- Picking a major/Career guidance/Job search

- Linking college and career

- Developing life skills

General information

College Rules! How to Study, Survive, and Succeed in College. Sherrie Nist, Ph.D., and Jodi Patrick Holschuh, Ph.D. Berkeley, CA: Ten Speed Press, 2002.

This is a comprehensive guide to vital topics: the transition from high school, starting out strong, finding help, handling stress, constructive interaction with professors, questioning grades in a tactful manner, choosing a balanced course load, contemplating the relation between a major and a career, and time management. The authors also offer fine advice about when to drop courses, how to take notes, and how to read actively. Some of the strategies I offer from personal experience find confirmation in these authors' excellent chapters on memory, active reading, test-taking outlines, and mastering the difference between memorization and conceptualization. Essential, moreover, is the chapter on reading and annotation.

How to Succeed in College. Barbara Mayer. Lincolnwood, IL: VGM Career Horizons, 1993.

Urging self knowledge and personal and internal definitions of success—and especially valuable for anybody working up the courage to attend college—this book emphasizes change, stress, attitude, independence, finances (avoid credit cards!), study skills, realistic class loads, note taking (learning what's noteworthy), choosing classes and professors, managing change, student independence, and the importance of asking questions. Also covered are such topics as roommates, peer pressure, building great memories, friendships, and the benefits of having your professors know who you are.

Major in Success: Make College Easier, Fire Up Your Dreams, and Get a Very Cool Job (Third Edition). Patrick Combs. Berkeley, CA: Ten Speed Press, 2000.

This book urges students to undertake a quality college career that leads to long-term, vocational happiness. The author covers such topics as drive, passion, positive thinking, and happiness in relation to salaries. Among its many positive emphases are journalizing, positive thinking, overcoming fear, action plans, the benefits of studying abroad, the importance of internships, and campus involvement in clubs and other organizations. The author urges students to place grades in perspective, to network within a framework of professional association, and to seek out success coaches.

Making the Most of College: Students Speak Their Minds. Richard J. Light. Cambridge, MA: Harvard University Press, 2001.

This is a very helpful book that offers insights and conclusions emerging from the perspectives of Harvard undergraduates. Emphases range from forming powerful connections with faculty (in supervised research environments), to letters of recommendation, to group associations and volunteerism, to effective classes, to course sequencing, to study groups, to handling academic problems. This book also describes the benefits of multiple writing assignments, leading up to the challenge of a senior honors thesis. Then there are emphases on campus diversity, learning differences, and leadership.

Strategic Learning in College. Trent A. Petrie, Hugh G. Petrie, Lisa Landy, Kim B. Edwards. Denton, TX: RonJon Publishing, Inc., 2002.

An admirable example of applied psychology, *Strategic Learning* covers such vital concerns as self-regulation, multiple learning styles, memory, note taking, test taking, time management, goal setting, motivation, creative solutions, types of communication, stress and coping, big campuses and their social settings, personal health, and careerism. The book also offers suggestions for smooth transitions to college, balancing school and work, handling finances, study groups, and study methods in relation to varied learning styles. Invaluable are the book's emphases on goal-setting, active learning, and getting involved in extracurricular activities or groups.

Hobson's College View (online)
www.collegeview.com/campuslife/index.html
Wide array of information covering college searches, college life, and financial aid.

nextSTEP Magazine (online)
www.nextstepmagazine.com
Contains online articles about the full spectrum of college life.

College admissions

Lists of colleges
"American Universities"
www.clas.ufl.edu/au/
University of Florida's comprehensive, alphabetical index of all American universities having web page links. Very useful for university research.

Web U.S. Higher Education section
www.utexas.edu/world/univ/
University of Texas at Austin Web Central links to American universities
and community colleges having websites.

Standardized tests (SAT/ACT) and test preparation

The College Board
www.collegeboard.com
Multi-purpose website for college students. Frequently used for SAT
registration.

ACT Information for Life's Transitions
www.act.org
Emphasizes educational planning and career decisions.

Kaplan Test Prep and Admissions
www.kaplan.com
A trusted authority on SAT/ACT preparation, among other services.

Triumph College Admissions
www.testprep.com
Offers SAT/ACT/PSAT preparation.

Admissions process helpers (timetables, national organization, etc.)

Mapping Your Future™
www.mapping-your-future.org
Contains a number of helpful get-ready hints about selecting
and paying for college, or planning a career.

College prep

High-school level
Preparing Your Child for College
www.ed.gov/pubs/Prepare/index.html
A U.S. Department of Education website. An excellent overview of high-
school level preparation for the college experience.

College level (College 101 courses)
College Prep 101: Helping Students Prepare for College
http://collegeprep.okstate.edu/homepages.nsf/toc/precollege/
An Oklahoma State University service that offers multiple helpful hints
about a wide range of college matters and issues. Very helpful.

Paying for your college education

College Costs/Calculators/Budgeting

Educaid™ "Budget Calculator"
www.educaid.com
Click the Budget Calculator link under Resource Center. Hard facts, figures, advice about loans and college finance.

Esther Maddux, *et al.* "Making it on a College Budget"
www.fcs.uga.edu/extension/survivalguide/collegebudget/
The University of Georgia College of Family & Consumer Sciences Cooperative Extension Service. Handy worksheets for college budgeting.

Mapping Your Future™
"Ten Steps to Paying for School"
www.mapping-your-future.org/paying/

EssayAdvice.com
www.essayadvice.com/bookstorescholarship.asp
Links to top books on scholarships and financing college. Includes very good annotated commentary on each book.

Deborah Fowles, "Money and the College Student"
http://financialplan.about.com/cs/college/a/MoneyCollege.htm
This article will help you leave college without credit card debt, a problem many students experience.

Scholarship search engines

CollegeBoard.com Scholarship Search
apps.collegeboard.com/cbsearch_ss/welcome.jsp
An online tool to help you locate scholarships, internships, grants, and loans that match your education level, talents, and background.

Broke Scholar
www.brokescholar.com
A free website that puts students in contact with over 650,000 scholarship opportunities.

FastWeb!
www.fastweb.com
A search engine for hundreds of thousands of scholarships.

Financial aid to go to college

FAFSA (Free Application for Federal Student Aid)
www.fafsa.ed.gov/
You must fill out the FAFSA form to qualify for most internal university scholarship and loan assistance.

FinAid
www.finaid.org/calculators/
Links to scholarships and to loan and loan-payment calculators.

Prestigious national scholarships

National Association of Fellowships Advisors
www.nafadvisors.org/scholarships.htm
Provides links to leading prestigious scholarships, including Rhodes, Marshall, Mitchell, Javits, NSF, Udall, and Goldwater.

Cornell University Graduate Fellowship Database
http://cuinfo.cornell.edu/Student/GRFN/
A fine search engine, containing descriptions of over 650 prestigious scholarships and fellowships. Search by field of study or by major.

Scholarship list for the Office of Pre-Professional Advising and Fellowships, Vassar College
http://deanofthecollege.vassar.edu/fellowships/scholarshiplist.html
Excellent links to nationally competitive scholarships and to a number of college websites directing students to various national scholarships.

University of Maryland National Scholarship Office
www.scholarships.umd.edu/descriptions.html
Chart of the top national scholarships, showing the number of awards given each year, dollar value, and a brief summary of eligibility.

University of North Carolina at Chapel Hill,
Office of Distinguished Scholarships
www.distinguishedscholarships.unc.edu/scholarships.html
Distinguished scholarship opportunities, listed by availability to sophomores, juniors, and seniors, with a link to a comprehensive list of brief summaries for each scholarship.

Specialty scholarships (minority, veteran, disabled, international, and women)
DFW International
Scholarships for Minorities and Internationals
http://www.dfwinternational.org/assistance/ (Click "Scholarships for Minority Students and Int'l Study" to download a Word document.)

Reference Service Press
www.rspfunding.com (Click Books & More in the navigation menu. Then click the link, "complete alphabetical list of all RSP publications.")
A superb collection of financial-aid books, including books devoted to minority students, women, disabled students, and veterans, among others.

Scholarships for Women
www.college.ucla.edu/UP/SRC/women.htm
A helpful resource from the UCLA website.

Microsoft College Careers Scholarships
www.microsoft.com/college/ss_overview.mspx
Excellent scholarships for women and minority students in computer science or related engineering fields.

International Education Financial Aid
www.iefa.org
Scholarships and grants for studying abroad.

Writing essays and completing applications for scholarships
Writing Personal Statements and Scholarship Application Essays: A Student Handbook. Joe Schall. Eden Prairie, MN: Outreach Publishing, 2006.
Schall's book offers advice about content and form—across many academic disciplines—for application essays spanning a wide range of national scholarships. The sample essays and advice are splendid. This book is a must.

Live to Learn™
www.livetolearn.com
Live to Learn™ is a free online educational service coordinated by recent graduates and high academic achievers for students interested in applying for top academic programs and awards worldwide. This website offers, for instance, general information about specific top scholarship awards, "frequent reasons applicants were not advanced" tips, and some sample

application essays and interview questions. The site managers also seek to help applicants connect with past fellowship and scholarship winners.

The college experience

Selecting professors
Pick-A-Prof
www.pickaprof.com
This website offers student comments about professors, as well as their grade distribution. Students would do well to consult this website before enrolling in a professor's course.

Ratemyprofessors.com
www.ratemyprofessors.com
A growing resource, akin to pickaprof.com.

Note: There are many other similar websites besides the two mentioned above. Some of these websites may charge fees for some or all of their services.

Note taking
"Lecture Note Taking"
Saint Benedict's and Saint John's University
www.csbsju.edu/academicadvising/help/lec-note.htm
A number of splendid tips.

"In the Classroom - Listening and Note Taking"
Saint Benedict's and Saint John's University
www.csbsju.edu/academicadvising/help/clasroom.htm
Nicely integrates the listening and note taking processes.

Studying
"University Learning Center's Study Skills Handouts"
University of North Dakota
www.und.nodak.edu/dept/ULC/handout.html
A wonderful list of handouts, many relating to studying and test taking.

"Preparing for Exams"
Homework Spot
www.homeworkspot.com/tips/preparingforexam.htm
Brief but helpful tips.

"How to Take on College Studying: Your Cramming Days Are Over"
College Board
www.collegeboard.com/article/0,3868,2-10-0-961,00.html
Sound advice about when, where, and how to study.

Test taking

Getting Straight A's: A Proven System for Achieving Excellence in College and Graduate School by Becoming Test-Wise and Making the System Work for You. Gordon W. Green. Syracuse, N.J.: Lyle Stuart, 1985.
Includes advice about takingn the many different types of exams.

"Tips on Writing the Essay-Type Examination"
Saint Benedict's and Saint John's University
www.csbsju.edu/academicadvising/help/essayexm.htm
Helpful suggestions for essay-type exams.

"Math: Test Taking Strategies "
Lynchburg College
www.lynchburg.edu/academic/math/mathlab/TestStrats.htm
Useful tips about preparing for and taking math exams.

"Test Taking Strategies"
EMC Paradigm website
www.emcp.com/college_resource_centers/resourcelist.php?GroupID=1338
Useful and insightful tips, including those for multiple-choice exams.

Critical thinking and reading

Critical Thinking Across the Curriculum Project
Longview Community College
www.kcmetro.cc.mo.us/longview/ctac/toc.htm
Excellent overview of arguments, premises, and reasoning.

Thinking Critically about World Wide Web Resources
www.library.ucla.edu/libraries/college/help/critical/
UCLA College Library Help Guides. Very informative and useful advice about the relative merit of various web resources.

"Critical Reading Links," CRC Competency Resource Center
http://academic.udayton.edu/crc/faculty/CriticalReadingLinks.htm
University of Dayton links to over thirty other university websites concerned with critical-reading skills. Superb resource.

John Lye, "Critical Reading: A Guide"
www.brocku.ca/english/jlye/criticalreading.html
Excellent guide to critical reading of literary texts.

Citation
"Using and Citing Information"
Bowdoin College Library website
http://library.bowdoin.edu/1st/citation.shtml
Basic, necessary advice on citation.

"Turabean Samples for a Bibliography: Library Resources and Methods of Research"
Ithaca College website
www.ithaca.edu/library/course/turabian.html
Excellent overview of citation for books, periodicals, doctoral dissertations, web pages, government documents.

Relationships with professors and teaching assistants
"How to Get Along with Your College Professor"
Montana State University, Counseling and Psychological Services office
www.montana.edu/wwwcc/docs/professor.html

Dr. Ed Witse, "Negotiating Relationships with Professors"
Nazareth College/Freshman Seminar Program website
www.naz.edu/dept/frs/relationships.html
Helpful suggestions for meeting with professors outside of class and negotiating extensions and other problems.

Free speech on campus and related issues
Beating College Discipline: When the Thought Police Come Knocking. Jeffrey M. Duban. 2002.
A student/faculty due process guide to understanding and surviving the excesses of campus political correctness.

Writing and communication skills

College-level writing and essay writing
Most recent editions of:

Harbrace College Handbook. Winfred B. Horner and Suzanne Strobeck Webb.
Excellent on grammar, punctuation, citation.

The Little, Brown Handbook. Fowler and Aaron.
Splendid on grammar, punctuation, citation. See, especially, its guide to researching with computers.

Writing with Style. Strunk and White.
A wonderful brief guide that offers the best advice in the least number of pages.

Writing helpers (online dictionaries, thesauruses, etc.)
Merriam Webster Online
www.m-w.com
Online dictionary and thesauruses search.

OneLook® Dictionary Search
www.onelook.com

Public Speaking
Toastmasters International
www.toastmasters.org
Toastmasters: A wonderful organization devoted to improving public-speaking skills and building confidence.

Tara Kuther, "Public Speaking: Conquer Your Anxiety About Speaking"
gradschool.about.com/cs/presentations/a/speak.htm
Tips for graduate students anyone can learn from.

Morton C. Orman, "How to Conquer Public Speaking Fear"
www.stresscure.com/jobstress/speak.html
Splendid suggestions about how to relieve stress and succeed.

Ron Curstis, "Be Valuable to Your Audience"
www.school-for-champions.com/speaking/value.htm
A concise perspective on why audiences value a speaker

Listening
"Tips for College Listening Skills," Quinnipiac College website
www.quinnipiac.edu/x2917.xml
Excellent suggestions.

"Be a Great Listener!"
www.campusblues.com/studentoflife_5.asp
Campusblues.com. Fine suggestions on how to focus and how to listen.

College-level research

The Council for Undergraduate Research
www.cur.org
Encourages undergraduate research—summer research and fellowship opportunities.

NASA Undergraduate Student Research Programs
www.nasa.gov/audience/forstudents/postsecondary/learning/
Click the link for "undergraduate student research" to learn about opportunities for summer research at NASA space centers.

Summer Undergraduate Research Opportunities
University of North Carolina
www.med.unc.edu/pmbb/sure/
Chapel Hill summer research opportunities.

The National Science Foundation website
www.nsf.gov
Enter "undergraduate research" into the search engine for a number of entries describing NSF commitment to undergraduate research endeavors.

Getting published or "presenting" in public

List of undergraduate journals and publications
Council on Undergraduate Research
www.cur.org/ugjournal.html
An excellent overview of various journals publishing undergraduate research.

Alternative college learning environments

Honors programs

Indiana University website
www.indiana.edu/~iubhonor/nchc/other.php
This comprehensive page provides a link to all other university honors programs.

Distance learning

"Distance Learning Resources for Continuing Your Education"
Quintessential Careers website
www.quintcareers.com/distance_learning/

A treasure trove of links to the pros and cons, the dos and don'ts of distance learning, along with other distance-learning resources.

"What you need to know about Distance Learning"
Montgomery County Community College
www.mc3.edu/aa/DISTLRN/know-dl.htm
Excellent points to consider before enrolling in a distance-learning course, including personality traits of successful distance learners.

National Student Exchange
National Student Exchange website
www.nse.org
For students interested in exchange arrangements at U.S. universities. Expand your horizons and, perhaps, get letters of recommendation from famous professors at other universities.

Buffalo State University
www.buffalostate.edu/depts/nse/memcam.asp
Links to all universities offering National Student Exchange Opportunities.

Picking a major/Career guidance/Job search

How to Choose a College Major. Linda Chase Andrews. Chicago: VGM Career Horizons, 1998.

Finding careers/jobs in your major
The College Majors Handbook: The Actual Jobs, Earnings, and Trends for Graduates of 60 College Majors. Paul E. Harrington, et al. Indianapolis, IN: Jist Works, 1999.

Most Lucrative College Degrees
CNN Money website
http://money.cnn.com/2004/02/05/pf/college/lucrative_degrees/
Check it out to see what you stand to earn with your college degree in different fields of study.

Professional and graduate schools
The Law-School Exchange™: One-to-one consulting for applicants to top law schools
www.law-schools.net
Assessment, planning, LSAT Prep., Application Development, etc.

Association of American Medical Colleges (AAMC) website
www.aamc.org/medicalschools.htm
Comprehensive guide to assessing medical schools.

Medical College Admissions Test (MCAT®)
www.aamc.org/students/mcat/start.htm
Information about the main test required for admission to medical school.

Jobs, careers, salaries
U.S. Department of Labor, Bureau of Labor Statistics website
www.stats.bls.gov
Has numerous links to vocations, benefits, and salaries.

Multnomah County Library home page
www.multcolib.org
Click Job Seekers on the website's home page for multiple helpful links to career information, websites, and bibliographies.

Jobstar Central website
www.jobsmart.org
Career, salary, and résumé information.

Career Journal
The Wall Street Journal Executive Career Site
www.careerjournal.com
Covers multiple issues pertaining to jobs, the economy, and job hunting.

Hobson's College View
www.collegeview.com/careers/
Great review of cover letters, job profiling, salary information.

Résumés
Jobstar Central website
www.jobsmart.org/tools/resume/
Contains links for résumé writing, among other job-related concerns.

Résumés, Job Search Letters, & Interview Skills
www.bc.edu/offices/careers/skills/
Boston College website. Terrific advice and examples of résumés, cover letters, thank-you letters, etc.

Interview skills
"Interview Skills," Boston College website
www.bc.edu/offices/careers/skills/interview/
Great suggestions for various aspects of an interview, including research
before the interview, questions to ask, proper dress, and dealing
with anxiety.

"Interview Preparation," Western Career Services
www.western.edu/career/interview/Interview_skills.htm
Splendid advice on interviewing, including what you should know about
the company with whom you are interviewing.

Résumés, Job Search Letters, and Interview Skills
Boston College
www.bc.edu/offices/careers/skills/interview/
This section covers many aspects of the job search process.

Linking college and career

Internships
"Internships and Co-op Opportunities for Undergraduates"
American Mathematical Society
www.ams.org/employment/internships.html

Carter Center Internships
www.unis.org/pdf/college/interview.pdf
Unique opportunities for meaningful internships for students interested
in domestic and international issues.

Developing life skills

Time management
How to Get Control of Your Time and Your Life. Alan Laekin. (Mass Market
Paperback, 1989)

The 7 Habits of Highly Effective People. Stephen R. Covey. (New York: Simon
& Schuster, 1989)

Mindtools—Essential Skills for Excellent Careers website
www.mindtools.com/pages/main/newMN_HTE.htm
Excellent overview of several time-management techniques, including
work priorities, costing your time, and prioritizing responsibilities.

Steve Randall's "Time Management Guide"
www.members.aol.com/rslts/tmmap.html
A site about anxiety, planning, goals, procrastination, and scheduling.

"23 Time Management Techniques"
College of Saint Benedict and Saint John's University
www.csbsju.edu/academicadvising/help/23tmt.htm

"Time Management"
University of Illinois at Urbana-Champaign Counseling Center
www.couns.uiuc.edu/brochures/time.htm
Excellent tips on time management, including how to safeguard blocks of
time and how to organize priorities and goals.

Physical and mental well-being
"Going to College"
TeensHealth website
http://kidshealth.org/teen/school_jobs/school/college.html
Numerous categories of interest, including sexual health and diseases.

"Alcohol and Student Life"
Facts on Tap website
www.factsontap.org/collexp/Collmain.htm
An excellent resource on alcohol abuse on college campuses.

Keeping up with current events
You should read a variety of newspapers and magazines to benefit from
multiple perspectives across the political spectrum. Most campus libraries provide a comfortable area for students to read current newspapers,
magazines, and other periodicals. Many of these same publications' make
some or all of their articles and opinions available on the Internet, too.
What follows is merely a sample "multiple-perspectives" reading list:

- *The New York Times*
  www.nytimes.com
- *Wall Street Journal*
  www.opinionjournal.com
- *The Economist*
  www.economist.com
- *The Christian Science Monitor*
  www.csmonitor.com

Notes

Library Book Request Form

Name:_____

Department:_____

I am: _____ Faculty   _____ Staff   _____ Student

E-mail:_____

Day phone:_____Cell phone:_____

Additional information:

Note: Please notify me when the book is received.

Book Information

Title: Be a College Achiever: The Complete Guide to Academic Stardom

Author: James Duban

Publisher: Trafford Publishing

Online ordering URL: www.trafford.com/robots/04-2554.html

Binding: quality trade paperback (softcover)

Edition: 1st ed

Publication date: August, 2005

ISBN: 1-4120-4746-3

Price: U.S. $29.95

Pages: 300 pp

Size: 6 x 9 inches

Categories:
- Study Aid
- College
- Success
- Career
- Nationally Competitive Scholarships

Copies requested: _____

The Be A College Achiever™ Seminar Series Is Here for You!

Bring a Be A College Achiever™ seminar to your high school, educational group, college, house of worship, or community organization to get the ultimate insider track to college success.

Dr. James Duban, author of *Be A College Achiever™: The Complete Guide to Academic Stardom*, also offers multi-media, interactive seminars that will show college-bound students how to:

- Make a smooth transition to college
- Greatly improve your study skills
- Write A+ essays
- Ace tests
- Impress professors
- Schedule your day to make best use of your time
- Get on a research team
- Think "outside the campus"
- Go the extra mile to get your future career off to a fabulous start
- Maximize your graduation options with an ideal college education
- Build the credentials for national scholarship competitions
- Prepare and interview for competitive scholarships and graduate school fellowships

To inquire about group rates for a Be A College Achiever™ seminar, e-mail seminars@college-achiever.com, call 972-533-4254, or write to James Duban Consulting, LLC, P. O. Box 270922, Flower Mound, TX, 75027-0922. Also, please visit the Be A College Achiever™ website, www.college-achiever.com for a schedule of Dr. Duban's seminars and presentations. Thank you for your interest!

Purchasing Information and Order Form

Online 🖥️

You can order this book online from Trafford Publishing at: www.trafford.com/robots/04-2554.html or you can order directly from James Duban Consulting, LLC (options below).

Phone ☏

Call 972-533-4254. If we're not in, we'll call you back during regular business hours.

E-mail ✉️

Send an e-mail to orders@college-achiever.com

Mail completed form to: 🖅

James Duban Consulting, LLC, P. O. Box 270922, Flower Mound, TX USA 75027-0922.

___ **Yes**, please send _____ copies of *Be a College Achiever*™: *The Complete Guide to Academic Stardom* for $29.95 each.

___ **Yes**, I'm interested in the Be a College Achiever™ seminars for schools, companies, and other community organizations. Please send more information.

First Name:_____ Last Name:_____

Company name (if any):_____

Address:_____ Apt #_____

City:_____State/Province:_____

Country:_____ Postal/Zip code:_____

Phone:_____ E-mail:_____

Sales tax

Add 7.75% sales tax for book(s) shipped to Texas addresses.

Shipping & handling

U.S.: Add $4 shipping and handling for one book; $2 for each additional book. Please allow 3 weeks for delivery.

International: Please e-mail orders@college-achiever.com for an estimate before ordering.

$	+	$	+	$	=	$
Book total (# of books x $29.95)		8.25% tax if shipping to Texas		Shipping & Handling		**Total**

Payment

Payment must be in U.S. funds and accompany order. Thank you!

_____ Enclosed is my check or money order in the amount of $_____ payable to James Duban Consulting, LLC.

_____ Please charge the above **Total** to my:

___VISA ___Mastercard ___AMEX ___Discover

Card number:_____

Name on card:_____ Exp. Date: _____/_____

Signature:_____

Note for credit card sales: If the address above does not match the credit card's billing address, we may have to contact you for additional information for verification before completing the credit card transaction.